THE CLOSING OF THE GATES

N'ilah

PRAYERS OF AWE

THE CLOSING OF THE GATES

N'ilah

Edited by
Rabbi Lawrence A. Hoffman, PhD

JEWISH LIGHTS Publishing

Turner Publishing Company
Nashville, Tennessee
New York, New York
www.turnerpublishing.com

The Closing of the Gates: N'ilah *(Prayers of Awe Series)*

Cover design: Maddie Cothren
Book design: Tim Holtz

Library of Congress Cataloging-in-Publication Data available upon request

Printed in the United States of America
17 18 19 20 10 9 8 7 6 5 4 3 2 1

For Gayle

Who Opens Gates

Contents

Introduction to N'ilah
THE CLOSING OF THE GATES (AND OF THE SERIES)

Rabbi Lawrence A. Hoffman, PhD

Earlier volumes in this series featured just one or two individual prayers as their subject matter. That proved too limiting for *N'ilah* because the message of *N'ilah* comes through only in the service as a whole. Unable to reproduce all of *N'ilah*, however, we settled for its most representative parts, what a reader would have to know to appreciate the service's uniqueness. Rather than produce a road map of the entire service, that is, we have provided just a guidebook of the landmarks along the way. We paid little attention, therefore, to prayers that are transplants from the normal service structure elsewhere and focused instead on those that are unique to *N'ilah*, the ones that convey the message that we are supposed to carry home with us, as the gates of Yom Kippur close.

Three prayer units stand out in that regard:

Rabbi Lawrence A. Hoffman, PhD, editor of this entire series (Prayers of Awe)—and the ten-volume series prior, *My People's Prayer Book*—has written or edited over forty books on prayer, spirituality, and synagogue transformation and maintains a blog, *Life and a Little Liturgy*. His writings appear in five languages and on four continents. Rabbi Hoffman, who lectures widely for popular audiences and consults with synagogues desirous of meaningful change, is the Barbara and Stephen Friedman Professor of Liturgy, Worship, and Ritual at Hebrew Union College–Jewish Institute of Religion, New York, and cofounder of Synagogue 3000, a pioneering initiative to transform synagogues spiritually and morally for the twenty-first century.

1. *A lengthy prayer in two parts: "You Extend Your Hand"* (Atah Noten Yad) *followed immediately by "You Set Humans Apart"* (Atah Hivdalta Enosh): We think of prayer as theological—centering on God. But this prayer is both theological and anthropological: theological in that it says something about God ("God extends a hand"), but anthropological too, because it affirms an understanding of human nature (as a species, we are "set apart"). The anthropology (the uniqueness of human moral consciousness, but also human fallibility) goes hand in hand with the theology (even when we fail, God extends a hand to help us start anew).

2. *Poetry* (piyyutim) *on the metaphor of "gates":* Jewish services are technically known as *seder t'fillah*—not just *t'fillah* ("prayer") but also *seder* ("an order"), because they follow a prescribed pathway from beginning to end. Despite the many changes in wording and content that vary with the time of day—morning as opposed to evening, for example—the overall structure remains intact.

   On holy days, however, this structure is augmented by *piyyutim* (singular: *piyyut*), poetry on the themes that the days represent. The liturgy of any particular holiday stands out because of the selection of *piyyutim* that it has accumulated over time.

   The prevailing image of *N'ilah* is "gates," so poem after poem explores "gates" as a master metaphor for human life. We choose here a representative sample of such poetry, including *El Nora Alilah* ("God Whose Deeds Are Awesome"), a particularly well-known medieval poem characteristic of Sephardi liturgy but now part and parcel of many Ashkenazi congregations as well.

3. *The grand conclusion of the service: congregational acclamations shouted aloud, followed by the blowing of the shofar:* The acclamations are known as *Sh'mot*, "Names"—more precisely (in context), "Names of God."

We begin this volume with overviews of *N'ilah*, three general ones (part 1) and two specific observations on what Jewish law (halakhah) has to say concerning *N'ilah* practices that inevitably evoke curiosity (part 2): keeping the ark open throughout the entire service, and hammering in the first nail for the sukkah the minute we return home (after *N'ilah* ends). With these two introductory sections behind us, we provide "Opening Meditations: As *N'ilah* Begins" (part 3) and then move to the centerpiece of the book (part 4), an annotated translation of the liturgy, divided according to the threefold understanding described above ("You extend your hand"; poetry on gates; the concluding acclamations and shofar). Each of the three units begins with an editorial introduction that provides the history, theology, and significance of the prayers in question. Each is similarly followed by a set of essays that expand on the unit's significance. Essays on *El Nora Alilah* ("God Whose Deeds Are Awesome") are grouped separately from the other essays on gates, however, because enough contributors focused on it that it seemed to deserve its own section.

As we introduced the liturgy (part 4) with "Opening Meditations: As *N'ilah* Begins" (part 3), so too we end it with "Concluding Meditations: As *N'ilah* Ends" (part 5).

In addition, we provide something that none of the other books in this series has: two detailed accounts entitled "Appendices: Going Deeper." Readers interested in the fullness of Jewish liturgy, its origins in antiquity and evolution through the Middle Ages, will enjoy the appendices, which break new ground in that they are scholarly accounts, unavailable elsewhere—but composed so as to be comprehensible not just to scholars in Judaica, but also to interested readers who lack technical background in Jewish sources.

If this final volume is "the closing of the gates," the series as a whole represents the "opening of the gates": the gates of understanding, that is, gates to comprehending the magnificent depth behind High Holy Day worship. Each volume, this one included, is the combined work of over forty contributors—from Australia, Canada, England, France, Germany, Israel, and the United States. Geographically, then, but ideologically as well, they represent the true diversity of the Jewish People.

I am indebted to each and every one of these contributors, but also to so many others who made this eight-year project possible. At a book a year, it has demanded a great deal of a great many.

The production side begins with Stuart Matlins, the visionary who founded Jewish Lights and took special interest in providing an entire library on Jewish liturgy, including especially the ten volumes on daily and Shabbat liturgy (*My People's Prayer Book*), the two volumes on the Passover seder (*My People's Passover Haggadah*), and the High Holy Day service that this volume concludes (*Prayers of Awe*). Deserving of special mention is Emily Wichland, the editor who worked closely with me on practically all the volumes in both series. With the acquisition of Jewish Lights by Turner Publishing, a second production team entered the process, represented by general editor Jon O'Neal, whose exceptional competence I gratefully recognize as well.

My People's Prayer Book began in 1997; the final volume in *Prayers of Awe* was completed in 2017, two decades later. I am privileged to have worked with so many wonderful minds and hearts and am grateful to God for the opportunity to explore the depths of Jewish prayer all these many years.

⟨∞⟩

Part I
Overviews
of *N'ilah*

The History and Symbolism of *N'ilah*

A THICK DESCRIPTION OF LIFE AND DEATH

Rabbi Lawrence A. Hoffman, PhD

The word *n'ilah* has two separate but interrelated meanings. It is, first of all, the name of a synagogue service, the closing service for Yom Kippur. But its original context was the Jerusalem Temple, where *n'ilah* (literally, "closing" or "locking shut") was short for *n'ilat sh'arim*, "the closing [or locking] of the gates," a reference, presumably, to the closing and locking of the Temple's doors at nightfall. When Roman armies destroyed the Temple (in 70 CE), all that was left was the synagogue service.

But synagogue worship was still just coming into existence, and Rabbinic writing on both topics—the Temple and the early synagogue service—was composed well after the fact with no guarantee of historical accuracy and little or no hard evidence to go on. So we know very little about *n'ilah* in those early years. Although the earliest Rabbinic source (the Mishnah, c. 200 CE) takes it for granted, most of what actually occurred then remains a mystery. That dearth of reliable detail is true of both the Temple ritual (*n'ilah*), which had ceased over a century earlier (in 70), and the synagogue service (*N'ilah*—we capitalize it when naming the service), which was still in its infancy.

Both the Babylonian and the Palestinian Talmud expand on the Mishnah in significant ways, but they don't add historical clarity on what originally happened at the Temple, a matter that existed, by then, only as a distant (and unreliable) communal memory. Their focus, therefore, is not so much *n'ilah* at the Temple, but *N'ilah*, the service, for their own day.

3

Still, Talmudic discussion at least speculates on what is meant by "the Temple gates" that were said to close. They were not the outer gates to the entire Temple structure, but a set of inner gates to a freestanding building within the Temple complex called the *heikhal*.[1] Among other things, an incense offering is said to have taken place there in the afternoon, after which the doors were closed. The Temple's *n'ilah* (the closing of the gates) would then take place during late afternoon—rather than at nightfall, when our own *N'ilah* (the synagogue service) occurs.[2] Alternatively, one Talmudic opinion identifies the closing gates of *n'ilah* not as any Temple gates at all, but instead as "the gates of heaven," another way of saying "nightfall," the close of day.[3]

More significantly, for our purposes, we find Rav and Samuel, the two most important authorities of early- to mid-third-century Babylonia, engaged in a discussion about the essence of *N'ilah* as it was practiced in early synagogues.[4] Rav assumes it to be an extra *Amidah*, as indeed it is for us. We call *N'ilah* a "service" precisely because it contains that central prayer. To be sure, contemporary Jews sometimes refer to other things as services: a "shofar service" for Rosh Hashanah or a "memorial service" for Yom Kippur. But technically, these are additional prayers inserted into already existent services (Rosh Hashanah *Musaf* [additional service] or Yom Kippur *Shacharit* [morning service] in traditional synagogues). For convenience sake, some modern prayer books have detached these from their original context and relabeled them, conveniently, as "services" in their own right. But the word "service" is properly reserved for those occasions when an *Amidah* is said, and ever since the Talmud, if not before, the bulk of *N'ilah* (like the bulk of the other services—*Shacharit, Musaf, Minchah,* and *Ma'ariv* [morning, additional, afternoon, and evening]) has been an *Amidah*.

Rav's opponent to the debate, Samuel, disagrees. The closing of the gates, he says, is not an *Amidah*; rather, it is a prayer that begins with the words "What are we, what are our lives . . ."[5]—something we now recognize as the second part of our prayer, "You extend your hand" (see liturgy, p. 67–69). Could it be that as late as the third century, some Jews marked *N'ilah* not with any *Amidah* at all, but just with one last parting reference to human mortality? The Talmud rejects Samuel's contention on halakhic ("legal") grounds, believing that halakhah ("Jewish law") demanded an *Amidah* then. But Jewish law often arose after the fact and was then applied retroactively to practices already in place. Historically speaking, therefore, we should consider the possibility that *N'ilah* was not necessarily the kind of service we now have. It may just have been this final confession-like statement of human fallibility. By the time the Talmud was codified, however—circa seventh century—halakhah did indeed demand an *Amidah* for *N'ilah*, so if it wasn't already there at the outset, it had indeed been added, giving us *N'ilah* more or less as we now have it, extra *Amidah* and all.

But suppose we take Samuel seriously and assume that the *Amidah* was added only eventually, for halakhically technical reasons (a "service" was considered incomplete without it). This is not to discount the *Amidah* as unimportant. But knowing that the *Amidah* was added after the fact helps us focus elsewhere for the essence of what *N'ilah* is about. This book tries to capture that essence.

But it tries also to do more. The traditional study of liturgy focuses solely on the liturgical text, the words of the prayers. It looks historically at the textual origins and variants: how they began in antiquity and what they became in the many versions of the traditional service that have come down to us. It analyzes the words theologically, asking what they mean for us today. It is all about "words, words, words" (to quote Shakespeare's Hamlet).

But Hamlet speaks sarcastically here; he knows that life is so much more than words—and so too is worship. We appreciate our worship only when we arrive at the significance of those words in ways that literary analysis alone cannot accomplish—when, that is, we grasp its underlying symbolism.

Studying worship with no attention to symbolism is like surveying the landscape of North America or Europe and paying no attention to the Rockies or the Alps. Worshipers would be like dwellers in a valley, their eyes firmly looking downward at the words in their prayer books but missing the mountains of meaning all around them.

The "words, words, words" of our liturgical texts are unlike those in Jewish literature generally, because they exist to be prayed. What really matters, therefore, is how those texts are rendered in the act of prayer we call worship. What is sung and what is whispered? What is emphasized and what gets passed over? Studying liturgy purely as a text is like reading an operatic libretto with no regard for the music. The libretto comes to life only in performance. Liturgy too takes on meaning only when it is "performed."

Think, then, of *N'ilah*'s extraordinary "performance," and compare it to the "performance" of *Kol Nidre* the night before. *N'ilah* stands out as being the only service where the ark stays open the entire time; *Kol Nidre* too features an open ark—not for the entire service, but for the duration of the *Kol Nidre* chant. Yom Kippur is therefore "bookended" by an open ark: we begin it with the open ark of *Kol Nidre*; we end it with the open ark of *N'ilah*. Think also of the *tallit*, the special prayer shawl that is normally worn only in the morning—except on Yom Kippur, when we don it the night before (at *Kol Nidre*) and leave it on until the concluding service (*N'ilah*) the night following. And consider the music of *N'ilah*— bracketed by the *Kaddish* sung to uniquely individual tunes that are heard at no other time in the year.

This book properly explores the many meanings of the liturgical words. But it also unravels the deeper symbolism of which most worshipers are unaware: the way the liturgical performance is staged (the open ark), the costumes of the players (a *tallit* donned the night before and removed for *N'ilah*), and the music (the opening and closing *Kaddish* melodies).

When I describe worship as a "performance," I do not mean a concert or play performed for an inactive, albeit attentive, audience. I mean a performance in which everyone who comes has a role—like the "cultural performances" that attract anthropologists, who visit societies and cultures and watch the rituals there. Worship is a ritual, after all. If we are to understand its message, we need to see ourselves as anthropologists within our own tradition, watching ourselves play out our liturgical scripts in our own act of worship. An anthropologist well known for modeling this sort of study is Clifford Geertz (1926–2006), who calls what he does "thick description."

Geertz would attend the rituals of native peoples in such places as Bali and Morocco, not just watching what happens, but paying special attention to the symbolic use of gestures, words, and movements. "Thick description" is the process of "sorting out the structures of signification," figuring out, that is, what things *really mean* to people in the know. His example is a mock sheep raid that he studied in Morocco.

> The thing to ask about a burlesqued wink or a mock sheep raid is not what their ontological status is [not just *what they seem on the surface to be*, that is]. It is the same as that of rocks on one hand and dreams on the other—they are

things of this world. The thing to ask is what their import
is . . . *what in their occurrence and through their agency is
getting said* and why.[6]

An anthropologist observing *N'ilah* would notice the *Kaddish* melodies,
the open ark, and the "missing" *tallit*—but also the redundant imagery
of closing gates, symbolized by the ark doors that are finally closed as the
service ends—as well as the blowing of the shofar immediately afterward.

The insistence on symbolism assumes that all of this runs deeper than
it looks. But the symbolism is not necessarily overt. Sometimes even those
who know and even lead the service may not know it. It sometimes takes
the insider-outsider viewpoint of the participant-observer to point out
lessons that those who mechanically run through the service may miss.
To get at it, therefore, we have to distance ourselves from such rote participation. Like anthropologists, we must watch the drama of what we
do, looking for meaning in the "play" of the prayer-book drama the way
careful theatergoers look for lessons in a play by Shakespeare.

From 1991 to 1994, I encouraged some rabbinic students to experiment with this method. They were to become experts in one service or
another, reading it through thoroughly, again and again, and familiar-
izing themselves with the performative instructions provided by rabbinic
commentary over time. They rounded out their knowledge by reading
rabbinic traditions relevant to the prayers and to their contents. They then
imagined a properly played out performance where all the instructions
on what to do and all the hidden meanings buried in the text came alive.
They would be like omniscient observers of a play, voracious readers of the
script, who recognize such things as foreshadowing of plot, hints at major
themes, and how the staging underscored what the play was all about.

The first such experiment (1991), by Rabbi Helaine Ettinger,
focused on *N'ilah* itself.[7] Thereafter (1993), Rabbi Eleanor Smith studied
Kol Nidre and the traditional rituals that individuals go through in preparation for it.[8] Finally (1994), Rabbi Lisa Edwards looked more closely at
the latent symbolism of the shofar "service" for Rosh Hashanah.[9] Taken
together, the three studies revolutionize the way we should see the message of the High Holy Day liturgy.

Rabbi Ettinger saw *N'ilah* as the final act in a drama best described
as a "rite of passage," a term invented by a French anthropologist Arnold
van Gennep in 1909. Much of life involves moving from place to place,

job to job, and status to status, and van Gennep described such changes as a three-part transformative process: "separation" from what we were; "reincorporation" into what we are becoming; and, in between, a transition stage in which we are neither one nor the other, neither here nor there. Yom Kippur turns out to be Judaism's transformative day *par excellence*. Rabbi Ettinger has summarized her fascinating findings here, in the introductory essay that follows this one ("Closing Lines, Closing Gates: How the Yom Kippur Drama Ends").

What drew Rabbi Edwards to her subject was her discovery of rabbinic texts that compared the sound of the shofar to the cries of a woman giving birth. The various sounds (*t'ki'ah*, *sh'varim*, and *t'ru'ah*) are said to be her moaning; the final drawn-out sound—the *t'ki'ah g'dolah* ("the great *t'ki'ah*")—is her last cry as the child is born. No wonder these shofar blasts are followed by a prayer announcing *hayom harat olam*, "This is the day of the world's conception." Rosh Hashanah becomes a woman's holiday, a memory of the way the world was birthed into being. Most people associate Rosh Hashanah with the Torah reading called the *Akedah*, "the binding of Isaac," but actually, that is just the additional reading added in Babylonia when it became customary to celebrate Rosh Hashanah for two days. The original reading, and still the traditional selection for day one, is the tale of God's appearing to Sarah to announce her pregnancy; and the haftarah accompanying it is Hannah's prayer that she might bear children.

Kol Nidre, meanwhile, as Rabbi Smith discovered, is not simply the beginning of Yom Kippur; it is also the last of several preparatory acts that precede the fast, and its importance can be seen in the symbolism of all those acts taken together. Among other things, parents offer their children—even if they are already grown—an extended blessing, replete with mandatory tears, the goal being, in effect, to bid them a final farewell, in case the Yom Kippur trial turns out poorly for the parents, who would then not merit being sealed in the book of life. A set of other Jewish traditions, however, offers parents whose merit is wanting the saving grace of their innocent children, which is said to pull them through—so that the blessing is, in part, an insurance policy for the people offering it. If that is not enough, however, the parents also visit the graves of their own departed parents with the implicit hope that they (who have passed safely into the next world) may intercede with God on their behalf. In addition, traditional practice includes bathing in the *mikveh* (the ritual bath) to wash away sin and then dressing in white, the color of purity.

But ritual washing of the body accompanies our deaths as well; and the traditional white garment for Yom Kippur is a *kittel*, the "shrouds" in which we are buried. As we saw, we also wear a *tallit* from *Kol Nidre* to the beginning of *N'ilah*, and the *tallit* too is a garment used for burial. In sum, we spend the hours prior to *Kol Nidre* preparing for our death and then put on burial clothes to symbolize the fear that the Yom Kippur trial will find us guilty. We remove the burial garb only at the *N'ilah*, where the ritual is designed to return us safely back to life.

What emerges from all these studies is Rosh Hashanah as the celebration of birth, Yom Kippur as our ritualized preparation for death, and the ten days in between—the Ten Days of Repentance, as they are called—as the opportunity to review our lives: where we have come since our birth and what we still must do before we die.

All of this is possible, however, precisely because what we are describing is a ritual. We know in advance how it all ends. The gates will stay open long enough for us to pass through them into life renewed. So we arrive at *N'ilah* once again, Yom Kippur's ritual ending, and our topic in this volume.

One of the striking features of *N'ilah* is the *Kaddish* that begins and ends the service. The *Kaddish* is regularly used that way, but not with the melodies for *N'ilah*. The introductory *Kaddish* is even called "the *N'ilah Kaddish*," so striking is its melodic texture.

As the service begins, we have dispensed with our *kittel* and *tallit*. We are dressed as we normally would be for an evening service—in our street clothes, ready for a brief service before going home to dinner. But the day is not over; we are still fasting; the final moments of trial have yet to occur. The opening *Kaddish* still conveys the possibility of a dire outcome, but it does so hesitatingly, as if knowing that the service just beginning will, in the end, announce the joy of being reborn to another year of life after all. Cantor Benjie Ellen Schiller describes it this way:

> An opening phrase of any given mode in a service usually consists of a range of five steps within a scale. The notes in the opening phrase of the *N'ilah* mode span seven notes. This signature note pattern is uniquely expansive and far-reaching. The feel of these notes (upward major second followed by a leap of a minor sixth) is also unsettling, possibly foreboding, most certainly dramatic and intense.[10]

By contrast, the concluding *Kaddish* is sung in the most optimistic, joyous, and upbeat melody imaginable, as if heralding our safe passage through the long day of trial. The ark doors will close behind us, but as the new day dawns, we will not be left outside.

We return then to the image of gates opening and closing, of the ark itself, which opened wide for *Kol Nidre* the night before and is now left open for the entire final service of *N'ilah*. All the symbolism of transformation, life, and death is bound up with the visual experience of these ark doors.

Rabbi Smith's study of Yom Kippur preparations reached its most compelling point when she considered the open ark of *Kol Nidre*. Not only are the ark doors opened, the Torah scrolls are taken from them at the time, so that the ark is emptied out for the entire *Kol Nidre* chant. At no other time in the year does that occur. Technically, as it happens, the ark is referred to as the "holy ark" (*aron kodesh*); tradition actually frowns on calling it just an "ark" (*aron*) without the modifying adjective "holy" (*kodesh*), partly because the word *aron*, by itself, can also mean the "coffin" or "casket" in which we are buried. Intent on observing what Geertz called the symbolic "structures of signification"—what things really mean—Smith thought more deeply about the open ark without the scrolls within them. It is the scrolls that make the ark "holy." Remove them, and you get just an ark, just an *aron*, just a coffin. So there we are: we have blessed our children one last time and visited our deceased parents to get all the help we can muster. We are dressed in a *tallit* and shroud-like white, preparing for our death, just in case we fall short in the trial just beginning. As warning of what may come, we stare into the empty ark, the *aron*, the casket, *our* casket, a symbol of the ultimate transitional status that Yom Kippur ritualizes: our transition from life to death.

But the story is not over; it is just beginning. We reach the tale's end only at *N'ilah*, when the ark is again opened wide; for the entire service, we stare into it. The Torah scrolls are back. No longer a coffin, it is again the "holy ark." The covenant with God has been reclaimed. We are about to be forgiven. With the tentative strains of the opening *Kaddish* behind us, we anticipate the joyous sound of the *Kaddish*'s final melody. We will end the service by shouting aloud the *Sh'mot*, the affirmations of God that reestablish our place in the covenant, after which we have one more sound in store for us, the final shofar blast that ends the day— none other than the *t'ki'ah g'dolah*, the sound that announces life itself. The whole point of Yom Kippur is this rebirth into life renewed.

Closing Lines, Closing Gates

HOW THE YOM KIPPUR DRAMA ENDS

Rabbi Helaine Ettinger

N'ilah is a ritual, a form of art that expresses what cannot be conveyed in words alone. But *N'ilah* is not just any ritual. As the concluding moments of the long Yom Kippur fast, it elevates our deepest yearnings and confronts our greatest fears through the medium of sacred drama.

All worship is such drama, replete with a prayer-book script, staging, props, costumes, and players. The sacred drama of the High Holy Days is just one example, but it is the most elaborate example of the entire year. Familiar worshipers know the script (*Kol Nidre, Avinu Malkeinu,* the confessions, and so forth) as well as the score (the traditional High Holy Day

---

Rabbi Helaine Ettinger earned her B.A in English Literature from Princeton University, her rabbinic ordination from HUC-JIR in 1991 and her Masters in Jewish Education from HUC-JIR in 2017. In her rabbinate she has served in small congregations in New Jersey and Pennsylvania as well as serving as the Synagogue Outreach Coordinator for the MetroWest Jewish Health and Healing Center. She currently serves as the rabbi of Philipstown Reform Synagogue in Cold Spring, NY. Her work has been published in *The Women's Torah Commentary, The Women's Haftarah Commentary* both published by Jewish Lights, and she has a chapter about *Ne'ilah* as a rite of passage in Lawrence A. Hoffman's next book in the "Prayers of Awe" series. She has taught the Melton Adult Mini-Course in its regular format, in a pilot format for parents of younger children and in a graduate class. She is a Past President of the Women's Rabbinic Network.

melodies and the distinctive sound of the chant—the *nusach*). Costumes include the *tallit* (worn all day long on Yom Kippur, and even the night before) and *kittel*, the white linen tunic reminiscent of the shrouds in which we are buried. For staging, the congregation variously rises, sits, bows, and manipulates sacred props: the shofar, the scrolls of Torah, and even the doors of the ark, reminiscent of gates that open or close. And the drama is played out against the natural backdrop of autumn twilight, as reflected in the room we call a sanctuary, the place where God is assumed to dwell, as if even God is a player in the drama, waiting to make an appearance at key moments along the way.

N'ilah is the culmination of this sacred drama. Its very name, according to the Mishnah (Ta'anit 4:1), alludes to finality: *n'ilat sh'arim*, "the locking of the gates," either the Temple's gates or heaven's gates, the Talmud adds (Jerusalem Talmud, Ta'anit 7c), but either way, the marking of something momentous that cannot be undone. At stake is nothing less than human transformation, as if we hope, somehow, to pass through the gates before they close in order to come out the other side into life renewed.

Way back in 1909, the French anthropologist Arnold van Gennep (1873–1957) saw the importance of such rituals of renewal, calling them *rites de passage* ("rites of passage"), the ritualized transitions we all make from one stage of life to another. He had probably never even heard of *N'ilah*, but Yom Kippur in its entirety, including this final service, is the Jewish People's classic example of the ritual van Gennep described.

He isolated three distinct stages to these rites of passage: *separation* from what we were before; *reincorporation* into whatever we are slated to become; and, in between, the state of being separate from both—no longer what we were, but not yet what we will be. The middle stage is the most interesting. It is like standing in a doorway, looking back at the room from which we have emerged but not yet in the room to which the doorway opens up. From the Latin *limen*, "doorway," van Gennep called the middle, or transitional, stage "liminal."

Rites of passage allow individuals or groups to move successfully from one defined position in society to another. They thus surround any major life event that changes a person's status: pledging a sorority or fraternity, attaining political office, or graduating college, but also birth, marriage, pregnancy, and death itself. The three rite-of-passage stages are not always equally emphasized. Funerals highlight separation; marriages accentuate incorporation; pregnancy stresses transition.

The image of the doorway is especially apt for *N'ilah*, Judaism's rite of passage from the old year to the new one. Think again of standing in a doorway, this time at a job interview, transitioning from the waiting room to the potential employer's office (and, we hope, from candidate to new hire): we pause in the doorway to survey the larger office and wonder about where this moment may lead—will they offer me the job, and do I want to work here? So too in life itself: only rarely and with difficulty do we move directly from one stage to another. We prefer time to pause and take stock before leaving one status behind and before moving on to another.

Yom Kippur is the Jewish People's time par excellence for taking stock. At *Kol Nidre* (stage 1: separation) we separate from the former year, and even from our former selves, as we undertake the voyage into the new and better person we hope to be. The rest of Yom Kippur (stage 2: transition, liminality) perches us betwixt and between, awaiting whatever it is that we will become. *N'ilah* (stage 3: reincorporation) launches us on our way back to life, life renewed. Its final shofar blast announces the return to routine, which is symbolically represented by the regular, ordinary, weekday *Ma'ariv* (evening) service immediately following *N'ilah*. The closing gates are the metaphoric threshold where we pause one last time before moving on.

Van Gennep's insights were deepened by those of others, particularly anthropologist Victor Turner (1920–1983), who was fascinated by the liminal, or transitional, stage particularly. He noticed that people in that stage are often stripped of any distinguishing personal characteristics so as to eliminate any distinctions of rank or status—they all dress the same, for example. Also, their behavior is typically humble to the point where they are expected to be self-effacing, even self-denying, while obeying their superiors without question. So too, on Yom Kippur, the traditional dress for all adult males (and females in some settings) is the same white *kittel* and *tallit*; and our behavior then is decidedly humble and passive: although no human authority instructs us in how to behave, we do have a heavenly figure whom we obey absolutely, as we spend the day in penitential prayer and self-denial—we do not eat, drink, wash, or engage in sexual relations.

In sum, over the course of this one dedicated day, we act as if we are physically and spiritually not just passive, but dead. The pure white *kittel* suggests our burial shroud, as does the *tallit*, another burial garment, which is worn at *Kol Nidre* and all the next day, even though we usually wear it only for morning services. Like the dead, we have no need to sustain ourselves with food or drink or to seek satisfaction through sexual relations. With abstinence, too, we forgo even the possibility of creating new life. We return to our most basic state by not washing—dust to dust. Traditionally speaking, we also avoid leather shoes on Yom Kippur, for the dead need not worry about mobility. And we avoid bodily anointing, again a sign of treating our bodies as if they are already dead and buried. In addition, the act of anointing is normally a way of conferring status on an individual. In death, all are equal.

Liturgy, as well, plays a role in homogenizing our status and de-emphasizing our individuality. The confessions that we recite all day are written in the first-person plural, making them anything but private and personal. They anticipate, as well, the confession we will say on our deathbeds as we prepare to pass from this world to the next. By analogy, the Yom Kippur confessions too raise the specter of passing to what might be our death if we are not pardoned. Yet despite all this existential uncertainty, we know in advance how this Yom Kippur drama will end: we dare to hope that this year, like the last, we will indeed be pardoned, in which case confession moves us not to the grave but to a new self. "Our rabbis, of blessed memory, said that the Holy Blessed One makes new creatures of those who repent, so their words of confession are the cause of a powerful and great act of creation."[1]

This fundamental sense of insignificance characteristic of liminality builds to a climax at *N'ilah*. On the one hand, the long confession, *Al Chet*, is curiously absent from *N'ilah*, as if to say that we are finally coming out of our liminal state and preparing to enter the new life that awaits us in the year following. On the other hand, the prayer that takes its place ("You [God] extend your hand") emphasizes the utter worthlessness of life, as if the message of Yom Kippur has finally come home in all its severity.

> What are we? What are our lives? What is our love? What is our righteousness? What is our salvation? What is our strength? What is our might? What can we say before You, Adonai our God and our ancestors' God? Are not all mighty ones as though they were nothing before You, men of fame as though they never existed, the educated as though without knowledge, and the wise as though without insight, for most of their acts are without value and the

days of their life worthless before You? Man barely rises
above beast, for everything is worthless.

And the paragraph following the short confession (*Ashamnu*) that we do
include at *N'ilah* makes the connection between confession, death, and
re-creation:

My God, before I was formed I was of no worth, and now
that I have been formed it is as if I had not been formed.
Dust I am in life, and all the more so in death. In your
sight, I am like an object filled with shame and disgrace.
May it be your will, Adonai my God and God of my ancestors, that I sin no more.

N'ilah concludes what *Kol Nidre* began the night before began. As the first
stage in the rite of passage ("separation"), the *Kol Nidre* service initiates
our transformation to a deathlike state. The service begins at dusk, itself
a transitional time of day. We wear a *tallit* on top of our *kittel*, as though
preparing for burial. And then comes *Kol Nidre* itself, a formula that
invalidates all oaths, pledges, and promises of the past year, as if to cut off
all social contracts that make us human. The introductory paragraph, "By
the authority of the heavenly court . . ." (*Biy'shivah shel ma'alah*), pictures
us on trial before a heavenly tribunal, as if all our promises, to people and
to God, are under review.

No promise is more important to the Jews than the covenant made
at Mount Sinai, the pact that gives Israel its identity, and without which
Israel is just like any other nation. By canceling all our social contracts,
even, possibly, our promise to God, we face the frightening possibility
that everything we counted on is now null and void. We are, as it were,
"nobody," stripped of all uniqueness, both as individuals and as Jews.
The liminal state is upon us.

The moment is so fraught with significance that we actually act it
out as if the heavenly court were in session. One person invokes the court
and chants *Kol Nidre* while the Torah scrolls, which have been removed
from the ark, are held by at least two others standing alongside, forming a
bet din (a "rabbinic court") of three individuals. The ark remains open—
and empty—as worshipers are left to contemplate the unoccupied places
where the scrolls usually stand: there, in starkly visible form, is the implicit
symbolism of God's withdrawal and the suspension of the covenant.

When *Kol Nidre* ends, the Torah scrolls are returned to the ark and the *bet din* is dissolved. But the verdict awaits *N'ilah* the following evening, so until then, we remain fully immersed in the liminal space, suspended between life and death.

Only with *N'ilah* is the covenant renewed; only then do we end our liminal waiting and transition back from death to life. This service also takes place at dusk; again we face the open ark, which is generally left open throughout the service. Now, however, the Torah scrolls are back in place. As *Kol Nidre* introduces us to the liminal, deathlike state of Yom Kippur day, so *N'ilah* reintroduces us to normality.

As in all rites of passage, safe passage is guaranteed from the start. A rite, after all, is designed to carry us through difficult transitions, precisely to avoid the possibility of failure. As van Gennep himself put it, "Life . . . means to separate and to be reunited, to change form and condition, to die and to be reborn. It is to act and to cease, to wait and to rest, and then to begin acting again, but in a different way. And there are always new thresholds to cross."[2]

So too, the gates close every year at *N'ilah*, but there is always another year in store for us. Every *N'ilah* we make our last pleas for forgiveness, and every year we meet with divine reassurance. Every *N'ilah* as the sun sets, we find the Torah scrolls securely positioned inside the ark, and every *N'ilah*, as well, the last sound we hear, even after the final verses that we shout aloud, is the shofar, announcing our exultation at having come through another Yom Kippur whole and renewed.

◦⟊⟊◦

God's Plea

A WORDLESS GESTURE AND A STILL SMALL VOICE

Rabbi Margaret Moers Wenig, DD

The gates of prayer do not close with the final shofar blast, nor do the gates of repentance or the gates of forgiveness. *N'ilah* marks only the "closing of the gates of heaven," meaning nighttime, when God figuratively closes the shutters on the light of day[1] and that in ancient times coincided with the literal closing of the gates of the Temple. The *N'ilah* service does not even conclude prayer. Immediately following it, many Jews pray *Ma'ariv*, the evening service, including this blessing recited every weekday throughout the year: "Forgive us, *avinu*, for we have sinned; pardon us, *malkeinu*, for we have transgressed; for You do pardon and forgive."

If our *t'shuvah* isn't complete by the end of *N'ilah*, we will not be struck by a divinely flung bolt of lightning. There is no divine deadline. There are only the deadlines human relationships and responsibilities impose upon us. And because there are consequences to our hurtful acts and words, there are good reasons to do *t'shuvah* in a timely fashion and not put it off. That urgency applies year-round, however, not only on Yom Kippur or by its close.

Rabbi Margaret Moers Wenig, DD, teaches liturgy and homiletics at Hebrew Union College–Jewish Institute of Religion (New York) and is rabbi emerita of Beth Am, The People's Temple in Washington Heights, Manhattan. Her longtime liturgical passion has been the prayers and music for the High Holy Days, and she has contributed to all the volumes of Prayers of Awe, the series on the High Holy Days that this volume, *N'ilah*, concludes.

God, who, we say, "neither slumbers nor sleeps," does not shut off the ringer on the divine cell phone following *N'ilah* and send our subsequent confessions and petitions to a voice-mail box black hole. God, we say, will "wait for us until the day of our death"[2] to turn from our harmful ways. So what changes when we leave the synagogue at the close of Yom Kippur? The busyness of life rushes in upon us once again: eating, washing, commuting, working, vacuuming, typing . . . once again our time is consumed with messages, meetings, news reports, laundry, and bills . . . and the full day of prayer, contemplation, listening, learning, physical rest, and emotional release afforded us by Yom Kippur comes to an end.

And perhaps, it is hoped, we change too, not from our desperate attempt to meet a deadline, but from the service's reassurance, profound and repeated, that the God we imagine prefers to forgive than to punish, prefers that we depart from our harmful ways rather than continue them, that we relinquish violence rather than perpetuate it.

The musical mode of *N'ilah* is distinctive, as are the service's *piyyutim* (liturgical poetry). Then, too, there are the final dramatic professions of faith (see liturgy, p. 174), the cathartic rhythms of the Hasidic *Kaddish* and the longest shofar blast of the High Holy Day season. There's drama too in subtler moments, especially the appearance of *Atah Noten Yad* ("You Extend Your Hand") and *Atah Hivdalta Enosh* ("You Set Humans Apart") in place of yet another *Al Chet*, the long confession that Yom Kippur services normally feature there. Rather than one more plea to God to forgive our long litany of sins, this time we imagine God reaching out a hand toward us and pleading with us.

God has no body, we say, but at times we allow ourselves to imagine God in physical terms—God's face, eyes, ears, voice, wings, and especially hands: "God brought Israel out of Egypt with a strong hand" (Psalm 136); "God holds the scales of justice in a divine hand";[3] "You open your hand and satisfy all the living" (Psalm 145); "Into your hand I entrust my spirit";[4] "Like clay in the hand of the potter . . . so are we in your hand."[5] Yet only in *N'ilah* do we picture God "extending a hand" to us, to the worst among us, to us at our worst, when we question our very worth:[6] "What are we?" we ask. "What are our lives? What is our love? What is our righteousness? What is our salvation? What is our strength? What is our might? What can we say before You? . . . Everything is worthless."[7]

Here in *N'ilah*, we imagine God not atop Mount Sinai amidst thunder and lightning, instructing the Israelites to stand far off; not as the creator, arranging the stars in the sky; not with a voice resounding above the crash of mighty waves; not as a king sitting on a throne or robed in light; but as a compassionate judge who sets down the ledger book, closes the depositions, removes the robe, steps down from the raised platform, approaches the one who has confessed, and extends a hand—simply holds out a hand. Though we may sometimes feel our life is for naught, God considers us worthy—and who are we to question God?

In this scene painted for us in *Atah Hivdalta Enosh* ("You Set Humans Apart"), a dialogue of sorts ensues between us and God:

We plead: "In your great mercy, have mercy upon us. . . ."

Then we imagine God beginning to stammer, to repeat again and again, to vow, to urge, to insist, and to plead: "As I live, do I desire the death of the wicked, or the return of the wicked from their ways that they live? Return, return from your evil ways. . . . Do I desire the death of the wicked? . . . I do not desire anyone's death, so return and live."

It is as if God is mirroring our very own prayer, uttered first on Rosh Hashanah in *Un'taneh Tokef*, when *we* said *to God*, "You will not desire / may you not desire the death of the wicked, but that we return from our ways and live." (Verbs in the imperfect tense, such as these, can convey either mood.) Now, in *N'ilah*, it is as if *God* is saying *to us*, "I've heard your petitions. Of course I don't desire the wicked to be punished with death! Now, you hear my petition: Don't suffocate your soul with sin. Don't murder your moral spirit. Please don't remain stuck in your stultifying ways. Please . . . here's my hand, take it. I'll help you cross over to the other side. The crossing is terrifying, but you don't have to make it alone. You need not spend your days incarcerated, isolated in a cell of shame. Here's my hand; take it, that I may lead you from your destructive ways into a life of meaning."

⟨✤⟩

PART II
The Halakhah
of *N'ilah*

The Custom of Standing Before *N'ilah*'s Open Ark

Rabbi Daniel Nevins

The custom of leaving the holy ark open for certain prayers is associated with moments of intensified petition. For example, on Sukkot, throughout the congregational prayers for "rescue" or "deliverance" (the *Hoshanot*), the ark is kept open. The idea goes back to the days when our farmer ancestors worried that their crops might be imperiled by drought, blight, or infestation. Sukkot came at the end of the autumn, and the spring crop, just being planted, depended on receiving proper rainfall during the winter months following. Looking ahead to the winter, with so much at stake, they opened the ark, circled the room, and implored God for salvation.

Likewise during *N'ilah*, at the end of Ten Days of Repentance, we worry that all we have done has not been enough, that we have failed to be inscribed in the book of life. Before the ink dries, as it were, and the books are sealed, we petition God to remember our merits one more time. The open ark reminds us that the final hours are upon us, that

---

Rabbi Daniel Nevins is the Pearl Resnick Dean of the Jewish Theological Seminary Rabbinical School and dean of the JTS Division of Religious Leadership. Upon his ordination by JTS, he served as rabbi of Adat Shalom Synagogue in Farmington Hills, Michigan, for thirteen years before returning to work at JTS. Rabbi Nevins is a scholar of contemporary Jewish law and a member of the Rabbinical Assembly's Committee on Jewish Law and Standards. He has written responsa on varied topics from bioethics to sexuality, disability, and technology. These and other of his writings may be found at www.rabbinevins.com.

the hour at hand remains propitious nonetheless, and that we should summon up the strength for a final surge of yearning to return to God's good graces.

But how old is the custom of keeping the ark open for the entire *N'ilah* service?

That is hard to say for sure, but already in the fourteenth to fifteenth centuries, German Jewish sources attest to the practice of doing so, while the congregation remains standing. Rabbi Isaac Tyrnau (fourteenth-century Austria) writes in *Sefer Haminhagim*, his book of Jewish customs, "We open the ark for the entire *N'ilah* service until the end of the *Kaddish*." Rabbi Joseph ben Moses (1423–c. 1490) dedicated his book *Leket Yosher* to the life and teachings of his teacher Rabbi Israel Isserlein (1390–1460), perhaps the leading Ashkenazi authority of the fifteenth century. He reports that the sage would hurry through *N'ilah*, perhaps because the ark was open and the congregation was standing for the entire service.

But why did this custom develop?

That too is uncertain. Most halakhic sources do not discuss it directly. Rather, they assume the ark is open at *N'ilah* and focus on the concern that the priests who ascend to bless the people during the service will necessarily have their backs to the open ark. This is considered a possible offense to the dignity of the Torah. True, the ark is usually closed when the priests offer their blessings, but on *N'ilah* it is open. Wanting neither to forbid the blessing nor to close the ark, they find precedent for the status quo. After all, in the Talmud (Sotah 40a), Rabbi Yitzchak says that a person should always revere the community, giving as proof the fact that the priests stand facing the congregation, with their backs to the divine presence (symbolized by the ark).

Still, the rabbis ultimately view the custom of standing for the open ark to be just that—a good custom, not a requirement, a surprisingly lenient view based on the commentary of the Ukrainian rabbi David ben Samuel Halevi (1586–1667), the *Turei Zahav* (or Taz) to *Shulchan Arukh, Yoreh De'ah* 242:13. In his responsa known as *Igrot Moshe* to *Orach Chayim* (vol. 5, no. 38), the twentieth-century Rabbi Moshe Feinstein (1895–1986) reiterates this view that standing for the open ark is a good custom, but not an obligation. Contemporary clergy often remind the congregants that if they are feeling faint, they should not hesitate to sit down, even with the ark open, since matters of health take priority over most other religious concerns. Still, in traditional synagogues anyway, most people attempt to stand, not only out of respect for the open ark but also from the desire to demonstrate the sincerity of their devotion.

As we have seen, then, our halakhic sources attest to the medieval origins of this custom of standing for *N'ilah*, but they do not provide an explicit rationale. Still, we can surmise what the answer must be. Surely this prayer at the end of the holiest day of the year acquired a sense of the great urgency entailed in submitting one final petition before the day's end. We instinctively stand at attention when something dramatic is occurring, and what could be more dramatic than our petition that God "open a gate for us when the gate is locked"!

In recent years, many congregations have encouraged worshipers to leave their place in the congregation and stand in front of the open ark with their personal petitions, even as the service continues as if they were not there. While the *chazzan* offers prayers for the community as a whole, individuals present God with their own requests and problems. Quite obviously, we intuit that something special is possible at the end of the day of Yom Kippur. Just as the third Shabbat meal is considered to be the moment when the divine presence is most accessible, so too the grand finale of Yom Kippur, the *N'ilah* service itself, invites our special attention. This is the time to seal the deal, so to speak—and so we stand. Similarly, when Yom Kippur falls on a Saturday, we leave out the recitation of *Avinu Malkeinu*, except at *N'ilah*. The sky has darkened, and the prayers have been said, but we open the ark for one last extended time as we stand, sway, and sing, asking that God regard us as beloved children once again.

After twenty-five hours of fasting and prayer, the open ark with its white-clad Torah scrolls standing upright inspires the congregation to stand a little taller, to pray a little harder, and to release whatever hesitations may have restrained their prayer until now. The gates are closing, but there is still time to pray—the waning hours of the day are the most poignant and powerful time to return. We hurry even while we tarry—allowing the tension to mount until the great moment of release when the shofar blast signals the gift of divine atonement and a fresh start to our lives.

◌⟆⟒⟆◌

Goodbye Yom Kippur, Hello Sukkot!

Rabbi Asher Lopatin

How do we bring the intensity of Yom Kippur to fruition without squandering its spiritual and moral momentum? *N'ilah* ends with such emotional passion, after all: its final affirmations shouted aloud—"Adonai is God!" "Hear, O Israel," and for many, "Next year in Jerusalem" as well—not to mention the shofar blast following. Some services even break out in dancing. And then what? How do we go from the high of *N'ilah* to the practical business of living the way God wants for the rest of the year?

Not surprisingly, the halakhic sources tell us. Particularly helpful are the *Tur* of Jacob ben Asher (1269–1340), the comments of the R'ma (Moses Isserles, 1520–1572), and the more contemporary *Arukh Hashulchan* (Yechiel Michel Epstein, 1869–1908). These sources draw on earlier midrashim to verses from Genesis, Psalms, and Ecclesiastes and reflect two opposite approaches to the problem. The first is: We've spent twenty-four hours praying, repenting, and fasting. Now, let's eat! The second cautions us not to deflate our spiritual balloons so quickly. Rather, we should build on the power of Yom Kippur, going, as it were, from strength to strength. Both approaches are mandated in the halakhic sources, and as frequently happens, the codes find a way of having us fulfill them both.

Rabbi Asher Lopatin has ordination from Rabbi Aaron Soloveichik and Yeshiva University and received his MPhil from Oxford University on a Rhodes Scholarship. He serves as president of the Modern Orthodox Yeshivat Chovevei Torah Rabbinical School, after having served as rabbi of Anshe Sholom B'nai Israel in Chicago for eighteen years. He and his wife, Rachel, are both Wexner Graduate Fellows and have four children.

We may think that the rush to a break-fast meal is just modern "bourgeoisification," but the idea that we may immediately eat and celebrate goes very deep in Jewish sources. The key verse here is Ecclesiastes 9:7: "Go, eat your bread in gladness, drink your wine in joy, because God has already accepted your deeds." The midrash to this verse believes these words emanate from a heavenly voice (a *bat kol*) whenever children leave their studies or adult Jews leave their synagogues and study halls.[1] Eventually, however, the verse and its midrashic lesson were seen particularly as applying to the end of Yom Kippur, and the *Tur* cites it that way.[2]

Of course we should celebrate—all is forgiven, after all! It might even be akin to the relief that the high priest felt when he made it out alive from his confession in the ancient Temple's Holy of Holies.

The R'ma quotes the *Tur*, as does the *Arukh Hashulchan*, whose author, incidentally, an actual rabbi in Lithuania, was not just an ivory-tower scholar; we shall see that he sympathized with the people's need to really celebrate as soon as Yom Kippur was over.

Yet the R'ma adds another custom, based on a *Zohar* interpretation of Genesis 33:16–17, when Jacob and Esau hugged and kissed after twenty years of enmity.[3] Their reconciliation implies that they had both repented for their respective sins: Jacob, for stealing Esau's blessing; and Esau, for wanting to kill Jacob. When they parted, however, the Torah says, "On that day Esau went back along his way to Seir, while Jacob moved on to Sukkot" (Genesis 33:16–17), a seemingly innocuous conclusion to which the *Zohar* accords great significance. "That day" was interpreted to mean Yom Kippur; and "Sukkot" is taken to be not just a place name, as it is in the Bible, but the *sukkot*—the flimsy booth-like structures—that we build for the festival of that name. Esau, representing the materiality of our superficial world, the anger and unrestrained passions from which we strive to extract ourselves on Yom Kippur, went back not just along the path to Seir, but, literally, "along his way," meaning "he returned to his old ways." By contrast, Jacob did not backtrack from his Yom Kippur atonement. Rather, he moved on and actually built *sukkot*, dwelling places for the new nation of Israel that he was creating.

The great Ashkenazi rabbi Jacob Halevi Moellin (the Maharil, 1365–1427) had drawn on this Zoharic interpretation to say, in effect, "Don't rest on your laurels after Yom Kippur! Be happy, eat, and rejoice, but keep moving on." The R'ma, following the Maharil, writes,

"Immediately after Yom Kippur, those who are scrupulous begin build-ing the sukkah, in order to go from *mitzvah* to *mitzvah*."[4] Like Jacob, we do not halt our journey toward living a more godly life just because Yom Kippur is over. We make a point of continuing that journey by imme-diately commencing the next *mitzvah*, building our sukkah for Sukkot.

The *Arukh Hashulchan* makes the case more compelling. Not only are we meant to go from *mitzvah* to *mitzvah*, but as Psalm 84:8 puts it, we thereby "go from strength to strength" (*meichayil el chayil*). Yom Kippur repentance is an accomplishment whose "strength" is not to be demonstrated by merely sitting back and eating when *N'ilah* ends. Only by attending to the next great *mitzvah*, building the sukkah, can we demonstrate how "strong" we really are: not exhausted by Yom Kippur, but strengthened by it to take on the next task! The Hebrew *meichayil el chayil* evokes the metaphor of a soldier (*chayal*). Living the righteous life is equivalent to being at war with the forces of evil! We leave Yom Kippur committed never to rest from the ongoing fight to be better people, to be closer to God, to be the moral human beings we were meant to be.

And yet, as we are ready to jump from a powerful *N'ilah* service right into the hammer and nails of building a sukkah, the smell of freshly cooked food pulls us in the direction of eating rather than struggling with hammer and nails in the dark. Moreover, if *N'ilah* really moved us, as it should, we may wish to linger on the experience a bit, to discuss what inspired us, perhaps, or to recommit ourselves to the people we love, over our break-fast meal—not just move immediately to the task of banging together the pipes and boards that compose our sukkah.

The *Arukh Hashulchan* helps us do both. Whereas the R'ma had implicitly recommended that we too should act like "the scrupulous" who "begin immediately to *build the sukkah*" (*b'asiyat hasukkah*), *Arukh Hashulchan* interprets the R'ma to say only that we ought to "make *some preparations for the sukkah*" (*la'asot hakhanat hasukkah*)—and that can be done, he says, by studying Tractate Sukkah or even just some laws of Sukkot, presumably from some other more accessible source. Yes, there should be some Sukkot element in our lives right after Yom Kippur, but these need not detract unduly from the celebratory meal following.

Arukh Hashulchan actually goes so far as to postpone the *mitzvah* of building to the next day—only then do we go "from *mitzvah* to *mitz-vah*"—not the night before, which is devoted to celebrating our accom-plishments and making sure we are ready to jump to the next *mitzvah* and go "from strength to strength." In a sense, the *Arukh Hashulchan* asks us to test our spiritual muscles as we coast with joy down the mountain of Yom Kippur ("Trucks: test brakes!") rather than to leap to the next thing without fully taking in the enormity of the day just ended.

So we complete *N'ilah* by properly appreciating what we have accomplished on Yom Kippur. As we eat and drink once again, we may spend the evening thinking through the highs of the day, the miracle of repentance, and our commitment to transform ourselves. Only then do we find the confidence to do more, to go from the "strength" of the *mitzvot* of Yom Kippur to the "strength" of other *mitzvot* too, starting with the sukkah.

Like Jacob, that is, we "move on to Sukkot," but rather than leaving Esau to return to his old ways, we might consider inviting all our brothers and sisters in the world, the Esaus as well, to join us in the *sukkot* we construct, the lives we hope to lead, and the task of walking together with all humanity to the world we dreamed about on Yom Kippur.

Part III

Opening
Meditations

As *N'ilah* Begins

"We Barely Rise above Beast, for Everything Is Worthless," but "You Can Because You Must"

Rabbi Walter Homolka, PhD, PhD, DHL

Immanuel Kant's "Ethics of Obligation" culminates in a most optimistic view of human nature: "You can because you must," by which he means that since we are obligated ethically, we must also have within us the capacity to act upon our ethical impulses. Similar rigor applies when Judaism singles out humankind to participate in God's creation and bring it to perfection. Yom Kippur makes this its central message; yet it also declares us to be existentially dependent on God's undeserved

Rabbi Walter Homolka, PhD, PhD, DHL, is full professor of modern Jewish thought and executive director of the School of Jewish Theology at the University of Potsdam. The rector of the Abraham Geiger College, Germany's Reform rabbinical school, Walter Homolka is also chairman of the Leo Baeck Foundation and of the Ernst Ludwig Ehrlich Scholarship Foundation. In addition, in 2013, he became executive director of the Zacharias Frankel College Potsdam (Masorti). In 2017, the congregations of the Union of Progressive Jews in Germany elected him president. Rabbi Homolka is a member of the French Legion of Honor, an officer of the German Federal Merit Order, and a Knight Commander of Austria. In 2018 he edited with Aaron Panken *Engaging Torah—Modern Perspectives on the Hebrew Bible* (HUC Press).

grace and forgiveness, thereby confronting us with our utter insignificance. This dichotomy between "little lower than angels" (the rest of the year) and "just dust and ashes" (during the Days of Awe) differentiates Judaism from Protestant Christianity. Jews see ourselves as dependent on God but *nonetheless* part of the healing process of the world. Martin Luther, by contrast, thought it ultimate vanity to imagine that human endeavor can ever be justified by the good it achieves.

That difference is highlighted particularly now—sixty years after Rabbi Leo Baeck's death (1956) and five hundred years since Martin Luther is said to have tacked his ninety-five theses onto the door of the Wittenberg Schlosskirche (1517). How did Baeck's approach differ from this Protestant doctrine?

As a leading liberal rabbi living a good part of his life in Berlin, Baeck had a lifelong relationship to the Jewish-Christian dialogue. His celebrated masterpiece *The Essence of Judaism* (1905) was written as a refutation of a similarly named book, *The Essence of Christianity* (1900), by Lutheran theologian Adolf von Harnack, who had portrayed Judaism as an irrelevant cult of outmoded ritual and law. Then in 1922, Baeck continued his response with his essay "Romantic Religion," which is his description of Christianity, as opposed to Judaism, which he called "classic." Classic religion is active, intent on changing the world. Romantic religion is passive, dependent on divine grace.

Judaism stands out, therefore, as the religion of the prophets, whose mandate to better the world remains central. The church, by contrast, lacked the dynamic nature and forward-looking impatience that is embodied in Judaism. It became characterized by passivity and an immobile self-centered sense of salvation.

Baeck continually contrasts the active ethical monotheism of Judaism with the passive mysticism of grace in Christianity—two different types of religious experience. The one, "classic," is positive, outgoing, spontaneous, ethical, social, action-oriented, and rational. The other, "romantic," is passive, receptive, individualistic, self-centered, inward, concerned with faith, rooted in "feeling," and emphasizing grace. Of course, such pure types only exist in abstraction, but Baeck saw Judaism as coming closest to the classic type and Christianity as the most conspicuous example of the romantic alternative. "In classic religion," Baeck says, "man is to be freed by the commandment, in romantic religion he has become free through grace."

Baeck associates "romantic" with "mystery," and "classic" with "commandment." In "mystery," the individual is shown the deeper reality that is hidden below life's surface. While "mystery" thus raises the question of life's meaning, "commandment" raises the question of its goal. Judaism exists in the tension between the two.

Christianity, however, sheds "commandment" and is left only with "mystery"; rather than the commanding laws of God, it relies on the anticipated gift of God's grace. Luther accepted this sharp dichotomy. In the certainty of salvation, Luther seemed to deny any value to work and human action; everything was reduced to dependence on grace and faith.

In Baeck's view, the experience of "mystery" and faith is what gave birth to religion in the first place, but it alone does not make up religion, just as birth does not constitute the entirety of life. Human life, Baeck insists, requires individual moral action informed by the duty of shaping a better world. As Kant had said, "You can because you must." For Baeck, salvation through moral behavior is humanity's most glorious and optimistic possibility.

One may ask, though, Where is this moment of mystery in Judaism? To be sure, Baeck assumed it, but I see it better described by Moses Hayyim Luzzatto's *M'silat Y'sharim* (*The Path of the Upright*, 1740). It is the very striving for righteousness that serves as the path to encounter holiness:

> Holiness is of a twofold nature; it begins as a quality of the service rendered to God, but it ends as a reward for such service. . . . But since it is impossible for human beings to attain this status through their own efforts—for we are, after all, only physical beings, mere flesh and blood—holiness has to be finally granted to us as a gift. The best that one can do is to strive to attain true knowledge, and to be assiduous in the study of what may sanctify our actions. But, in the last resort, it is the Holy One, blessed be He, who leads us in the path He has chosen, and who imparts to us some of His own holiness, thereby rendering us holy. It is only then that we succeed in being in continual communion with God, blessed be He; for whenever nature might deter us, God comes to our help and grants us His aid.

In endeavoring to become holy, we inevitably realize the enormity of the human task of "commandment." Just then, however, the mystery occurs, as we experience God lifting us up to sanctify us.

N'ilah is that most intimate moment when "mystery" takes over from "commandment." It is the moment when we Jews can step back from our workbench and take time off from the rigorous demands being made by commandment. At *N'ilah*, we face our imperfection and take refuge in the ultimate insight: we "barely rise above beast, for everything is worthless." Imperfection, we see, is ingrained in the human condition. In our striving after holiness, but realizing we cannot fully attain it by ourselves, *N'ilah* reveals the soothing message that God comes to our aid, imparting divine holiness to us, that we may eventually complete the work of creation.

༄

The Case of the Inverted Birdcage

Rabbi Karyn Kedar

What are we? What are our lives? What is our love? What is our righteousness? What is our salvation? What is our strength? What is our might? What can we say before You, Adonai our God . . . ?

On my writing desk sits a candleholder, kind of an inverted birdcage, delicate metal bars, golden on the inside, burnished on the outside, no more than eight inches high. When the candle is lit, a shadow is cast upon the wall, the bars of the cage are elongated, stretching as the flame moves to and fro. Especially during the early dawn, there is a dance. The light dances and the shadows flicker . . . it is quite alive, this interplay of darkness and light.

Quite alive.

Within every caged-up, closed-off, locked-down, remote, and hidden soul burns a light, I suppose. An animated play of good and not so

Rabbi Karyn D. Kedar is an author, poet, spiritual counselor, inspirational speaker, and the senior rabbi at Congregation BJBE. Her published books include *God Whispers, The Dance of the Dolphin (Our Dance with God)*, *The Bridge to Forgiveness*, and *Omer: A Counting*. She is also published in numerous anthologies and has created liturgy, rituals, and ceremonies. Rabbi Kedar teaches courses and designs retreats on finding meaning and purpose in our busy lives, creating a prayerful and intentional life, spiritual awakening, forgiveness, and intentional leadership. She offers workshops in engagement, vision, and creating the synagogue for the 21st century. A meaningful and purposeful life, is revealed by vision and imagination, the persistent pursuit of light and the practice of kindness. She and her husband, Ezra, are the proud parents of Talia, Moti, Shiri, and Ilan and grandparents of Lihi, Maya, and Eliya, all who live in Israel.

good. Of well-intentioned and unaware. Of moral courage and of fear. Our lives flicker, dance upon a backdrop of circumstance, of personal story, of challenge, of defiance, of despair. Good days and bad days make up a life, my daughter reminded me—a phrase I would say when she was a young girl filled with the angst that accompanies life.

How consequential is this invitation to consider and to contemplate? On Yom Kippur we are invited to enter into the holy of holies of our complexities. *What are we?!* Our souls are so complex, a mysterious gnarl of purity and not. We are vulnerable, bare, pondering, wondering, sometimes confused. We are often sad that our humanity has kept us from living our highest good.

What are our lives? we ask out loud to the God of eternity, to the God of mortality. Shall I live another year? Shall I die?

What is our love? Open the gates of righteousness, that I might enter. Open. Open. Love and righteousness are found in the outer orbs of self-obsession. It is the very meaning of a purposeful life: one who stretches beyond the boundaries of self and interacts with the world, with others, and with God's creation, anchored by compassion.

What are we? What are our lives? What is our love? What is our righteousness? The law of kindness. To touch the shoulder of another and ease their pain; to work for a just society; to give away time, money, and kindness, for they are the abundant natural resource of an open heart.

Open the gates of righteousness, that I might enter. Open. Open. I fear that I may be left out of a life well lived.

Nothing is permanent; nothing stays the same. Amidst the blessings of my life there is so much loss. The book of life opens and it closes. Some people have vanished quickly to a sudden death and some to old age. And some people just drift away. Relationships change because of indifference, or infidelity, or distraction. Or just because it's like that sometimes. I just know that I stand before the gate empty, vulnerable, wondering, and in supplication . . .

What is our salvation? What is our strength? Is loneliness my destiny? Must I tarry in my inadequacies? In this moment I begin to see the truth of myself. I turn away. In this moment of naked awareness, I prefer the shadows that keep me covered.

What is our might? As the gates begin to close, I search for the caged light within. *Dear God, by your light, may I see light.* Courage, I say. Resolve, I promise. Resilience, I pray. I'm sorry, I whisper. I forgive you, I whisper. My strength comes from the sounds and senses of this moment. *N'ilah*. Standing at the entrance, I know that legacy resounds in the words and deeds of my life, in compassion and moral courage. In the way I choose to live.

And I choose to live. With every breath I have a choice. O source of life eternal, *What can I say before You, my God? Open, open the gates of righteousness and I will enter.* Open my heart, for it has been caged too long. Crack me wide open, O God of rescue, God of redemption, God of salvation. In You I trust. Steady. Steady.

And then . . . just at the moment of despair, of desolation, I hear *Sh'ma yisrael*, "Hear, O Israel!" We exclaim that all is one. The holy and the human. The ordinary and the extraordinary. The earth and transcendence. The purity of soul and transgression. All is one. Everything possible. Redemption and destruction. I turn toward the light, the sun is setting, the shadows are upon the wall. I feel quite alive, and aloft. Floating toward some awareness, some prayer of gratitude. For within every cage, every remote and hidden soul, beyond every closed gate, there is a light. Hope takes over. Anticipation takes over. And then one long breath. The single sound of *t'ki'ah g'dolah*; a sustained groan of yearning. I will. I promise. Help me.

Open, open.

Chasing God

Rabbi Noa Kushner

All year long God chases us, like a parent chases a child. But on *N'ilah*, we chase God.

All year long God chases us. God tries to catch our attention in every imaginable way. Look at the natural world, practically in competition with itself, each entry another mind-blowing matter. God made color and variety, shape and size, just so that we might notice, just so we might make a connection from that one leaf to the One who somehow brought the idea of "leaf" into the world.

And some say that God plants lures for us, choices, so that we might grow into who we need to become. I like the idea of God creating these elaborate scavenger hunts and finding the right moment to hide the right clue. I imagine God scribbling on a piece of paper, then folding it over, concealing the message. Sometimes the clue is beyond subtle, half a breath, more than easy to ignore, and sometimes it is a knock, a pounding on the door, a blatant interruption, a shaking of our foundations. Sometimes the lure works—we bite, look up, and change immediately. Other times, it doesn't. We ignore the clue and go back to where we were. No matter though, because just like a parent watching a child, whether from close or from far away, God goes back to chasing us all the same.

Rabbi Noa Kushner is the Founding Rabbi of The Kitchen, a religious community in San Francisco. Since its inception in 2011, The Kitchen has engaged thousands of Gen X and Millenials in an exploration of Jewish life. After graduation from Brown University, Kushner was ordained by Hebrew Union College–Jewish Institute of Religion (New York) and then served as the Hillel Rabbi for Stanford University. She speaks nationally and her work has been profiled in *Newsweek*, *SF Magazine*, *Haaretz*, and *Tablet*. She is married to Rabbi Michael Lezak of GLIDE and the proud mother of three daughters.

God goes back to chasing us, except on *N'ilah*. On *N'ilah*, God is tired from all the chasing and wants to be chased—wants, needs to be pursued by *us*. And so, as the prayers would tell it, God hides behind the heavenly gates and starts closing them slowly, slowly: a one-act play. In repeating the liturgy over the past twenty-four hours, we've begged God to be forgiven, we've recited those confessions over and over again, and now we realize all the words are true. We want to forgive each other and to right past wrongs; we want to right even our future wrongs. We want to be like angels in white, somewhere far beyond the embarrassments of being human. We want to be written into the book of life; it finally dawns on us that to live is not our right but our blessing. We want all these things, but *N'ilah* is about something more.

I heard a story.

My friend and teacher Rabbi Tamar Elad-Applebaum told me about *N'ilah* in her community in Jerusalem. I don't have to tell you that Jerusalem is fraught with violence, and this had been a particularly bad year. There wasn't a person in the room untouched by grief. But this is a community that wants peace so badly it builds literal homes in the public square together with Muslims and Christians. They invite everyone in for a week to pray together as a way of building peace. While this would be a sweet but relatively benign gesture in ultra-pluralist San Francisco where I live, it is a truly radical and even dangerous act in a city like Jerusalem, where religious extremists and death too often go hand in hand. But Rabbi Applebaum's is a community that wants peace so badly they will risk and suffer for it, and yet they had suffered more than they could take that year. Their numbers were fewer, their collective soul had been trampled, desecrated. Tamar told me, "You know what I did toward the end of *N'ilah*? We had been praying and crying and we were still so angry. I don't know what came over me. I went up to the *aron* [ark] and I shouted, "I forgive You, God! For not being able to save us from ourselves, from each other, for all the things You have put us through, I forgive You. We forgive You. We forgive You."

All year long God chases us, like a parent chases a child. But on *N'ilah*, we chase God. On *N'ilah*, we finally stop ignoring the flurry of divine prompts, God's clever hints, only to realize we are momentarily, unmistakably alone. God has left the room. "Come back," we hear ourselves implore. "Do not shut the gates. We will do whatever it takes; we will find our way back to You."

Now we are in no position to turn a deaf ear, for we are the ones who knock. We press our hands on the gates, try to peer through the bars. "We forgive You for everything," we say. "Let us back in."

We remember with embarrassment that the big question of the High Holy Days has always been directed from God to us. *Ayeka?* God has asked us again and again, "Where are you?"

By *N'ilah* we have found our answer: *Hineni,* "I'm here; we're still here."

But even as we say it, we realize it's our turn now to ask that question of God, for the tables have turned. We screw up our courage and ask into the evening night, *Ayeka?* "God, where are *You?*"

All year long God chases us, like a parent chases a child. But on *N'ilah,* we learn to chase God. The shofar is blown one final time, and our great need for God is buried within its cry.

They say there's a kind of heartbreak that can rush past any guard, break down every door, and directly reach God. And maybe they're right, because just like that, at the end of *N'ilah,* the gates swing open and we begin our new year, exhausted, thankful, with our answer from God in the form of our lives.

൭〰〰൭

Recapturing *Piyyut*

MUSIC AND POETRY IN JEWISH TRADITION

Cantor David Lefkowitz

High Holy Day worship has connected generations of Jews for over two thousand years—an amazing achievement and a constant challenge! Jewish leaders today often see an unbridgeable chasm separating us from our predecessors, but earlier disjunctions in history teach us that successful uniting of "modern" and "authentic" is indeed possible by balancing the simple and the sacred—and thereby connecting spirited joy with serious and consecrated religious depth.

Throughout the Middle Ages, from the fourth or fifth century on, the liturgical art of *piyyut* (plural: *piyyutim*) was created by skilled poets (*payyetanim*) who were at home in biblical language and Rabbinic concepts and were masters of such poetic devices as rhythm, rhyme, alliteration, litany, and acrostic. Their various forms of religious poetry flourished in numerous Jewish cultures and lands all the way into the

---

Cantor David Lefkowitz, celebrated cantor, singer, and composer, was senior cantor of New York City's Park Avenue Synagogue for thirty-three years and cantorial faculty member at Hebrew Union College–Jewish Institute of Religion (New York) for twenty-seven. As emeritus, he has been documenting, digitizing, and archiving the thousands of works he and his predecessors at Park Avenue created and commissioned. His academic interest has been researching, editing, and arranging nineteenth-century unpublished musical treasures and investigating early and medieval liturgical poetry (*piyyutim*) as models of liturgical participation for today. For *N'ilah*, in particular, he has revived *piyyutim* through congregational melodic litanies that intensify the spiritual metaphors of "opening" and "closing" our personal "gates of possibility."

43

seventeenth century, enabling long-term attractive insertions in, or alternatives to, the familiar prayers of the service.

This "balancing" of the service successfully reached congregants of many sorts. The complex linguistic forms of *piyyutim* and their esoteric allusions to biblical and Rabbinic literature appealed mostly to the very learned, but because the traditional musical rules of liturgical chant (called *nusach*) did not apply to *piyyutim*, they could be rendered in diverse *melodic singing* that effected widespread *congregational appreciation* and *spirited participation* by all worshipers.

From the outset, *piyyutim* specially characterized the High Holy Days, including *N'ilah* with its powerful imagery of closing gates: a realistic acknowledgment of *time and opportunity* slipping away, but also a recognition of new possibilities opening up. Some of life's gates do close, but others can open. *N'ilah* confronts us with the need to recognize our self-imposed habits that often block the gates within us, impeding the realization of our full potential and obstructing the possibility of even finding the open gates of opportunity that are before us!

This emphasis on self-fulfillment would sound foreign to traditional Rabbinic tradition, which defines sin as wrongful behavior in the eyes of God; we repent, avoid punishment, and receive divine forgiveness. *Piyyutim* of the past naturally convey this more traditional message. But they can also support more modern perspectives, because music allows for interpretive horizons beyond what words alone can convey, especially at *N'ilah*, when a hallowed, spiritual atmosphere is so highly charged by the custom of keeping the ark doors open throughout the service, a visible symbol of the service's dominant image, "gates." The *piyyutim* elaborate on that powerful image.

The theme of "gates" is sounded early in *N'ilah* with *Sha'arei Armon* ("Quickly open the gates of the palace"; see p. 102–103). This poem—which we shall highlight shortly—is called a *siluk*, a poetic climax, akin to *Un'taneh Tokef* in the *Musaf* service for Rosh Hashanah and Yom Kippur.[1]

The *N'ilah Amidah* anticipates the Thirteen Attributes of God (see pp. 105–106), an accent on God's compassion, but only after another *piyyut*, *P'tach Lanu Sha'ar* ("Open a gate for us"; see p. 104–105),[2] evoking the hope that God will hold the gates open just a bit longer. Throughout that poem, the thirteen attributes are reiterated, as they are in the next *piyyutim*, *Enkat M'saldekha* ("May the cry of worshipers ascend your throne") and *Ezk'rah Elohim* ("I remember your mercy, God")—two poems (not included in this book because of spatial limitations) that accentuate *N'ilah's* final plea for compassion and culminate with a dramatic repetition again of the Thirteen Attributes.

These powerful poems cannot be properly appreciated without consideration of their music. They reach the heights of passion through their musical interpretation and cantorial fervor, a genuinely Jewish art form that has uplifted the souls of worshipers for centuries. *Sha'arei Armon* is a particularly awesome example.

Sha'arei Armon portrays our need to pass through gates: the gates of the ancient Temple in Jerusalem, but also heaven's gates, as if we (like Jacob's angels) are "climbing a ladder" of gates all the way to God, whom the *piyyut* portrays with a *keter ham'yuman*, a "mighty crown." Each of the poem's six lines designates a separate gate, and the poem's power lies in the naming of each one (e.g., "the gates of hidden treasure . . . of the glorious courtyard . . . of the camp on high"), punctuated by forceful energy of the congregation crying out, *M'heirah tiftach* ("Quickly open!"). Much as this imagery may have moved medieval worshipers, however, it may lack some metaphoric resonance today; hence the need for music that conveys this poetic impact, as in figure 1.

I referred above to the perceived chasm between ourselves and our tradition, and the challenge of uniting the "modern" and the "authentic" to meet the needs of today's congregants. Historically speaking, it was precisely the *piyyut*—the expression of meaningful themes through spirited rhythm and litany—that accomplished that end. A vast expansion of congregational melodies made dozens of the most beloved texts, including *B'rosh Hashanah* and *Avinu Malkeinu*, survive all these centuries![3]

When liturgical reformers (who pioneered all our modern-day denominations) sought to update our services, they sought to shorten the liturgy, however, not expand it through "optional" poetry! Also, they often favored the vernacular, not Hebrew; and even those who liked Hebrew looked disapprovingly at the complex Hebrew of the *piyyut*. Not only was new poetry discouraged, even traditional *piyyutim* were excised.

In our current time too, the *piyyut* has been under attack. Most Orthodox congregations either race through them perfunctorily or bypass them as non-halakhic and unnecessary intrusions in the service. Conservative liturgies often include only those *piyyutim* that are most popularly sung (like *B'rosh Hashanah*) and absolute staples (like *Avinu*

Sha'arei Armon

Cantor-Congregation Antiphonal Chant
for
Yom Kippur N'ilah Service

[shortened version]

Liturgical Piyyut by:
Eleazar Kalir – 7th Century
English Translation:
David Lefkowitz

Music composed by:
Cantor David Lefkowitz
September 24-30, 1995

© 1995 David Lefkowitz

Figure 1

Malkeinu and *Kol Nidre*). The tradition of liturgical poetry that has dramatically inspired congregants for over fifteen hundred years is now threatened with virtual extinction.

Recent decades, however, have seen a resurgence of *piyyutim*, especially from Israel, composed enthusiastically by secular Jews and enhanced with the advanced Hebrew language of Jews who actually speak it. This is an extraordinary opportunity to unite *secular* and *sacred* in a more open and spiritually minded atmosphere! Simultaneously, prayer-book editors are discovering older material that had been lost, forgotten, or limited to just one tradition. *Sha'arei Orah* ("Gates of light"), for example, from the Sephardi *Tei'anu V'tei'atru* ("May you be answered and may your request be granted"; see pp. 106–108), was included in the Reform Movement's *Gates of Repentance* (1975) and is now in the newest Conservative Movement's *Mahzor Lev Shalem* (2010)—albeit as a replacement for the traditional *Sha'arei Armon*, because its list of gates seemed more attuned to contemporary consciousness.

But writing new or recovering old *piyyutim* will come to naught without proper accompanying music, which invites congregational engagement through litany-like responses, as we saw in *Sha'arei Armon*. Without such music, we have words—mere words—especially if they are in Hebrew and literally translated without even the poetry of the original! However compelling their meaning to the mind, they will never enter the heart without the proper engaging music, which alone is the vehicle for transforming objective ideas into emotionally charged realities.

N'ilah has been, for me, the most thrilling and inspiring moment of my being a cantor! It can be that for everyone.

☙

There and Back Again

Catherine Madsen

After confession and tears and the day's starving,
compassion lengthens our days past our deserving.
Pure and unwashed we crowd the sidewalks, but in the gloom
God, our old partner in the sin trade, follows us home.

The emotional intensity of *N'ilah* is a collective state. Packed like sardines among a crowd of tired, hungry, thirsty, and exalted people, we pick up the exaltation; even for someone in the habit of alienation, it is not easy to stay alienated. It doesn't matter that the emotion is in some ways contrived—that fasting and dehydration heighten emotion, make us vulnerable to exalted states. We can know that and still be vulnerable. The contrivance calls to the real emotion, plunges its artificial hands down into our warm and squishy physical shame. On the other side of that shame is a sense of purgation and potential, and there's not a thing we can do to resist it.

A prescribed physical ordeal is a tried method of transcending ordinary consciousness; ours is nothing to the Sun Dance or the walkabout or the angakoq's[1] journey. Ours lasts a day; it is uncomfortable rather than painful or life-threatening; its purpose is moral realignment, not a visionary state or a major shift in identity. Yet it is ritually orchestrated and thus effective. If even a largely symbolic form of suffering gets real results, it is worth undergoing. "Axioms in philosophy are not axioms," wrote Keats, "until they are proved upon our pulses."

What is the emotional intensity of *N'ilah* for? It doesn't last—neither the feeling nor its effects; we are pretty much back to gossip and idle speech halfway through the break-fast. That doesn't make the experience

---

Catherine Madsen is the author of *The Bones Reassemble: Reconstituting Liturgical Speech*, the novel *A Portable Egypt*, and many essays. She has recently retired after eighteen years at the Yiddish Book Center and is studying Norwegian and working on a long poem.

false, any more than after-theater small talk falsifies *King Lear* or the *Oresteia*. It simply means we cannot easily transfer orchestrated communal intensity to a social setting. The experience was true, but we immediately have to work within the accustomed parameters of social speech and subdue strong emotion. Whatever was proved upon our pulses does not readily transform our relations with other people. It may continue only obscurely, subliminally, in our pulses and not in our conscious thought.

If the intensity is true but nevertheless very temporary, what is it for while it lasts? Or *who* is it for? A quiet little memoir of a lost pregnancy, Paula Saffire's *Tender Miscarriage*, makes an unsettling suggestion. Saffire writes:

> I had once read a book which presents the view that we humans are kept by Someone as cows are kept by humans—for our milk. The "milk" that Someone wants, and uses for his own purposes, is our emotions—the purer and more intense, the better. Anger, jealousy—any emotion will do. But the prime emotion is love, which is given the name "loosh." I can remember getting out of bed one day [during pregnancy] and realizing that this was loosh. Suddenly I understood the author's point of view. If I were Someone, I, too, would want to harvest this. It was the highest-octane fuel, the most powerful human love, that I had ever known.[2]

The word "loosh," as far as I can discover, comes from Robert Monroe, a writer of New Age books on out-of-body experiences. However one reacts to the sound of the word (or to books on out-of-body experiences), the idea is striking—not altogether consonant with the Jewish notion of a God who wants us to be disciplined and morally deliberate, yet not altogether dissonant with the jealous God who gets angry and who wants our unwavering love. Elias Canetti, in his book of aphorisms *The Human Province*, says a similar thing: "Men's voices are God's bread."[3] He feeds on us.

Emotional intensity is easy to indulge for its own sake, and that can happen at *N'ilah*: a rush, a gush of mellow fellow-feeling, a crowd of hungry Jews swaying together to the strains of Debbie Friedman's *Havdalah*. The shofar has sounded, all's right with the world! If God has a sweet tooth, this may be good for dessert. But the entree leading up to *N'ilah* is more astringent fare. The substance of the ordeal is the repeated confessions, the confrontation with our own pettiness and failure, the descent into shame. If liturgists functioned less within the accustomed parameters of social speech and more on the frontiers of raw introspection, they might meet us there with lines like these from Gerard Manley Hopkins:

> I am gall, I am heartburn. God's most deep decree
> Bitter would have me taste: my taste was me.

Hopkins' ordeal—the prolonged double misery of his vocation as priest and his vocation as poet—was worse than ours on Yom Kippur; like the angakoq, he was stripped to the skeleton in his journey to achieve those sonnets. But it is a difference in degree, not in kind. Ordeals have a common structure. We descend, and at the bottom of the descent we find strength. "Mine, O thou lord of life, send my roots rain," demands Hopkins in another sonnet. The angakoq's task, in the old pre-missionary days, was to go in times of starvation (in an out-of-body journey) to the bottom of the sea to make Sedna release the sea animals that she had withheld in anger at the people's faults. "Forgive us, pardon us, grant us atonement," we chant over and over; over and over we revert to the story of God's pardon after the sin of the golden calf. The purpose of an ordeal is to compel God.

Having done so, we are naturally exalted: not only by fasting and dehydration, but by the power of our own insistence. We have stood up to God. There has even been an exchange: if God has harvested our emotions, we have harvested his response. We have *won* our forgiveness.

In a culture that compels us to move immediately away from every shame and failure, every urgent and unresolvable question, every half-starved private longing—a culture that exhausts us continually with the exaggerated urgency of the next client's claim on our attention, the next disturbing news item, the next retail transaction—there is little exaltation to be had. How to bring either moral or emotional power back into daily life from *N'ilah* is a dispiriting puzzle. It is the riddle of ritual action in general: how to bring the transcendence of ordinary consciousness to bear on ordinary consciousness. We can compel God; can we compel ourselves?

To the Point of No "Return"— and Back Again

Rabbi Nicole K. Roberts

"*M*ommy! *Daddy! Wake up! You only have thirty or forty years left to live!*" pleads the wise-beyond-his-years, pajama-clad toddler, as he stands on his parents' bed, tugging at his mother's arm. His persistence and urgency, depicted so deftly by the *New Yorker* magazine cartoonist,[1] reflects the tenor—and core message—of *N'ilah*: *Time is running out— wake up before it's too late!* The *machzor*, of course, prefers poetic and liturgical artistry to pictography and cartoon captions—and appropriately so. *N'ilah*'s message is no laughing matter; it is as serious as life and death, for it is, in fact, just that: life and death, an annual confrontation with our own mortality.

Until *N'ilah*, the gates of repentance and forgiveness have been flung wide open for us to reflect and commit to the reconciliation of soul that we call "turning" (*t'shuvah*). But, as with everything else in life, there

Rabbi Nicole Roberts is the first woman to be appointed senior rabbi in Australia. She has served the North Shore Temple Emanuel in Sydney since ordination in 2012 from the Hebrew Union College–Jewish Institute of Religion (Cincinnati), where she was awarded prizes for excellence in Midrash and class standing. An alumna of the Tisch Rabbinical Fellowship, her writing has been published in the Prayers of Awe series and in several "Rethinking" guides issued by Jewish Women International, on whose Clergy Task Force she serves. She is treasurer of the Council of Progressive Rabbis of Australia, New Zealand, and Asia and travels regularly to the United States for conferences and family visits.

does come a point of no "return"—where *t'shuvah* is unlikely, if not altogether impossible. When do the gates close once and for all?

Presumably they close when we can no longer change how we live, which is to say, at our death. The liturgy anticipates that moment with its image of *sha'at han'ilah*[2]—literally, "the hour of closing"—the point at which we are closed off from becoming a different person, living with different values, and being remembered for different things. *N'ilah* presents our *dead*line (pun intended). We've just mourned our parents with *Yizkor*, confronting the fact that *we* are next in line. Our abstention from food for the past twenty plus hours has slowed and weakened us, and standing throughout the final prayers makes us feel the weight of our years. We are dressed in white, like the shrouds in which we will be buried. The service concludes with *Sh'ma yisrael*, the same words found in the deathbed confession (the *Vidui*). At the end of the day, some even wish each other *Tizku l'shanim rabot*, "May you be worthy of long life."[3] The message is clear: the final gate *will* one day shut and lock behind us, and that day may come sooner than we think.

Depending on our stage of life, we may be no stranger to the way gates close. At a certain point, life seems to stop expanding with endless possibility. We begin to see that certain achievements will never be ours. I've grown too old to be "young and successful." I'll never live where I dreamt I would. I'll never be an Olympic athlete, a professional musician, an owner of my own business. I was not the parent I wanted to be, and the children are now grown. At my age, no one wants to interview me, much less hire me. One by one, the gates close on us as we get older.

In our senior years, they close with greater frequency and poignancy as we begin to see our end in sight. We retire, and a gate closes on our income potential. We relinquish our driver's license, and a gate closes on our freedom. We move into a nursing home, and a gate closes on our independence. We lose our eyesight, and a gate closes on our ability to read our favorite novels or see our grandchildren's artwork. We lose our life partner, and a gate closes on intimacy. We lose our only sibling, and a gate closes on our past. We lose our final friend, and a gate closes on companionship. One day, *N'ilah* reminds us, the final gate will close on *all* that we have loved about this world.

To age is to grieve the succession of closing gates, our own personal equivalents of the *sha'arei armon* ("gates of the palace"), *sha'arei g'nuzim* ("gates of hidden treasures"), and *sha'arei heikhal hanechmadim* ("gates of the glorious courtyard")[4] that *N'ilah* pictures as our entryways to all that we thought made life worth living. *N'ilah* sounds differently in our senior years. We hear the haunting refrain "as the gates begin to close"[5] and wonder, what hope still remains for us? Are our best years behind us? Is what's left of life worth living?

But ending Yom Kippur with these questions alone misses the point, for much as *N'ilah* reminds us of our mortality, it does not leave us in despair. Yes, our time is running out, but there is always that second part of *N'ilah*'s message, the one conveyed by the cartoon child to his sleeping parents: *Wake up, before it's too late!* It is not that the best of life is behind us—it's just that we've been asleep! Moments after *N'ilah*'s deathbed-like final *Sh'ma*, its shofar blast awakens us to life renewed: a new array of gates lies open before us, not the transitory ones of secular promise (more money, success, power, and privilege), but the gates of spiritual satisfaction that never cease to gratify: *sha'arei orah, sha'arei v'rachah, sha'arei gilah* ("the gates of light, the gates of blessing, the gates of joy . . ."),[6] an entire *alef-bet* of hope that defies the death and futility we believed was at hand. With so many gates lying open before us, life once again expands with possibility!

N'ilah can change our mind-set. Time *is* running out, but not on the things that are eternally worthwhile.

N'ilah takes us to the point of no return, and back again. *L'shanah haba'ah birushalayim* ("Next year in Jerusalem!"),[7] we proclaim with new-found confidence—defiance even!—for indeed there *will* be a next year, and whatever our own life's age and stage, the time ahead *will* be worth living. The treasures of this life are not yet all behind us. Before us lies our own Jerusalem of gold.

⟨∞⟩

Come Back to Life

THE RESURRECTING POWER OF THE DAYS OF AWE

Rabbi Elaine Zecher

Resurrection. What can such an idea mean to people who are college educated, scientifically astute, fully modernized, and happily secularized, as they reflect on the final moments of the Yom Kippur experience? To the extent that it means anything at all, it is likely to evoke an image from the surrounding Christian culture. But it is authentically Jewish in origin, and perhaps it is time to reclaim it.

Our tradition weaves metaphor into our liturgy. We call God *avinu* and *malkeinu*, knowing God is neither "king" nor "father." "The Lord is my shepherd," Psalm 23 informs us, but how is God a feudal lord? And God's role in our life is not to gather sheep. Metaphor defies literal interpretation; it provides us with conceptual figures of speech that deepen the way we think.

"Resurrection" applied to human beings is no less metaphoric than "king," "father," and "shepherd" applied to God. The Mishnah teaches us that when we see a friend after an absence of a year or more, we recite a blessing of resurrection. *Barukh atah Adonai, m'chayei hametim*, "Blessed are You . . . who revives the dead" (Talmud, Berakhot). It certainly isn't

---

Rabbi Elaine Zecher has served Temple Israel of Boston since 1990 and became its senior rabbi in 2016. Her congregational work has emphasized finding meaning and purpose through spiritual practice, study, and righteous impact. She is honored to have been part of the editorial team of both *Mishkan T'filah* and *Mishkan HaNefesh*, the North American Reform Movement's current liturgies. The High Holy Days are Rabbi Zecher's favorite time of year because they bring the community together in prayer and rededication to the sacred work of introspection and confession.

because they have died, but because their presence is renewed in our own lives. Even traditional Judaism that believes literally in resurrection knows that here the blessing is offered because at least one High Holy Day period will have passed with the possibility of being erased from the book of life, so *it is as if* the person we see has been resurrected.[1] In similar fashion, although we recognize God does have the power to resurrect, we do not necessarily believe that resurrection literally happens. Yet even Reform Judaism has restored "who revives the dead" to its place in our daily liturgy, because of its metaphoric resonance.

This brings us to Yom Kippur and *N'ilah*.

On Yom Kippur, when we follow the Mishnah's instruction to refrain from eating and drinking, perfuming, bathing, wearing leather shoes, and engaging in intimate relations (Mishnah Yoma 8:1), we are depriving ourselves of most of life's necessities. Many also don the *kittel*, the white plain garment that is likened to burial shrouds. In essence, during Yom Kippur, we simulate our own symbolic deaths.[2] We turn our attention away from life-sustaining functions so that our souls, unencumbered by bodily needs, may engage in the work of *t'shuvah* (repentance). For that one day, we are neither living nor dead. We float in the ephemeral ether of our imagined demise on this most sacred day.

Jewish tradition teaches us to repent one day before our death, but since we don't know when we will die, we are to view each day as if it were the last. On Yom Kippur, however, it is as if we are told, explicitly, that our final day is at hand. Then, especially, we follow the instructions to "engage in *t'shuvah* on the day of your death."

By *N'ilah*, however, we turn to God who lifts up the fallen,[3] using the image of a hand reaching out to till the soil of our soul and plant within us the potential for rebirth. *Atah noten yad*, "You extend your hand to sinners." It is the ultimate act of healing to be brought back into life.

The Talmud emphasizes the healing power of a simple extended hand (Berakhot 5b). When Rabbi Chiya bar Abba was ill, Rabbi Yochanan paid him a visit. Recognizing that Rabbi Chiya was suffering, Rabbi Yochanan instructed Rabbi Chiya to give him his hand. He complied, says the Talmud, and was revived.

The story does not end there, however. Rabbi Yochanan then fell ill, and another rabbi, Chanina, visited him. The same encounter ensued, as this time Chanina asked for Yochanan's hand and revived him. The Gemara asks: Why did Yochanan need Chanina's assistance? He had already demonstrated his healing powers when he revived Rabbi Chiya. Couldn't he just revive himself? No, says the Gemara. "A captive cannot release himself from prison." This cryptic response reveals an important message. We all need people other than ourselves to be revived. Such is the power of *N'ilah*.

Slowly and assuredly, we walk *N'ilah*'s liturgical path back to life, surrounded by community and loved ones, and in vital need of one another. Ahead in the distance, as it appears that the gates of *t'shuvah* are closing, we plead, *P'tach lanu sha'ar tzedek!* "Open for us a gate of righteousness!"

Have we not earned righteousness with our *t'shuvah*? Alas, it too may begin to close, but immediately, yet another gate opens. And so it goes: there is always another way in—room somehow to squeeze through gates that are never entirely sealed shut. The shofar blasts and our resurrection appears as restoration to life's potential far beyond what we might have dared to imagine. Through the opening of the gates, we behold our greatest joy, *z'man simchateinu*, the "time of gladness" that we call Sukkot. Our first act as we move out of Yom Kippur, revived, is to begin building a sukkah.

Nature itself is the ultimate reminder of resurrection's reality. Every winter, it lies dormant until the rebirth of spring. Every parched flower can be quenched by rainfall. Our healing is secured by the act of creating the sukkah.

The sacred work of Yom Kippur may drain us, but *N'ilah* revives us. We turn back to life revitalized and ready to begin again, just as at the moment of our own birth, our souls return to the pure state of fresh possibility.

L'shanah tovah, we wish one another—"toward a good new year," with life renewed and ready once again to flower toward the future.

☙⊰⊱❧

Time-Out or Getting Back in the Game

Rabbi Daniel G. Zemel

For nearly a quarter of a century, Geoffrey Canada has been the educator, revolutionary thinker, and chief visionary at the celebrated Harlem Children's Zone. Every Yom Kippur morning, he becomes my chief visionary at Temple Micah, my chief commentator to the Isaiah haftarah portion, as I dutifully read the following words from his 2012 commencement address at the University of Pennsylvania to the congregation:

> Our country is desperate for . . . women and men who will fight to see through the veils of pure self-interest and half truths. . . . The poor fill our jails and prisons. They stumble into emergency rooms wheezing, limping, with blood leaking from holes never intended by God or nature. They sit in waiting rooms hoping for a sympathetic ear, which can stave off homelessness for another month, another week, another night. They stand on lines for food, or clothes, or whatever is being given away for free. Those who are poor in this country have the weight of poverty, violence and lack of education hanging over their heads, straining to break free and crush them, maybe

---

Rabbi Daniel G. Zemel graduated from Brown University, received rabbinic ordination from Hebrew Union College–Jewish Institute of Religion (New York, 1979), and has recently celebrated twenty-five years as rabbi of Temple Micah in Washington, DC. He has been involved in numerous community and Jewish organizations but derives greatest satisfaction from being a founder of Micah House, a group home for formerly homeless women. His twenty-year involvement with Synagogue 2000 was instrumental in shaping his vision of synagogue life. He has contributed an essay to each volume of the *Prayers of Awe* series.

kill them. And when the weight crashes down, you will not be under it. . . . My question to you is, do you care about those who won't make it without real help? You [are] . . . preparing to enter the big game of life, and I have a most wondrous proposition for you. Come join our team. We're losing. Yes, that's right, we're losing.

Mr. Canada's call, the call of Isaiah for our time, is the call of God for every time, ever since the biblical Cain first asked the question "Am I my brother's keeper?" At every *N'ilah*, that question echoes, haunts, and challenges.

The Holy Days ask the impossible. Honesty, introspection, clarity. What do I love? Whom do I serve? What am I? Why?

As a congregational rabbi I am occasionally asked when I begin preparing my Holy Day sermons. My usual answer is the day after Yom Kippur. It takes a year. The question about sermons is the question about life itself. The High Holy Days are the ritual of the examined life. *N'ilah* closes the door on the ritual but not on the life.

For the last twenty years in my synagogue, as we open the ark doors for *N'ilah*, we invite anyone in the congregation who wishes to come forward silently and pray before the open ark. Throughout the service that continues as if oblivious to their presence; they come forward, stand silently in line to await their turn, and then stand there at the ark for as long as they wish. Mothers with children, couples together, lawyers, accountants, academics, writers—they stand and pray whatever it is that they care about most. Everyone present is in some way deeply touched by this public, yet private, outpouring.

I wonder: what is it that this invitation unlocks within us? Is there something that Yom Kippur's *N'ilah* draws out in us that no other day or time can match? What is it? Why?

I wonder: to what should *N'ilah* be compared?

Few of us have ever played the final game in a championship series of any sport. Is *N'ilah* like the final out or winning goal of that last game? If so, having stayed in the synagogue to the final blast of the *t'ki'ah g'dolah*, are we winners? Is this a victory celebration—the celebratory exhaustion of crossing a cosmic, spiritual finish line or home plate?

Or is Geoffrey Canada right to remind us we are losing? The big game, he says, is just about to start all over again. The High Holy Day heavy lifting of self-examination, self-judging, and grueling introspection just sends us back into the field, with the reminder that we play on a team, the Jewish People: "We are your people, You are our God." It is all well and good to take personal time out for prayer and introspection, but we do so in service of a larger purpose. We rejoin the battle in which we are losing.

We are not in the game for just a day or even a season, however. Our covenant is for the long haul. And we are not in it alone. I like to think that Temple Micah members leave together joining Jews from every synagogue who do the same; joining all good people, for that matter; joining Geoffrey Canada, for example, and Isaiah too, people past and present in the quest to be our "brother's keeper."

Yom Kippur is just halftime, an intermission to catch our breath; *N'ilah* is that halftime's final moment. That's where *N'ilah* gets its power. We know in our hearts that when the ark doors finally close, we reenter Geoffrey Canada's game of life.

Canada comments on the challenge of Isaiah (58:5): "Is this the fast I desire?" Does God want only the fast of our time-out? Or does God want us to return to the game? The answer comes with *N'ilah*'s final surging vision of universal human redemption: "Adonai is God." The shofar sounds its concluding clarion call for us to take the field again, to go out to face the world. We are still losing. Someday, we will win.

⌾∞∞⌾

PART IV

The Liturgy and Related Commentary

"You Extend Your Hand . . . You Set Humans Apart"

(*Atah Noten Yad . . . Atah Hivdalta Enosh*)

Editor's Introduction

Rabbi Lawrence A. Hoffman, PhD

The two prayers "You Extend Your Hand . . . You Set Humans Apart" (*Atah Noten Yad . . . Atah Hivdalta Enosh*), combined, are the very centerpiece of *N'ilah*. A detailed account of their message and development can be found in appendix A, "The Boldest Claim: God Reaches Out a Hand." Here we summarize their message.

All other services for Yom Kippur include two confessions: *Ashamnu* ("We have been guilty . . ."), known technically as the "Short Confession" (*Vidui Zuta*); and then *Al Chet* ("For the sin we have committed against You . . ."), called the "Long Confession" (*Vidui Rabbah*). They are recited privately by the worshiper at the end of the silent *Amidah* and then repeated aloud by the prayer leader in the middle of the reader's repetition of that prayer. Their acrostic format symbolizes the ubiquity of sin as part of the human condition.

For all other services, worshipers dress, traditionally, in a *tallit* and a *kittel* (a white shroud-like tunic), both of them reminiscent of burial garb, as if to emphasize the gravity of the moment: we are on trial for our sins, and our lives are at stake. By *N'ilah*, however, we appear before God dressed in ordinary clothes, as if we know already that we will be restored to life.

Indicative of this newfound optimism is the fact that when we get to the confessions in *N'ilah*, only the Short Confession (*Ashamnu*) is included. In place of the Long Confession (*Al Chet*), we get a treatise on human nature that admits the reality of human sin but highlights equally the miracle of human moral consciousness and the capacity to attain divine pardon.

A pair of images makes the message manifest. First, we get the remarkable metaphor of God "extending a hand" to us, as if to help us repent and then to draw us up and out of the anticipatory mourning mode that set in with *Kol Nidre*—to be cleansed and sealed in the book of life. Second, we get the picture of God "setting us apart," as the sole species with consciousness sufficient to know what sin and morality are in the first place.

The ark remains open throughout the service, a symbol of the Temple gates of old, but also gates to heaven, as if we might be able to see God's hand extended through them, drawing us up from our penitential state into life renewed.

⟩∿∿∿⟨

Annotated Translation

Dr. Joel M. Hoffman

You Extend Your Hand (*Atah Noten Yad*)

[1]You extend your hand to sinners, and your arm reaches out to accept those who repent. [2]Teach us, Adonai our God, to confess all of our sins before You, so that we cease to oppress with our hands, and You accept us before You in perfect repentance like fires and

¹אַתָּה נוֹתֵן יָד לְפוֹשְׁעִים,
וִימִינְךָ פְּשׁוּטָה לְקַבֵּל
שָׁבִים. ²וַתְּלַמְּדֵנוּ יְיָ
אֱלֹהֵינוּ לְהִתְוַדּוֹת לְפָנֶיךָ
עַל כָּל עֲוֹנוֹתֵינוּ, לְמַעַן
נֶחְדַּל מֵעֹשֶׁק יָדֵינוּ,
וּתְקַבְּלֵנוּ בִּתְשׁוּבָה
שְׁלֵמָה לְפָנֶיךָ כָּאִשִּׁים

[1] *You extend your hand*: Others, "You reach out," but we need the word "hand" here because it forms a continuing metaphor in the prayer. First God extends a "hand," then, below, we hope that we cease to "oppress with our hands."

Additionally, the Hebrew literally reads "give a hand," which is

---

Joel M. Hoffman, PhD holds a doctorate in linguistics from the University of Maryland and has served on the faculties of Hebrew Union College–Jewish Institute of Religion (New York) and Brandeis University (in Waltham, MA). He is the author of a wide range of books about Hebrew, translation, and the Bible, most recently *The Bible Doesn't Say That*. A frequent guest speaker at religious and educational venues, Dr. Hoffman has traveled to six of the seven continents speaking about his research, always with a camera in hand. This volume represents his nineteenth collaboration with his father, Rabbi Lawrence A. Hoffman.

fragrances, as you promised. ³Our
obligatory fires are endless, and
our guilt-offering fragrances countless, but You know that our end
is the maggot and the worm, so
you offer us increased forgiveness.

וּכְנִיחוֹחִים, לְמַעַן דְּבָרֶיךָ
אֲשֶׁר אָמָרְתָּ. ³אֵין קֵץ
לְאִשֵּׁי חוֹבוֹתֵינוּ, וְאֵין
מִסְפָּר לְנִיחוֹחֵי אַשְׁמָתֵנוּ,
וְאַתָּה יוֹדֵעַ שֶׁאַחֲרִיתֵנוּ
רִמָּה וְתוֹלֵעָה, לְפִיכָךְ
הִרְבֵּיתָ סְלִיחָתֵנוּ.

obviously the wrong translation, because of the idiomatic meaning of
that phrase in English. So we use "extend." We add the word "your"
in keeping with the general pattern in Hebrew, but not in English, of
omitting possessive pronouns for body parts when their owner is clear.
¹*Arm*: Or "right hand," for the single Hebrew word *y'minkha*. (That word
literally means just "your right." In much the way that "righty" means
"right-handed" in particular but also "right-leaning" in general, the
Hebrew means "right hand" in addition to "right" more generally.) We
prefer simply "arm" in English because the Hebrew juxtaposes three pairs
of near synonyms, expressed here as "extend/reaches out," "hand/arm"
and "sinners/those who repent." We omit "right" in English because its
inclusion in Hebrew is incidental to the point of using synonyms.
²*Teach us*: Or "you have taught us."
²*Sins*: Others, "iniquities" or some other synonym for "sins," to avoid
using the same English "sin" (here and above) for two different Hebrew
words. But while "confess . . . sins" sounds like English, "confess . . .
iniquities" does not.
²*Before You*: That is, "to confess before You," not "our sins that are
before You." Our English translation is unfortunately ambiguous in this
regard. The Hebrew is not, because it literally reads "to confess before
You about all our sins," a word order that English does not allow.
²*To oppress with our hands*: Others, "to do violence." We want to keep
"with our hands" in the translation because of the way "hands" here
mirrors the opening of the prayer.

4What are we? 5What are our
lives? 6What is our love? 7What is
our righteousness? 8What is our
salvation? 9What is our strength?
10What is our might? 11What can
we say before You, 12Adonai our
God and our ancestors' God?
13Are not all mighty ones as
though they were nothing before
You, men of fame as though
they never existed, the educated
as though without knowledge,
and the wise as though without
insight, for most of their acts are
without value and the days of
their life worthless before You?
14Man barely rises above beast, for
everything is worthless.

מַה אָנוּ? ⁵מֶה חַיֵּינוּ?⁴
מֶה חַסְדֵּנוּ? ⁷מַה⁶
צִדְקֵנוּ? ⁸מַה יְשׁוּעָתֵנוּ?
מַה כֹּחֵנוּ? ¹⁰מַה⁹
גְּבוּרָתֵנוּ? ¹¹מַה נֹּאמַר
לְפָנֶיךָ, יְיָ אֱלֹהֵינוּ וֵאלֹהֵי
אֲבוֹתֵינוּ? ¹²הֲלֹא כָּל
הַגִּבּוֹרִים כְּאַיִן לְפָנֶיךָ,
וְאַנְשֵׁי הַשֵּׁם כְּלֹא הָיוּ,
וַחֲכָמִים כִּבְלִי מַדָּע,
וּנְבוֹנִים כִּבְלִי הַשְׂכֵּל,
כִּי רֹב מַעֲשֵׂיהֶם תֹּהוּ,
וִימֵי חַיֵּיהֶם הֶבֶל לְפָנֶיךָ?
וּמוֹתַר הָאָדָם מִן¹³
הַבְּהֵמָה אָיִן, כִּי הַכֹּל
הָבֶל.

²*Fires and fragrances*: A reference to the sacrifices that God once
accepted.
²*As You promised*: Or perhaps the more literal "for the sake of the words
You spoke."
⁴*What are we?*: For notes to lines 4–14, see *My People's Prayer Book*,
vol. 5, Birkhot Hashachar (*Morning Blessings*), pp. 157–169, in which
this text also appears.

You Set Humans Apart (*Atah Hivdalta Enosh*)

[1]You set humans apart from the outset, considering them worthy to stand before You. [2]For who can ask You, What are You doing? [3]And though they be righteous, what can they give You? [4]But You, Adonai our God, lovingly gave us this Day of Atonement, an end to, and complete forgiveness and pardon for, all our sins, so that we cease to oppress with our hands, and return to You and observe your gracious laws wholeheartedly. [5]In your great mercy, have mercy upon us, for You don't want the world's destruction, as is said: [6]"Seek Adonai where He is found, call upon him where He is near." [7]And as is said, "The wicked leave their path, and the evil their thoughts, and return to Adonai who will have mercy upon them, and to God who will extend forgiveness to them."

אַתָּה הִבְדַּלְתָּ אֱנוֹשׁ[1]
מֵרֹאשׁ, וַתַּכִּירֵהוּ לַעֲמוֹד
לְפָנֶיךָ. [2]כִּי מִי יֹאמַר לְךָ
מַה תִּפְעַל? [3]וְאִם יִצְדַּק
מַה יִּתֶּן לָךְ? [4]וַתִּתֶּן לָנוּ,
יְיָ אֱלֹהֵינוּ, בְּאַהֲבָה אֶת
יוֹם הַכִּפֻּרִים הַזֶּה, קֵץ
וּמְחִילָה וּסְלִיחָה עַל כָּל
עֲוֹנוֹתֵינוּ, לְמַעַן נֶחְדַּל
מֵעֹשֶׁק יָדֵנוּ, וְנָשׁוּב אֵלֶיךָ
לַעֲשׂוֹת חֻקֵּי רְצוֹנְךָ בְּלֵבָב
שָׁלֵם. [5]וְאַתָּה בְּרַחֲמֶיךָ
הָרַבִּים רַחֵם עָלֵינוּ, כִּי
לֹא תַחְפּוֹץ בְּהַשְׁחָתַת
עוֹלָם, שֶׁנֶּאֱמַר, [6]דִּרְשׁוּ
יְיָ בְּהִמָּצְאוֹ, קְרָאֻהוּ
בִּהְיוֹתוֹ קָרוֹב. [7]וְנֶאֱמַר,
יַעֲזֹב רָשָׁע דַּרְכּוֹ, וְאִישׁ
אָוֶן מַחְשְׁבֹתָיו, וְיָשֹׁב
אֶל יְיָ וִירַחֲמֵהוּ, וְאֶל
אֱלֹהֵינוּ כִּי יַרְבֶּה לִסְלוֹחַ.

[1]*Humans*: Or "humankind." We prefer "humans" because the Hebrew is gender-neutral, and this lets us use the similarly gender-neutral "them" in the next clause.

[4]*Gracious*: Or "favorable."

⁸You are a God of forgiveness, gracious and merciful, endlessly patient, most kind and truthful, extending beneficence. ⁹You want the wicked to repent, and You do not desire their death, as is said: ¹⁰"Tell them—says Adonai, God—as I live, do I desire the death of the wicked, or the return of the wicked from their ways that

⁸וְאַתָּה אֱלוֹהַ סְלִיחוֹת, חַנּוּן וְרַחוּם, אֶרֶךְ אַפַּיִם וְרַב חֶסֶד וֶאֱמֶת, וּמַרְבֶּה לְהֵיטִיב. ⁹וְרוֹצֶה אַתָּה בִּתְשׁוּבַת רְשָׁעִים, וְאֵין אַתָּה חָפֵץ בְּמִיתָתָם, שֶׁנֶּאֱמַר, ¹⁰אֱמֹר אֲלֵיהֶם, חַי אָנִי, נְאֻם אֲדֹנָי יֱהֹוִה, אִם אֶחְפֹּץ בְּמוֹת הָרָשָׁע, כִּי אִם בְּשׁוּב רָשָׁע מִדַּרְכּוֹ

⁷*Extend forgiveness*: Literally, "increase forgiveness," an idiom in Hebrew that has no exact parallel in English. Others use "pardon abundantly," partially reflecting the literal meaning of the Hebrew. We use "forgiveness" here instead of "pardon" because the same Hebrew root appears here and immediately below (where again we use "forgiveness").
⁸*God of forgiveness*: Or "god of forgiveness." In proper English usage, the lowercase "god" is generic, and the capitalized "God" specific. So technically, "God is our god" would be the correct capitalization, as would, here, "you are a god of forgiveness." But common usage sometimes capitalizes "god" even in these instances.
⁸*Gracious and merciful*: Hebrew, *chanun v'rachum*, an inversion of the "merciful and gracious" at the start of the Thirteen Attributes (see Prayers of Awe, *Encountering God*, p. 7).
⁸*Extending beneficence*: We use "extending" here for the same reason we did above (see line 7, "Extend forgiveness"). Instead of "beneficence" we could use "goodness."
¹⁰*As I live*: A Hebrew idiom whose exact meaning we do not know.

they live? [11]Return, return from your evil ways; why should you die, House of Israel?" [12]And as is said, "Do I desire the death of the wicked—says Adonai, God—or rather their return from their ways that they live?" [13]And as is said, "I do not desire anyone's death— says Adonai, God—so return and live." [14]For You are Israel's for- giver, and pardoner to the tribes of Jeshurun in every generation, and we have no king who pardons and forgives other than You.

[11]שׁוּבוּ, שׁוּבוּ וְחָיָה?
מִדַּרְכֵיכֶם הָרָעִים,
וְלָמָּה תָמוּתוּ בֵּית
יִשְׂרָאֵל? [12]וְנֶאֱמַר,
הֶחָפֹץ אֶחְפֹּץ מוֹת
רָשָׁע, נְאֻם אֲדֹנָי יֱהֹוִה,
הֲלֹא בְּשׁוּבוֹ מִדְּרָכָיו
וְחָיָה. [13]וְנֶאֱמַר, כִּי
לֹא אֶחְפֹּץ בְּמוֹת הַמֵּת,
נְאֻם אֲדֹנָי יֱהֹוִה, וְהָשִׁיבוּ
וִחְיוּ. [14]כִּי אַתָּה סָלְחָן
לְיִשְׂרָאֵל, וּמָחְלָן לְשִׁבְטֵי
יְשֻׁרוּן בְּכָל דּוֹר וָדוֹר,
וּמִבַּלְעָדֶיךָ אֵין לָנוּ מֶלֶךְ
מוֹחֵל וְסוֹלֵחַ אֶלָּא אַתָּה.

[13]*Anyone's death*: Literally, the "death of the dead" or the "death of the dying." The point may be "the death of people who, if they don't take action, will die."

☙

Commentaries on "You Extend Your Hand . . . You Set Humans Apart"

(*Atah Noten Yad . . . Atah Hivdalta Enosh*)

"Heart Surgery" in the Bible

GOD IS ON OUR SIDE

Dr. Marc Zvi Brettler

"You extend your hand to sinners" expresses a remarkable theology—that God not only wants people to repent (*shuv*), but facilitates repentance. God is, in other words, actually on our side, as we come to *N'ilah*'s opportunity for last-minute repentance. But where does this image of God extending a hand come from? Is it a Rabbinic innovation, or is it based on the Bible?

At first glance, this poem seems to have no biblical precedent. A major image of prophetic literature is the prophet summoning Israel to return, and Israel having to take the first step of heeding the divine summons. In Ezekiel 33:11, for example, where God says, "Turn back, turn back [*shuvu shuvu*] from your evil ways, that you may not die,"[1] the initiative is Israel's; God offers an ultimatum, but no help, no hand.

A closer look at the biblical corpus, however, reveals a small number of instances where God proactively facilitates repentance to one degree or another. The idea is developed primarily during the Babylonian exile (early sixth century BCE) and beyond, a time of great despair, when

Dr. Marc Zvi Brettler is the Bernice and Morton Professor of Judaic Studies at Duke University. He contributed to all volumes of *My People's Prayer Book: Traditional Prayers, Modern Commentaries*; to *My People's Passover Haggadah*; and to all volumes of the Prayers of Awe series. He coedited *The Jewish Annotated New Testament* and *The Jewish Study Bible* (a National Jewish Book Award recipient), coauthored *The Bible and the Believer*, and is sole author of (among many books and articles) *How to Read the Jewish Bible*. He was interviewed by Terry Gross on National Public Radio's *Fresh Air*.

Israel may well have imagined that it needed divine assistance to return to its God.

A good beginning point is the well-known verse from Lamentations (the collection of exilic poems commemorating the destruction of the Temple in 586 BCE). In 5:21, the poet says, "Take us back [*hashiveinu*], Adonai, to Yourself, so that we may come back [*v'nashuvah*]; renew our days as of old!" Reiterating the central verb of repentance, *shuv*, the verse implores God to "take us back" (the first step) "so that we may come back" (the second, following step). This same structure is found in Jeremiah 31:18, where Israel, chastened, pleads, "Take me back [*hasheiveni*] so that I may come back [*v'ashuvah*], for You, O Adonai, are my God." Here in Jeremiah ("Take me back"), as in Lamentations ("Take us back"), God initiates human repentance.

A similar idea is found in Isaiah 44:22, from a unit (Isaiah 40–55) usually attributed to an anonymous prophet writing in the Babylonian exile. That verse, which appears several times in the Yom Kippur liturgy, reads: "I wiped away your sins like a cloud, your transgressions like mist—come back [*shuvah*] to Me, for I have redeemed you." Only *after* God beneficently cleanses Israel of its sins does God demand that it return (*shuv*).

A more radical idea of what a helping hand might be comes from Jeremiah 24:6–7 and Ezekiel 36:25–27, both of which express the notion of a helping hand through "heart" imagery. The Jeremiah passage is probably datable to after 597 BCE, when exile had begun but had not yet reached its pinnacle in the destruction of 586 BCE. Jeremiah writes from the throes of despair, anticipating the worst. Speaking of exile-in-process, Jeremiah 24:6–7 notes:

> I will look upon them favorably, and I will bring them back to this land; I will build them and not overthrow them; I will plant them and not uproot them. And I will give them a heart to know Me, for I am Adonai. And they shall be my people and I will be their God. Indeed they will turn back to Me with all their heart.

Ezekiel, who was exiled to Babylonia in 597 BCE and lived through the destruction of Jerusalem in 586 BCE, uses even more radical heart imagery. After insisting that God will take Israel back for God's, not Israel's, sake (so that God's name will no longer be profaned among the nations), the prophet notes (36:25–27):

> I will sprinkle clean water upon you, and you shall be clean: I will cleanse you from all your uncleanness and from all your fetishes. And I will give you a new heart and put a new spirit into you: I will remove the heart of stone from your body and give you a heart of flesh; and I will put my spirit into you. Thus I will cause you to follow my laws and faithfully to observe my rules.

The promise of a new heart is critical. Biblical men and women thought the heart was the organ with which people think and understand. It is as if, therefore, God has given up on Israel's capacity even to think independently and in some sense impels them to follow the divine laws and rules.

These texts may recognize the idea found in Genesis 8:21, where after the flood God says, "The devising of people's mind [literally, "the heart," *lev*] is evil from their youth." Only by changing their "heart" do these prophets believe that people's "devisings" may become good rather than bad.

A similar (although not identical) idea to Jeremiah and Ezekiel comes from Deuteronomy 4:29–31, also from the exilic period. So far, we have seen God actively take the initiative. Here, as part of Israel's situation in exile, we see God not exactly holding out a hand, but offering assurance that repentance will occur. This passage as well uses the image of "heart" to express the need for a new understanding:

> You shall search there [in exile] for Adonai your God, you will find Him, for you will seek Him with all your heart [*l'vav*, a variation of *lev*] and soul. When you are in distress because all these things have befallen you, in the end, you shall return [*v'shavta*] to Adonai your God and obey Him. For Adonai your God is a compassionate God: He will not fail you nor let you perish; He will not forget the covenant that He made on oath with your fathers.

The passage assumes that Israel will necessarily "search" and "find" God in exile, just as the "compassionate God" will inevitably remember the covenant. So too, later, in Deuteronomy 30:1–3:[2]

When all these things befall you—the blessing and the curse that I have set before you [in Deuteronomy 28]—you shall take them [*v'hasheivota*, from the root *shuv*, "to turn"] to heart [*l'vav*] amidst the various nations to which Adonai your God has banished you. You shall return [*v'shavta*] to Adonai your God, and you and your children shall heed his command with all your heart [*l'vav*] and soul, just as I enjoin upon you this day. Adonai your God will then restore [*v'shav*] your fortunes [*sh'vutkha*] and have compassion upon you. He will turn [*v'shav*] and bring you together from all the peoples where Adonai your God has scattered you.

This is a remarkable passage in its repeated use of the verb *shuv*, "to turn" or "return," and hence, "to repent." Repentance is not just offered as an option, nor even just advised. Rather, it is assumed to occur as a matter of course. It is a bit softer in its "helping hand" than Ezekiel, however: Israel needs no new heart here; it will heed the divine command with its original one.

What type of helping hand is imagined in *N'ilah*? Is it God offering a gentle nudge toward repentance, or, as in Ezekiel, is God more actively holding our hand and pulling us up toward repentance—the equivalent of a new heart of flesh? Which of the two models did our anonymous poet have in mind? In either case, it is an optimistic response to counter the human predisposition to be "evil from . . . youth"—the same God who has created us will help us repent at the most crucial hour we call *N'ilah*.

⟨❧⟩

Please Remove Your Shoes

Rabbi Joshua M. Davidson

N'ilah derives from the same root as *na'al*, "shoe." When at the burning bush God commands Moses to remove his shoes and feel the sacred ground beneath him, Moses must decide whether to make himself vulnerable to the pain that life can bring—all those sharp stones that pierce and cut—knowing that only if he does can he experience all the fulfillment that life can bring.[1]

God's command to "put off your shoes from your feet" (Exodus 3:5) was intended for us as well.[2] We can become too comfortable in our old shoes, old outlooks, and old estimations of others and of ourselves. Only if we cut away the protective hardening on which we depend to shield us from disappointment and hurt can we hope to reconcile with others, with ourselves, and with our lives.

We have been hurt by others.

On Rosh Hashanah we read of Abraham taking Isaac up the mountain to slaughter him, until an angel cries out, "Stop." Isaac does

---

Rabbi Joshua M. Davidson graduated from Princeton University, was ordained by Hebrew Union College–Jewish Institute of Religion (New York), and serves the HUC–JIR National Board of Governors. From 2002 to 2013 he was senior rabbi of Temple Beth El of Northern Westchester in Chappaqua, New York, and is now senior rabbi of Congregation Emanu-El of the City of New York. Rabbi Davidson holds a Corkin Family Fellowship at the Herbert D. Katz Center for Advanced Judaic Studies at the University of Pennsylvania and Clal—The National Jewish Center for Learning and Leadership. His articles have appeared in the *Jewish Week*, *Commentary*, the *New York Post*, and the *Huffington Post*. His work includes anti-death-penalty advocacy, gay/lesbian inclusion, and interfaith dialogue.

not return home with his father. The Torah records no further contact between them. Some would say Isaac never forgives Abraham.

How many of us nurture resentment for times we felt sacrificed on the altar of a parent's expectations, a spouse's career, a good friend's ignoring our pain? How does one forgive when the bitterness runs deep and percolates through the years?

The Midrash tells us that after Sarah's death, Isaac journeyed to find Hagar,[3] the mother of Abraham's first son, Ishmael, whom Sarah had chased away, to reunite Hagar with Abraham lest his father remain alone. Despite all that Abraham has done to Isaac, the son performs this act of compassion. Why?

Isaac never receives an explanation for what transpired on the mountaintop so many years before. But he comes to accept that he never will. Acknowledging that there is a part of his father he will never understand, Isaac is able to give their relationship another chance.

We learn: there is a part of the people we love that we may never understand. They will never be exactly as we want them, yet we cannot expect to change them. Sometimes we simply have to set aside the past and reach out a hopeful hand again.

As tough as we may be on others, we often save our harshest condemnations for ourselves.

We are like the high priest Aaron approaching the altar on Yom Kippur to seek forgiveness for himself and for his people. But when he sees the altar's horned shape, he recoils in guilt, for it calls to mind the horns of the golden calf he had made when Moses had disappeared on Mount Sinai.[4] Sighting the golden calf from afar, Moses had smashed the tablets of the covenant in fury. It was as if Aaron had been carrying around their broken fragments ever since.

Our past mistakes weigh heavily upon us. Yet too often we hold ourselves to unattainable standards of perfection and then punish ourselves when we fail to meet them.

According to the Midrash, as Aaron trembles in shame for his sin, Moses places an arm around his shoulder, saying, "You should know that God accepts you as you are."[5] We learn: if God forgives us, surely we can forgive ourselves.

Sometimes we choose the wrong fork along life's complicated pathway. And sometimes misfortune chooses us. There are times when we feel empty and alone, and we can almost touch the darkness.

How do we lift ourselves up when we have fallen in despair? A Rabbinic legend begins to answer in the tale of the Israelites standing pinned between the Red Sea's swirling currents and Egypt's ever-approaching army. The tribes argue over who will dare march first into the waters God has not yet parted. In one version of the story, Nachshon ben Aminadab bravely leaps in of his own accord. In another, he panics and falls in. Only as the waves envelop him does he summon the strength to forge ahead.

Often we do not know our own mettle until we are tested.

Once I officiated at a wedding, an elegant affair in one of New York's fine hotels. Standing beneath the *chuppah*, I watched with tears in my eyes as the two flower girls marched down the aisle. Neither could have been more than ten. One of them suffered from a deeply debilitating muscular disease and labored with every step. But you would not have known it from the smile on her face. With her young cousin holding her tightly by the hand, she cast rose petals about her with the other.

We too can brace ourselves against the waves and forge ahead. As a rabbi, I am in awe of the way so many muster the fortitude to carry on through uncertainty, illness, suffering, and loss. Somewhere within, they find a bravery that not only strengthens them, but buoys the spirits of those who need them. We too can take hold of another's hand.

At *N'ilah*, God extends a divine hand to us, but do we have the courage to accept it? Standing as Moses stood, on holy ground, we must choose between entrenchment in old attitudes or openness to new ones, between certainty in our disappointments or the possibility of newfound fulfillment and joy. For the sake of our lives and our relationships, Yom Kippur entreats to unburden our resentments, forgive others and ourselves, grasp the hands reaching out to us, and enter the gates of a new year.

⊙⟩⟩⟩⟩⟩

"You Extend Your Hand"

Rabbi Edwin Goldberg, DHL

When the editorial team for the new CCAR Reform *machzor*, *Mishkan HaNefesh*, began to discuss our philosophy of the *N'ilah* service, we quickly decided to favor the image of God's holding out a hand, over the notion of the gates of repentance closing. It is commonplace to see the end of Yom Kippur through the frightening lens of scarcity, the rapidly approaching time when the divine window of forgiveness closes. But we preferred the reassuring image of abundance that is the hallmark of "You extend your hand."

To be sure, the traditional imagery of the day leads easily to accenting God as a judge and time running out for us, the defendants; but if God is a judge, God is a defense attorney's dream. God desperately *wants* to acquit us of our crimes and transgressions. It is as if God is saying to the defense attorney, "I want to let your client go, but you've got to give Me *something*—some way to justify announcing, 'The prisoner is free to go; court adjourned.'"

We wanted a metaphor to end Yom Kippur with the hopeful feeling that despite reasonable regrets from the year gone by, there was also much to build on for a good year ahead. The choice went beyond purely pastoral considerations. At stake was our core theology (or, more properly, our

---

Rabbi Edwin Goldberg, DHL, is senior rabbi of Temple Sholom of Chicago, received his doctorate in Hebrew letters from Hebrew Union College–Jewish Institute of Religion (Cincinnati), and served as the coordinating editor of the current Reform *machzor*, *Mishkan HaNefesh*. His field of interest is Jewish texts and their application to the modern world. Among his publications are *Saying No and Letting Go: Jewish Wisdom on Making Room for What Matters Most* (Jewish Lights) and *Divrei Mishkan HaNefesh*, a commentary on the Reform *machzor*.

religious anthropology). We broke sharply with the medieval insistence that human beings are so thoroughly steeped in sin that we have nothing good to recommend us. Indeed, throughout the afternoon our prayer book features not only the traditional recitation of sins but also a recognition of the good that we have done and that we hope still to do (*hakarat hatov*). This is not to say that we are faultless. But as much as we may be sinners, we are also virtuous enough to deserve God's help, while God is merciful enough to offer us a hand at maximizing that very virtue.

When I was growing up in Kansas City, at a then classical Reform temple, most congregants were not interested in *N'ilah*. They came for *Yizkor*, however, so the rabbi arranged services with *N'ilah* first, until the second to last page—and *then* we would have *Yizkor*. The message I took away was that *N'ilah* was the price to pay for *Yizkor*.

I probably never even read page 338 of the *Union Prayer Book* (the liturgy we used back then): "Thou puttest forth Thy hand unto those who go astray, and Thy right hand is extended to take back in love those who turn again unto Thee." Nor do I remember paying much attention to *Gates of Repentance*, page 514, and its version: "You hold out Your hand to those who have rebelled against You; Your right hand is stretched out to receive those who turn back to You." *Mishkan HaNefesh*, however, puts the image of God reaching out for us into a prominent place. Indeed, it is *the motif* for the service.

Our *machzor* editorial team (Rabbi Sheldon Marder, Rabbi Janet Marder, Rabbi Leon Morris, and myself) spent, literally, years together in conversation, building up our understanding of the High Holy Day liturgy and the worship that flows from it. Our notes on *N'ilah* include these insights on *Atah noten yad*, "You extend your hand":

1. In place of *Al Chet* (the long enumeration of sins), *N'ilah* provides a passage emphasizing God's desire to reach out to those who have done wrong. The symbolic act of "holding out a hand" suggests that God takes the initiative when we are too weak to extricate ourselves from sin.

2. The prayer focuses on God's constant presence and compassion, even in the face of sin and alienation. "Your right hand opens wide"[1] recalls Psalm 73:22–23, "I was senseless and ignorant, like a brute beast before You. Yet I was always with You; You held my right hand." In the Bible, the right hand symbolizes the favored

position, conveying a sense of safety, protection, and refuge (as in Genesis 48, when Jacob places his right hand on Ephraim's head to offer his blessing). Note also Psalm 16:8, "God is at my right hand; I shall never be shaken."

As these comments demonstrate, "You extend your hand" implies divine realization that compassion is the most important trait. By extension, we are to leave Yom Kippur with the recognition that compassion is the most important trait for us to practice—toward others, and ourselves as well.

The first Hebrew prayer book ever printed is *Machzor Minhag Roma* ("Prayer Book of the Roman Rite"), completed on August 21, 1486 / 20 Elul 5246 by Joshua Solomon Soncino in Casalmaggiore, Italy. *Atah noten yad* appears there in Hebrew characters twice the normal size, unlike any other prayer in the entire book. It may be that the printer was thinking of the Spanish conversos (called also Marranos), Jews who converted to Christianity following the anti-Jewish riots of 1381. The enlarged letters were then meant to encourage their *t'shuvah* (return to Judaism) by assuring them that God's hand remained stretched forth to them despite their baptism.[2] Alternatively, the printer may just have thought, as we do, that the key message of the High Holy Days is the offering of God's compassionate hand, even to sinners.

To underscore this central message of God's compassion and acceptance, *Mishkan HaNefesh*, three times, spreads the Hebrew words *Atah noten yad* wide across the page. By this point in the long day's liturgy, we have prayed, fasted, confessed, and asked forgiveness—all to the best of our ability. Now, instead of the long confession, *Al Chet*, we say, "You extend your hand"—"You reach out to us." The word *yad* can also mean "power." Thus *Atah noten yad* ("You give us *power*") can also suggest that as Yom Kippur concludes, God offers us the freedom and strength to turn our hands into instruments of blessing, to transform our myriad words of atonement into deeds of goodness.

Hence, we finish the day not with thoughts of closing gates, but with helping hands and open hearts. Ultimately the gates of prayer and repentance are not closing; they are always open.

⟨∿∿⟩

The Guy with the Butter

Rabbi Shira Stutman

New Jersey senator Bill Bradley recalls being the keynote speaker at a fancy fundraising dinner. The meal had just begun, and a waiter was circling, asking guests if they wanted a pat of butter for their bread. Senator Bradley said that yes, he would, in fact, like *two* pats of butter.

"Unfortunately, Mr. Senator, I'm only permitted to give out one pat of butter," the waiter said.

"Do you know who I am?" responded Bradley, fumingly. "I am an American Hall of Fame basketball player, Rhodes scholar, and former three-term Democratic U.S. senator from New Jersey."

"I know," said the waiter calmly. "And do you know who I am? I'm the guy with the butter." Then he walked off.

Sometimes, when I reach the heart of *N'ilah*, I feel like the guy with the butter.

N'ilah comes at the end of a very long day—a very long period of forty days, in fact, since the start of Elul, when we started our petitioning and penitential reflecting. Come the end of Yom Kippur, we're tired of the effort and tired physically too. Since early morning, not to mention

---

Rabbi Shira Stutman graduated from the Reconstructionist Rabbinical College in 2007 (as a Wexner Graduate Fellow) and is now senior rabbi at Washington, DC's innovative Sixth & I Historic Synagogue, where she works with her colleagues to create a spiritually connected, reflective, intellectually challenging and engaging Jewish community for the area's large millennial population. Rabbi Stutman also serves as the scholar-in-residence for the National Women's Philanthropy Program of the Jewish Federations of North America, teaches for the Wexner Heritage program, speaks nationally on a wide variety of topics, and chairs the board of directors of Jews United for Justice.

the night before, we have been standing before God, vulnerable and begging for our lives to last yet one more year. Our ears still ring with the *Un'taneh Tokef* and its terrifying reminder of the ways we might die—some of them quite painful—even before our time.

At *N'ilah*, we come upon another sobering reminder of who we are. *Mah anu*? What are we?

Meh chayeinu? What are our lives? What are we doing here?

Mah chasdeinu? What is our love? What do we love? How much love do we actually show?

Mah tzidkeinu? What is our righteousness/justice? How much justice do we actually do?

Mah yishu'ateinu? What is our salvation/help? What will save us?

Mah kocheinu? What is our strength? How much strength do we actually have?

Mah g'vurateinu? What is our might/power? How much power do we actually have?

To be clear, this is not the first time we have seen this litany of our human meagerness. It is in three other Yom Kippur services as well. Indeed, we say it every single morning in *Birkhot Hashachar*, the "morning blessings" that begin our day.

But at *N'ilah*, with the gates about to close, the questions become more desperate—perhaps because of how the prayer continues:

> *Mah nomar l'fanekha* . . . ? What can we say before You, Adonai our God . . . ? Are not all mighty ones as though they were nothing before You, men of fame as though they never existed . . . for most of their acts are without value [*tohu*] . . . ? . . . Everything is worthless [*havel*]."

The word *tohu* ("without value") evokes the formless confusion of the first days of creation, while *havel* ("worthless") evokes the powerlessness of Ecclesiastes. The intent of this passage seems clear enough: recognition that we are but a speck before God.

This prayer was sufficiently important for the early Talmudic authority Samuel to declare (Yoma 87a) that the entirety of *N'ilah* is contained within it. But why? Is it because our lives really are worthless? Are we really *nothing* before God? That cannot be, for if we truly were so utterly impotent, then why all the *t'shuvah* ("repentance") these past forty days?

To be sure, on Yom Kippur, with our failings so clearly brought to mind, it must *seem* to us that we are nothing. But by *N'ilah*, we are entitled to have second thoughts on such morbid self-abasement. As the gates close, we begin to talk back: "We'll tell you who we are, God. We're the guy with the butter."

Anu amekha, "we are your people." And we are deserving. Although we have missed the mark in many ways, we have done much good as well. We *have* acted justly—albeit not often enough. We *have* acted lovingly—and we'll do so even more next year. We speak in the plural, just as we do when we confess, because the whole is greater than any of its parts. *Mah kocheinu?* "What is our strength?" When viewed from a communal perspective: quite a lot.

If we view this prayer as a prayer of empowerment, we stand directly with Rebbe Levi Yitzchak of Berdichev, who famously cited the holy acts of his congregation at *N'ilah* to negotiate with God one last time. First, he pleaded, and the gates opened a bit; then he led a confession unlike any God had ever heard before, and they opened some more. And finally:

> He raised his head and cried out to the heavens. "Let them speak, not me," Levi Yitzchak boomed. "Remember the two rubles the widow Sarah paid her son's teacher, instead of spending them on the dresses she had longed for? Remember the bowl of soup the Yeshiva student shared with his classmates in spite of the fact that he was starving himself . . ." And so Levi Yitzchak went on and on, listing one by one the simple acts of loving-kindness, unselfishness, and mercy the ordinary men and women of his congregation had performed in the past year. As the congregation raised their eyes, they could see the gates of heaven open completely.[1]

The gates open fully not to petitions and supplications alone, but to standing with pride at all that we have accomplished, even as we know there is so much more still left to do. God is omniscient, but God needs us. We are the guys with the butter, the only ones around with the power to effectuate change.

The Metaphor
of Gates

Editor's Introduction

Rabbi Lawrence A. Hoffman, PhD

The master image of *N'ilah* is "gates": the gates of the ancient Temple (the inner sanctum, actually—the *heikhal*, as it was called); and the gates of heaven, as the Talmud puts it—meaning the end of daylight, as the sun finally sets. Essays in this book discuss other gates as well—the gates of prayer and the gates of repentance, for example.

N'ilah also features visible gates, the doors to the ark that holds the sacred Torah scrolls, which are purposefully left open throughout *N'ilah* so that we can appreciate their closing at *N'ilah*'s end. While Ashkenazi Jews call the ark the *aron*, Sephardi Jews name it the *heikhal*, an obvious extension of the Temple *heikhal*, whose closing doors (as we saw) were associated with *N'ilah* in Talmudic days. At no other time in the year do we keep them open that way. Of late, some congregations even invite congregants to walk up, one by one, and stand before the open ark in silent prayer. As if oblivious to the service going on around them, they take turns approaching the ark and speaking silently to God, whose presence they feel more acutely at that solitary solemn moment.

The theme of "gates" appears prominently throughout the poetic additions (the *piyyutim*) composed for the occasion. *Piyyutim* are a product of Jewish creativity all the way from the fifth century (or so) to the invention of printing, which effectively closed the traditional liturgical canon by providing mass-produced books to which it was difficult to make additions. The poetic impulse never entirely ended, however. Nineteenth-century Reform Jews, who revised the prayer books they inherited, composed many new prayers, some of them poetic, and in our time, liturgical poetry has flourished in many quarters worldwide, not just within the "progressive" Jewish camp, but within modern Orthodoxy as well, and even among secular Jews, especially in Israel.

The classical *piyyutim*, however, are those that preceded printing—beginning in the Land of Israel (c. fifth to eighth centuries) and then elsewhere. Those in *N'ilah* emphasize "gates."

We have included four such poems here:

91

1. *El Nora Alilah* ("God Whose Deeds Are Awesome")
2. *Sha'arei Armon* ("The Gates of the Palace")
3. *P'tach Lanu Sha'ar* ("Open a Gate for Us")
4. *Tei'anu V'tei'atru* ("May You Be Answered and May Your Request Be Granted")

El Nora Alilah ("God Whose Deeds Are Awesome") is by far the best known. Although Sephardi in origin, it is now standard fare in many Ashkenazi congregations too. Indeed, so many essays collected here cite it as the authors' favorite Yom Kippur prayer that it receives its own subsection of commentaries (pp. 139–167).

The author of *El Nora Alilah* was Moses ibn Ezra (c. 1055–1135), who etched his identity into his poetry for all time by an acrostic composed of the initial letters of each verse, spelling out MoSHeH CHaZaK, "Moses be strong." He is known particularly for poems on the theme of divine pardon, *s'lichah* (in Hebrew), to the point where he was known as Hasalach, "the author par excellence of *s'lichot* [poems on pardon]." Technically, this is such a poem, a *s'lichah*, that introduces Yom Kippur's final service with a reprise of its major theme, the certainty of God's forgiveness. The very first line lauds the "God whose deeds are awesome," but then identifies those deeds not as the creation of the universe, or the miracles of biblical history, but the incredible pardoning of human error.

Moses ibn Ezra spanned two eras, actually. He spent his early years in Granada, a center for Muslim and Jewish creativity in Spain's southern region of Andalusia. Among its best-known Muslim intellectuals of the next generation was the famed logician and philosopher Ibn Rushd (1126–1198), known more commonly to the West as Averroes, the man responsible for introducing Aristotle into Europe. By Averroes's time, however, this Jewish Golden Age was ending. Already in 1066, the bulk of Granadan Jews were massacred, and thereafter the weakening Spanish caliphate faced invasion from Christian forces in the north and more puritanical Muslims from Morocco in the south. The latter arrived first, the Almoravides in 1090 and the Almohades in 1148. They managed to delay the Christian reconquest, but their conservative approach to Islam led many Jews to flee. The best-known émigré was Maimonides, who escaped the later Almohades and settled in Egypt. Moses ibn Ezra, a victim of the earlier Almoravides, fled north to Christian Spain, where he wandered for the rest of his life, often in destitute financial circumstances.

The second poem included here, *Sha'arei Armon* ("The Gates of the Palace") is ascribed to Simeon bar Isaac bar Abun of Mainz (b. circa 950?), known also as Simeon the Great (Hagadol). As mentioned above, liturgical poetry arose in the Land of Israel from the fifth to eighth centuries. A second era of poetic greatness characterized Spain (Sepharad), where Moses ibn Ezra was representative. But medieval German Jewry also saw its share of poetic accomplishment and Simeon bar Isaac was part of that.

The German Jewish community (Ashkenaz) dates from the tenth century when Italian Jews crossed the Alps, settled the rich farming area of the Rhineland, and built a set of Talmudic academies that nurtured Ashkenazi rabbinic creativity ever after. The most famous of the "founding fathers" was Rabbenu Gershom ben Judah (c. 960–1040), "the Light of the Exile" (M'or Hagolah) as he is called—the jurist who, among other things, officially banned polygamy *de jure* (*de facto*, it had already ended throughout Ashkenaz), despite biblical precedent allowing it. He also facilitated international trade by prohibiting the reading of other people's letters, a decision that allowed Jewish traders to deposit business documents with one another along the trade route from Europe to the Byzantine east, without fear of having their bids and contracts read (and bettered) by competitors. Simeon bar Isaac bar Abun was an older contemporary of Rabbenu Gershom.

The image of gates plays a relatively minor role in Moses ibn Ezra's *El Nora Alilah*. The word *n'ilah* ("closing [of the gates]") concludes each stanza, but actual reference to *sh'arim* (the Hebrew for "gates") is lacking. By contrast, "gates" is the express topic of Simeon bar Isaac's *Sha'arei Armon*, which lists a series of gates associated with *N'ilah*—gates of the "palace," gates of heaven, and gates of prayer. The first two choices reflect the debate in the Palestinian Talmud (4:1 = 7b) over the identity of the gates that close when Yom Kippur ends. For Rav, these are the gates of heaven; for Yochanan, they are the gates of the *heikhal*, the inmost enclosure of the Temple. Our anonymous poet includes them both.

Sha'arei Armon is part of the cantorial repetition of the *Amidah*—just one of several poetic additions there. Such poetry is commonplace in holy-day versions of the *Amidah*—independent stanzas, actually, of a larger whole, an extended poem with nine parts called a *k'dushta*. We rarely have all nine parts nowadays, and what we have are usually a combination of stanzas from several poems rather than the original stanzas of

any single one. The stanzas are apportioned among the first three blessings of the *Amidah*, with six of the nine occurring in the third one, the
K'dushah—hence the name *k'dushta*, Aramaic for the Hebrew *k'dushah*.
The tenth and climactic stanza is known as a *siluk*. Here, we get only four
of those nine parts, and the first three are tiny, so that almost immediately
worshipers encounter *Sha'arei Armon*, the *siluk* itself.

We know it is a *siluk* from verse 1 (p. 102), the characteristic
introductory line to a *siluk* everywhere: "And so, let holiness rise up to
You, for You are our God, king." The "holiness" to which it refers is
the declaration of holiness that we find in the *K'dushah*—more properly
called *K'dushat Hashem*, the "Holiness of God's Name"—the place in the
Amidah where the *siluk* is embedded.

As verse 1 is the introduction to the poem, so verse 8 (p. 103)
is its conclusion, although unlike verse 1, it is specific to this *siluk*
alone: "And through them may You be revered and sanctified, as
the utterances of the assembly of holy seraphim." The poet pictures
us walking through the gates mentioned in the poem. As we do so,
God is to be "revered and sanctified" by our recitation of the *K'dushah*,
with its key phrase that acknowledges God's sanctity: "Holy holy holy"
(*Kadosh kadosh kadosh*).

P'tach Lanu Sha'ar ("Open a Gate for Us"), our third selection, is
less a poem than an exhortation, a fervent plea for God to open the gates
through which we wish to pass, the gates that represent emerging from
our trial of Yom Kippur to life renewed.

This poem occurs just prior to the Thirteen Attributes of God, a
topic important enough to have been assigned its own volume in this
series, *Encountering God:* El Rachum V'chanun—*God Merciful and
Gracious*. These attributes occur in the *Kol Nidre* service that introduces
Yom Kippur and then, again, as a concluding bookend here. "Open a
Gate for Us" thus anticipates the reprise of the Thirteen Attributes, which
promise God's merciful forgiveness as the central message of *N'ilah*.

That the attributes promise divine compassion is a story in itself.

They are biblical originally (from Exodus 34:6–7), within the larger
narrative of the golden calf, the classic example of the Israelites' foray
into idolatry. In context, Moses has climbed Mount Sinai to get the tablets of stone; anxious over his sustained absence, the Israelites construct
a calf to be their god. This failure of faith occasions God's wrath. But
the breach with God is redressed; Moses reclimbs the mountain and this

time receives not just a second set of tablets, but the revelation of God's true nature as well, God's thirteen defining attributes. This list becomes paradigmatic throughout the Bible, which cites them, at least in part, no fewer than sixteen times.

But the attributes as given in Exodus are not the same as the prayer-book version, which deliberately shortens them. The biblical original accents God's judgment as much as God's mercy. Initially God is indeed described as "merciful and gracious," but halfway through, we discover also that God will by no means cleanse the guilty—God even visits the sins of the fathers upon the following four generations of children!

> Adonai, Adonai, merciful and gracious God, endlessly patient, most kind and truthful, extending kindness to thousands, forgiving sins and transgressions and misdeeds. Yet He surely does not cleanse, but visits the iniquity of parents upon children and their children's children, upon the third and the fourth generations. (Exodus 34:6–7)

To arrive at a "prayer-book version," the Talmud omits the negatives. As the attributes appear in the liturgy, then, God is

> Adonai, Adonai, merciful and gracious God, endlessly patient, most kind and truthful, extending kindness to thousands, forgiving sins and transgressions and misdeeds, cleansing.

This liturgical shortening of the biblical original provides a God who is altogether compassionate. It is that revisionist version that becomes the "Thirteen Attributes" of our liturgy: first, in the *Kol Nidre* service (which introduces the fast) and then, again, at the *N'ilah* service (which ends it).

The Thirteen Attributes thus become their own set of gates, leading into and out of Yom Kippur. They function at the beginning (*Kol Nidre*) as a literary foreshadowing of the end: God's guaranteed pardon that awaits us in *N'ilah*.

In *N'ilah*, however, they are enlarged with the further message from the accompanying prayers that we looked at above (pp. 67–71), "You Extend Your Hand" (*Atah Noten Yad*) and "You Set Humans Apart" (*Atah Hivdalta Enosh*). As Yom Kippur begins, we wallow in our unworthiness; as it concludes, we take comfort in the fact that we mortals may be mere "nothings" in the grand scheme of things, but God has nonetheless marked us off as unique and worthy of being forgiven.

This concluding version of the Thirteen Attributes is announced by the exclamation "Open a gate for us" (*P'tach lanu sha'ar*), the gate, again, being only loosely specified. In some fashion, it is the gate of forgiveness, but here it refers also to the gate of the Thirteen Attributes, the gate that was opened at *Kol Nidre* and remains open at *N'ilah*.

Our fourth, and last, poetic inclusion, *Tei'anu V'tei'atru* ("May You Be Answered and May Your Request Be Granted") is also a product of Sephardi Jews. While we do not know for sure who composed the poem, medieval tradition, at least, ascribed it to none other than Judah Halevi (c. 1075–1141), the epitome of the philosopher/poet ideal so typical of Spain. Our information comes from Aaron ben Jacob Hakohen, a fourteenth-century authority who lived in Provence and then Spain. His reflection sheds light also on a related Yom Kippur custom of the time. At the end of *N'ilah*, he says:

> There are places where people wish each other well by saying *tei'aneh v'tei'ater* ("May you be answered and your request granted")—that is, "May your prayer be accepted [by God]." Thus the poet Rabbi Judah Halevi, may he merit long life, wrote *Tei'anu V'tei'atru*. In other places, people say to one another, *Teichatmu l'chaim* ("May you be sealed [in the book of life] for good"), and people respond [to this by saying], *Teichatmu l'chayim v'tizku l'shanim rabbot* ("May you be sealed [in the book of life] for good and may you merit long life").[1]

Tei'anu V'tei'atru is a more than apt summary of *N'ilah* and even comes, appropriately, in Sephardi ritual, just as the service is about to end. It is a Sephardi hallmark, but, of late, part and parcel of other communities as well. Indeed, the very terms Sephardi and Ashkenazi should nowadays be used with care. Reform rabbis, rooted firmly in nineteenth-century Germany, so admired the Spanish Golden Age that they regularly borrowed poetry from the Sephardi tradition, and by now, such borrowing is commonplace among all modern prayer-book editors who appreciate the way the various branches of Judaism can enrich one another. *Tei'anu V'tei'atru* is, therefore, included ubiquitously today, albeit not necessarily at the service's end, and not always with the opening lines intact. Editors tend to omit or shorten all but verse 6 (p. 107), the lengthy staccato alphabetic acrostic that gives the poem its vitality.

The opening poem, *El Nora Alilah*, merely suggests the theme of gates; *Tei'anu V'tei'atru*, by contrast, is a veritable riot of imagery. While other poems identify the gates with Talmudic prototypes (gates of heaven, of prayer, of the Temple, or even of the Thirteen Attributes), *Tei'anu V'tei'atru* invents gates for the entire Hebrew alphabet, from A to Z, as it were. We have other such poetry—the Yom Kippur confessions, for example, which do not stipulate specific sins so much as they imagine as many sins as there are letters. The impact in both cases is to amplify the imagery beyond the very possibility of confining it to any single set of actual examples. The redundancy of the imagery (gates or sins) suggests just how very many instances there are, as if to say they are altogether beyond counting. The Yom Kippur confession overwhelms us with just how much wrong there is in the world; here, at *N'ilah*, we are similarly overwhelmed with just how much blessing there can be as we pass through gates to life reimagined.

꘎꘎꘎

Annotated Translation

Dr. Joel M. Hoffman

God Whose Deeds Are Awesome (*El Nora Alilah*)

[1]God whose deeds are awesome, grant us pardon, as our prayers and the gates close.
[2]Those who are called "few in number" lift their eyes to You and worship in trepidation, as our prayers and the gates close.

¹אֵל נוֹרָא עֲלִילָה, הַמְצֵא
לָנוּ מְחִילָה בִּשְׁעַת
הַנְּעִילָה.
²מְתֵי מִסְפָּר קְרוּאִים לְךָ
עַיִן נוֹשְׂאִים וּמְסַלְּדִים
בְּחִילָה בִּשְׁעַת הַנְּעִילָה.

[1]*Our prayers and the gates close*: This long English phrase translates the two Hebrew words *b'sha'at han'ilah*—literally, "at the time of *n'ilah*." *N'ilah* is the word for "closing" in general, and also specifically the name of the closing Yom Kippur service. "The time of *n'ilah*" thus refers both to the metaphoric closing of the gates and to the prayer service in which the poem appears. The *N'ilah* service in English is just called "*N'ilah*," so we have no pithy way in English to capture this dual reference. Instead we spell out the two things that are closing: prayers and gates. Then, for the sake of grammar, we add "our" in English—unfortunately at the cost of mixing references later in the poem, where the gates are both "ours" and "theirs."

[2]*Few in number*: A reference to Genesis 34:30, where Jacob laments the trouble that Simeon and Levi have brought to the family, who are "few in number." The context is Simeon and Levi's violent defense of their sister, Dinah.

[2]*Worship in trepidation*: The Hebrew here, in a slightly different grammatical form, is from Job 6:10. The context is Job's feeling of

³They pour their soul out to You.
Erase their misdeeds and lies.
Grant them pardon as our prayers
and the gates close.
⁴Be their refuge. And save them
from curses. And seal them for
honor and joy, as our prayers and
the gates close.
⁵Be gracious and compassionate
to them. Execute justice on every
tyrant and foe, as our prayers and
the gates close.
⁶Remember the righteousness of
their ancestors, and renew their
days as of old, as our prayers and
the gates close.

³שׁוֹפְכִים לְךָ נַפְשָׁם מְחֵה
פִּשְׁעָם וְכַחֲשָׁם הַמְצִיאֵם
מְחִילָה בִּשְׁעַת הַנְּעִילָה.
⁴הֱיֵה לָהֶם לְסִתְרָה
וְחַלְּצֵם מִמְּאֵרָה וְחָתְמֵם
לְהוֹד וּלְגִילָה בִּשְׁעַת
הַנְּעִילָה.
⁵חֹן אוֹתָם וְרַחֵם וְכָל
לוֹחֵץ וְלוֹחֵם עֲשֵׂה בָהֶם
פְּלִילָה בִּשְׁעַת הַנְּעִילָה.
⁶זְכֹר צִדְקַת אֲבִיהֶם
וְחַדֵּשׁ אֶת יְמֵיהֶם כְּקֶדֶם
וּתְחִלָּה בִּשְׁעַת הַנְּעִילָה.

consolation that, despite his suffering, he did not deny God words.
Because the verb in the Hebrew phrase only appears once, we do not
know its meaning for sure. It has come to mean "praise" or "worship,"
so that's how we translate it here. Another understanding, probably
more faithful to the text in Job, is "leap" or "writhe."

⁴*Save them from curses*: That is, remove them from the effects of the
curses. It's tempting to use "shield" here, but the idea seems to be that
the curses have already taken effect, and the people have to be saved,
presumably by the refuge from the first part of the line. The Hebrew
for "curses" (which happens to be singular in Hebrew) is the rare word
m'ira, from the root *alef.r.r.*, "curse."

⁵*Execute justice on every tyrant and foe*: Literally, "on every tyrant and foe
execute justice"—a word order that is more successful in Hebrew than
in English—so the Hebrew has the effect of starting with tyranny and
reversing it.

⁶*Renew their days as of old*: An extension of a common phrase. Here the
Hebrew word *t'chilah*, "at first," is added to "of old," for the sake of

⁷Announce a year of favor, and restore the remnants of the flock to Jerusalem and Israel, as our prayers and the gates close.
⁸Michael, prince of Israel, and Elijah and Gabriel: Announce our redemption, as our prayers and the gates close.
⁹May you earn a long life, children and parents alike, in joy and in celebration, as our prayers and the gates close.

⁷קְרָא נָא שְׁנַת רָצוֹן
וְהָשֵׁב שְׁאֵרִית הַצֹּאן
לְאָהֳלִיבָה וְאָהֳלָה בִּשְׁעַת
הַנְּעִילָה. ⁸מִיכָאֵל שַׂר
יִשְׂרָאֵל אֵלִיָּהוּ וְגַבְרִיאֵל
בַּשְּׂרוּ נָא הַגְּאֻלָּה בִּשְׁעַת
הַנְּעִילָה. ⁹תִּזְכּוּ לְשָׁנִים
רַבּוֹת הַבָּנִים וְהָאָבוֹת
בְּדִיצָה וּבְצָהֳלָה בִּשְׁעַת
הַנְּעִילָה.

the ongoing rhyme. We leave that word untranslated, because we have already abandoned any attempt of mirroring the Hebrew rhyme scheme.
⁷*Jerusalem and Israel*: Represented by two somewhat rare proper names, Oholiva and Ohola—literally, "my tent is in it" and "its [own] tent." The former term refers to Jerusalem, while the latter to what is often called "Samaria." (It's tempting to use "Judah and Samaria" in English, but that phrase now carries strong political connotations that the original Hebrew does not.)
⁸*Prince of Israel*: Perhaps based on Daniel (10:21 and 12:1), where Michael is called the "prince" of Israel, in the context of unnamed princes of Persia and Greece.
⁸*Our redemption*: In Hebrew, just "the redemption."
⁹*Earn*: Others, "merit." "Be rewarded with" is another possibility.
⁹*In joy*: The slightly odd grammar here matches similarly odd grammar in the original Hebrew.
⁹*Children and parents*: Others, the more literal "sons and fathers." Perhaps in response to those other translations, the North American Conservative Movement's *Mahzor Lev Shalem for Rosh Hashanah and Yom Kippur* (2010) changes the Hebrew text here to "sons and daughters."

The Hebrew here follows a strict structural pattern. The chorus has three rhyming lines, each ending in *-ilah*. Each verse has four lines: two initial lines that rhyme with each other, a third line that rhymes with *-ilah* from the chorus, and a fourth line that repeats the last line of the chorus (and so also, of necessity, rhymes with *-ilah*). In addition, a weak assonance scheme in each verse connects the first word of each verse's third line to the rhyme from the end of the first two. Graphically, the pattern of the poem is as follows:

Chorus: A A "A"
Verse: B B bA "A"
Verse: C C cA "A"
etc.

where capital letters represent rhymes, lowercase letters represent more general assonance, and quoted letters represent exact duplication.

An English example on the same general theme as *El Nora Alilah* with the same rhyme scheme but with less metrical precision might be:

1. God of awe and might // You alone our sins requite // on this *N'ilah* night
2. Called "the numbered few" // we lift our eyes to you // through prayer and fright // on this *N'ilah* night

All three parts of line 1 (the chorus) rhyme. The first two parts of line 2 rhyme with each other. The third part of line 2 starts with the rhyme from the first two parts of that line; then that third part ends with a rhyme from line 1. And the fourth part of line 2 repeats the end of line 1.

In addition to the rhyming, a message of tribute to the poem's author, Moses ibn Ezra, appears in the first letters of the verses: MoSHeH CHaZaK, literally, "Moses, may he be strong," akin to the colloquial "Way to go, Moses."

Beyond the structure, the words themselves are laden with allusion and double entendres (see below, "our prayers and the gates close").

There is, obviously, no way we can capture the meaning, the references, and the rhymes in our English translation. Here we focus on the meaning and references at the cost of the structure.

Finally, our text here includes a verse that was added on to the original poem. Numbered 8 here, the line follows the same general rhyme scheme as the others, but does not contain the weak assonance we represent above with lowercase letters, and the line does not contribute to the acronym.

The Gates of the Palace (*Sha'arei Armon*)

¹And so, let holiness rise up to You, for You are our God, king.
²To those who faithfully expound Torah, quickly open the gates of the palace.
³To those who cling to your law, quickly open the gates of hidden treasure.
⁴To those who congregate, quickly open the gates of the glorious courtyard.
⁵To those with bleary eyes, quickly open the gates of the camp on high.
⁶To those who are beautiful and pure, quickly open the gates of purity.

¹וּבְכֵן לְךָ תַּעֲלֶה קְדֻשָּׁה
כִּי אַתָּה אֱלֹהֵינוּ מֶלֶךְ
מוֹחֵל וְסוֹלֵחַ.
²שַׁעֲרֵי אַרְמוֹן מְהֵרָה
תִּפְתַּח לְבוֹאֲרֵי אָמוֹן.
³שַׁעֲרֵי גְנוּזִים מְהֵרָה
תִּפְתַּח לְדָתְךָ אֲחוּזִים.
⁴שַׁעֲרֵי הֵיכַל הַנֶּחְמָדִים
מְהֵרָה תִּפְתַּח לְוֹעֲדִים.
⁵שַׁעֲרֵי זְבוּל מַחֲנַיִם
מְהֵרָה תִּפְתַּח לְחַכְלִילִי
עֵינָיִם.
⁶שַׁעֲרֵי טָהֳרָה מְהֵרָה
תִּפְתַּח לְיָפָה וּבָרָה.

²*Faithfully expound Torah*: In Hebrew, just "faithfully expound." We would prefer not to spell out the metaphor in English (because it's not spelled out in Hebrew), but, unlike in Hebrew, "faithfully expound" is ungrammatical, and "faithful expounders" is awkward.

³*Hidden treasure*: In Hebrew, just "hidden," a common poetic reference to hidden treasure.

⁴*Congregate*: That is, congregate in your name. But here we have the option of mirroring the terse Hebrew, so we do.

⁵*Bleary eyes*: Presumably, the eyes are bleary from studying Torah.

⁷To those who are not widowed, quickly open the gates of the mighty crown.
⁸And through them may You be revered and sanctified, as the utterances of the assembly of holy seraphim.

⁷שַׁעֲרֵי כֶתֶר הַמְיֻמָּן
מְהֵרָה תִפְתַּח לְלֹא
אַלְמָן.
⁸וּבָהֶם תֵּעָרֵץ וְתִקְדָּשׁ
כְּסוֹד שִׂיחַ שַׂרְפֵי קֹדֶשׁ.

⁷*Not widowed*: Marriage and widowhood are common metaphors for God's company or lack thereof.
⁷*Mighty crown*: Alas, "the crown" in English points in the direction of English royalty, not God's crown, but no better alternative presents itself.
⁸*Utterances . . . seraphim*: See *My People's Prayer Book*, vol. 2, *The Amidah*, p. 92.

The original Hebrew is a series of six lines of triplets. In each line, the first and third triplets rhyme. Structurally, the first triplet takes the form of "gates of . . . ," starting with "gates of the palace" in line 2, followed, in line 3, by "gates of hidden treasure." The second triplet, constant throughout the poem, is the imperative "quickly open." The third triplet is a group for whom the gates in the first triplet should be opened, staring with "those who faithfully " in line 2, followed by "those who cling to your law" in line 3.

Additionally, the first and third triplets, taken together, form an alphabetic acrostic. "Palace" in Hebrew starts with *alef*, and "expounders" starts with *bet*; "hidden treasure" starts with *gimel*, and "law" (which is the first word of the Hebrew phrase "those who cling to your law") starts with *dalet*. And so forth.

The genius of the poem is the combination of these three elements: image-laden vocabulary, strict rhyming in nearly strict meter, and the acrostic. Capturing any one of these elements would be difficult in English. We certainly cannot capture all three. Unfortunately, the poem loses most of its impact stripped of its rhythm and rhyme. But almost nothing rhymes with "palace" in English, and "castle" and similar words are similarly unhelpful. So we resort to prose. (We get a small sense of the original text with "The palace gates // be opened wide. // To devoted, faithful Torah guides.")

Also, for the sake of grammatical English, we transpose what would be the first and third triplets in each line. Otherwise, we'd be left with the dubious "the gates of the palace open quickly to those who faithfully expound Torah," which sounds more like a sentence about what the gates do than an imperative. Unfortunately, this step leaves us with "palace" at the end of the first line, robbing the translation of the impact of the Hebrew, which starts with "gates of the palace." Another translation option would be to ignore the imperative. For example, "let the gates of the palace be quickly opened" or even "the gates of the palace be quickly opened."

Open a Gate for Us (*P'tach Lanu Sha'ar*)

¹Open a gate for us when the gate is locked on us, for the day has passed.
²The day will pass; the sun will set and pass; we will come before your gates.

¹פְּתַח לָנוּ שַׁעַר, בְּעֵת
נְעִילַת שַׁעַר, כִּי פָנָה יוֹם.
²הַיּוֹם יִפְנֶה, הַשֶּׁמֶשׁ יָבֹא
וְיִפְנֶה, נָבוֹאָה שְׁעָרֶיךָ.

¹*On us*: We add "on us" to mirror the pattern of the Hebrew: The first two lines here are in triplets, of which the first and second triplets end with the same word. Some translations prefer to start "Open us a gate" or "Open for us a gate"—which makes it easier to end the second triplet with the matching "gate"—but we don't think those renditions are sufficiently within the bounds of standard English.
¹*Passed*: From the Hebrew *p.n.h*, not the root *ayin.b.r*, which forms the central metaphor of "passing" in other High Holy Day texts such as *Un'tanah Tokef.*

[3]Please, God, grant forbearance, forgiveness, pardon, absolution, mercy, atonement. Conquer sin and iniquity.

³אָנָּא, אֵל נָא, שָׂא נָא,
סְלַח נָא, מְחַל נָא, חֲמָל
נָא, רַחֶם נָא, כַּפֶּר נָא,
כְּבֹשׁ חֵטְא וְעָוֹן.

[2]*We will come before*: Or perhaps "we will enter." It's a big difference, unfortunately left ambiguous in the Hebrew.

[3]*Please, God*: The Hebrew has two words commonly translated as "please" here: *na* and the longer *ana*. Both are more accurately honorifics, in other contexts best translated as "sir." Here we use "please" for lack of a better option. We also miss the assonance and meter of the Hebrew's two rhyming trochaic feet: *AH-na EL-na*. (These same words appear in the famous Friday evening hymn *Y'did Nefesh*.)

[3]*Grant*: The Hebrew here is a sequence of verbs without objects. For instance (immediately below) "forbear" and then "forgive." Unlike Hebrew, English doesn't generally allow transitive verbs to appear without subjects, but it does with nouns. So we use "grant" to let us substitute nouns for the verbs in Hebrew, thereby preserving both the content and grammaticality of the Hebrew.

Each verb in Hebrew is followed by *na*—"please," in a sense, as described immediately above, but also a metrical placeholder to help the series of verbs flow better. We leave *na* untranslated here.

[Note: The Thirteen Attributes follow. We provide them here, without notes, for context. See pp. 94–96.]

[1]God is a king seated on a throne of mercy, governing graciously, pardoning the sins of his people, removing the irst, irst, extending pardon to sinners and forgiveness to transgressors, dealing

¹אֵל מֶלֶךְ יוֹשֵׁב עַל
כִּסֵּא רַחֲמִים, מִתְנַהֵג
בַּחֲסִידוּת, מוֹחֵל עֲוֹנוֹת
עַמּוֹ, מַעֲבִיר רִאשׁוֹן
רִאשׁוֹן, מַרְבֶּה מְחִילָה
לְחַטָּאִים וּסְלִיחָה
לְפוֹשְׁעִים, עֹשֶׂה

generously with all living beings.
[2]You do not treat them according
to their evil. [3]God, You instructed
us to recite the thirteen attributes.
[4]For our sake, remember the covenant of the thirteen attributes
today, as you once revealed them
to the Humble One, as is written,
"Adonai descended in a cloud,
and he stood with him there, and
he said God's name. Then Adonai
passed before him and said,
[5]'Adonai, Adonai, merciful and
gracious God, endlessly patient,
most kind and truthful, extending
kindness to thousands, forgiving
sins and transgressions and misdeeds, cleansing.'"

צְדָקוֹת עִם כָּל בָּשָׂר
וָרוּחַ. [2]לֹא כְרָעָתָם
תִּגְמֹל. [3]אֵל, הוֹרֵיתָ לָּנוּ
לוֹמַר שְׁלשׁ עֶשְׂרֵה. [4]וּזְכָר
לָנוּ הַיּוֹם בְּרִית שְׁלשׁ
עֶשְׂרֵה כְּמוֹ שֶׁהוֹדַעְתָּ
לֶעָנָו מִקֶּדֶם, כְּמוֹ שֶׁכָּתוּב
וַיֵּרֶד יְיָ בֶּעָנָן וַיִּתְיַצֵּב
עִמּוֹ שָׁם וַיִּקְרָא בְשֵׁם
יְיָ וַיַּעֲבֹר יְיָ עַל פָּנָיו
וַיִּקְרָא. [5]יְיָ, יְיָ, אֵל רַחוּם
וְחַנּוּן, אֶרֶךְ אַפַּיִם וְרַב
חֶסֶד וֶאֱמֶת, נֹצֵר חֶסֶד
לָאֲלָפִים, נֹשֵׂא עָוֹן וָפֶשַׁע
וְחַטָּאָה, וְנַקֵּה.

May You Be Answered and May Your Request Be Granted (*Tei'anu V'tei'atru*)

[1]May you be answered and
may your request be granted
in mercy from on high. [2]May
your cry be accepted. [3]May
your prayer be heard in favor.

[1]תֵּעָנוּ וְתֵעָתְרוּ בְּרַחֲמִים
מִן הַשָּׁמַיִם. [2]תְּקֻבַּל
צַעֲקַתְכֶם. [3]תִּשָּׁמַע
בְּרָצוֹן תְּפִלַתְכֶם.

[1]*Answered . . . request be granted*: Our translation misses the clear
Hebrew assonance: the first two Hebrew words are *tei'anu* and *tei'atru*.
Unfortunately, only words from the root "answer" begin "ans-" in English,
so we cannot capture this effect in English and still use the word "answer"
in our translation. We get a sense of the original Hebrew from the similar
"may you receive response and respite." The words "answer" and "request"
(in slightly different grammatical form) recur in line 4, below.

⁴And may the voice of your
request be answered. ⁵And may
Adonai our God open up for us
and for all of Israel:
⁶The gates of light, the gates of
blessing, the gates of joy, the gates
of gladness, the gates of prosper-
ity, the gates of good council, the
gates of merit, the gates of compassion, the gates of goodness,
the gates of salvation, the gates
of atonement, the gates of study,
the gates of expiation, the gates
of comfort, the gates of forgiveness, the gates of assistance, the
gates of redemption, the gates of
righteousness, the gates of acceptance, the gates of complete healing, the gates of peace, the gates
of tranquility, the gates of Torah,
the gates of prayer. ⁷And may He
remove from your midst jealousy

⁴וְיֵעָנֶה לְקוֹל עֲתִירַתְכֶם.
⁵וְיִפְתַּח יְיָ אֱלֹהֵינוּ לָנוּ
וּלְכָל יִשְׂרָאֵל.
⁶שַׁעֲרֵי אוֹרָה, שַׁעֲרֵי
בְרָכָה, שַׁעֲרֵי גִילָה, שַׁעֲרֵי
דִיצָה, שַׁעֲרֵי הַצְלָחָה,
שַׁעֲרֵי וַעַד טוֹב, שַׁעֲרֵי
זָכִיוֹת, שַׁעֲרֵי חֶמְלָה,
שַׁעֲרֵי טוֹבָה, שַׁעֲרֵי
יְשׁוּעָה, שַׁעֲרֵי כַּפָּרָה,
שַׁעֲרֵי לִמּוּד, שַׁעֲרֵי
מְחִילָה, שַׁעֲרֵי נֶחָמָה,
שַׁעֲרֵי סְלִיחָה, שַׁעֲרֵי
עֶזְרָה, שַׁעֲרֵי פְּדוּת, שַׁעֲרֵי
צְדָקָה, שַׁעֲרֵי קַבָּלָה,
שַׁעֲרֵי רְפוּאָה שְׁלֵמָה,
שַׁעֲרֵי שָׁלוֹם, שַׁעֲרֵי
שַׁלְוָה, שַׁעֲרֵי תוֹרָה,
שַׁעֲרֵי תְּפִלָּה. ⁷וְיָסִיר
מִתּוֹכְכֶם קִנְאָה וְשִׂנְאָה

⁶*Light . . . blessing . . .* : In Hebrew these form an alphabetic acrostic, a
feat we cannot duplicate in English without resorting to absurd words.
⁶*Torah . . . prayer*: These both end in *tav*, the last letter of the Hebrew
alphabet, as though the gates overflow the alphabet.

and hatred and contention. [8]And
may He establish among you what
is written: "Adonai your ancestors'
God will multiply you a thousand-
fold and bless you, as He promised you." [9]And may He seal you
in the book of good life. [10]May
this be his will. [11]Let us say,
Amen.

וְתַחֲרוּת. [8]וִיקַיֵּם
בָּכֶם מִקְרָא שֶׁכָּתוּב, יְיָ
אֱלֹהֵי אֲבוֹתֵיכֶם יֹסֵף
עֲלֵיכֶם כָּכֶם אֶלֶף פְּעָמִים
וִיבָרֵךְ אֶתְכֶם כַּאֲשֶׁר
דִּבֶּר לָכֶם. [9]וְיַחְתֶּמְכֶם
בְּסֵפֶר חַיִּים טוֹבִים. [10]וְכֵן
יְהִי רָצוֹן. [11]וְנֹאמַר אָמֵן.

Commentaries on the Metaphor of Gates

Ask Not for Whom the Gates Close

OR "WHEN" OR "WHAT THEY EVEN ARE"

Rabbi Bradley Shavit Artson, DHL

L ike the *grande finale* culminating a fireworks show, we expect something grand at the end of Yom Kippur. For twenty-four hours our souls have immersed in the flow of fasting, praying, singing, confessing, and absorbing scriptural readings. Like angels, we dress in white, refrain from eating or attending to bodily needs. And like angels, we seek to soar upward, purified from the distractions and dirt of daily life. The culmination of this packed day—filled with more *mitzvot* than any other twenty-four-hour stretch in the year, crammed with ample time for reflection, contemplation, and honest self-scrutiny—asks for something noble to drive its message home; and we get it—with *N'ilah*.

Rabbi Bradley Shavit Artson, DHL (www.bradartson.com), holds the Abner and Roslyn Goldstine Dean's Chair of the Ziegler School of Rabbinic Studies and is vice president of American Jewish University in Los Angeles. A member of the Philosophy Department, he is particularly interested in theology, ethics, and the integration of science and religion. He is also dean of the Zacharias Frankel College in Potsdam, Germany. A contributor for *Huffington Post* and *Times of Israel*, and a public figure on Facebook with about 50,000 likes, he is the author of 12 books and over 250 articles.

The Uncertainty

Yes, *N'ilah* definitely delivers that grandeur: in music that is a hit parade of the High Holy Day Top Ten; by asking us to stand throughout the entire final service, ark open, all eyes forward; and with the culminating liturgical affirmations recited responsively by cantor and congregation, and the final following blast of the shofar.

Small wonder that as the noise crescendos and then tapers away, we have the sense of completing a marathon—the marathon of our lives. We're sweaty, tired, worn, and hungry, but champions of the spirit.

Again and again, our liturgy suggests the image of gates closing upon us, as we rush to squeeze through in time; but which gates? The gates to our hearts, cracked open by intense prayer and introspection? The gates of God's compassion, flung wide open to welcome us home? The gates of heaven, inviting weary pilgrims to return? Perhaps even the gates of evening, as the setting sun meets a darkening firmament?

Or maybe these are the gates of time? Isn't part of Yom Kippur's distinctiveness the recognition that its promise is so time sensitive? Its opportunity for repentance, for changing our ways, for remapping our journey toward a more worthy destination is a once in a year thing—about to come to an end. If so, then the closing gates reflect our uncertainty as to whether we will succeed in our resolve in time.

The Gates: When and Where

Turns out that the liturgy doesn't help us resolve this ambiguity. "Where" are those gates? Inside our hearts? In God's ample love? At heaven's door? We never step outside the spatial metaphors to specify an answer. The choreography of keeping the ark open throughout *N'ilah* offers a visual that the gates that are closing are literally just before our eyes.

If that "where" is never nailed down, neither is the more obvious question of "when." The end of services (no matter when we end them)? The end of Yom Kippur (whether we have services or not)? Or, perhaps, actually, never? Paradoxically, the very tradition that rushes us to repent while there's still time is unambiguous in holding that God always welcomes our repentance. There is never a time when God's love is not greater than our shortcomings, never a time when God is too fatigued by our presence that we are not welcome to return. But if God is always eager to receive the sinner in repentance, then what's the rush now? Why must repentance coincide with the conclusion of Yom Kippur?

Unspecified gates in multiple time frames hardly sounds like a recipe for spiritual growth. Yet it turns out that precisely this uncertain swirl of multiple possibilities and shifting occasions is what makes human transformation possible.

Through Paradox to Growth

Were we only to believe that repentance is available at every time in general, we would never be motivated to change at any time in particular. Yom Kippur arises, to start with, because a general awareness of our mortality pushes us to seize one particular day to focus on it; the sense that Yom Kippur is a particularly favorable time for repentance inspires us to repent. But if all we had was a sense that we must repent today, that very repentance would be paralyzed by the ticking of the clock, by the desperation instilled by time running out. It is precisely the balance of "open-ended process" joining hands with "particularly favorable moment" that makes forward movement happen.

Similarly, were our tradition to identify the closing gates to just a single set of them, all the other valuable portals would be valueless. The gate of Torah is precious and vital, but not the only door through which we pass. We turn, in different moments of our lives, to other doorways: family, marriage, children, school, and career; spiritual discipline, pursuit of justice, adopting a cause—these are just a few. Each of these gates—in their own good time—manifests ways that the cosmos creates new possibilities for us, ways that the sacred offers a path to optimal greatness.

What gates close, then? Not just the symbolic doors of the ark, certainly, and not the gates of prayer. The gates in question depend on where each of us is in life's process from birth to death. Different doors open and close with regularity, depending on who we are and where we are in our life's journey. The gates must be specified, but not limited. There too, it is precisely the paradox that allows us to squeeze ourselves through, self-surpassing as is our God.

Our Challenge

IT'S UNLAWFUL AND UNJUST TO CLOSE THE GATES

Rabbi Tony Bayfield, CBE, DD

Nobel Peace Prize laureate Elie Wiesel was the spokesperson for the Survivors. In *Night*, his harrowing account of Auschwitz as a fifteen-year-old, he wrote:

> Some talked of God, of mysterious ways, of the sins of the Jewish people, and of their future deliverance. But I had ceased to pray. How I sympathised with Job! I did not deny God's existence, but I doubted his absolute justice.[1]

Through his subsequent writing, Wiesel became the spokesperson for our times, expressing the standoff between humanity and God in the shadow of tragedy and suffering—both collective and personal.

Not long ago, I reflected on the lengthy list of those whom the British Reform liturgy asks God to remember in *Yizkor*: "our ancestors

---

Rabbi Tony Bayfield, CBE, DD, is professor of Jewish theology and thought at Leo Baeck College in London; until 2011, he also headed up the British Reform Movement. His Lambeth Doctorate was awarded by the Archbishop of Canterbury, under ancient degree-giving powers, in recognition of his body of work on the theology of the Abrahamic faiths and their relationship. Published in May 2017, his latest book, *Deep Calls to Deep*, has been widely acclaimed both for the dialogical process out of which it is written and for the cutting-edge issues it addresses. He is currently completing *Challenging God: A Personal Theology*.

in their generations . . . the remnant of Israel . . . our martyrs . . . our pioneers . . . members of our community . . . our family and friends."[2] Why, I wondered, must God be reminded in such historical and sequential detail?

Are we not, in fact, reminding ourselves that far from being "sovereign selves,"[3] autonomous inhabitants of a historical and social vacuum, we are "situated selves"[4]—people with an inescapable past and a communal present, links in a battered but unbroken chain. The list connects us to those who, in the words of Ecclesiasticus,[5] "wielded authority . . . gave counsel . . . composed melodies" and also those who "have no memorial"—except us; those "who perished as if they had never been"—but were, nevertheless, "fathers, mothers, family"[6] to us.

If we are to remember who we are, what about You, silent, face turned away, indifferent to justice?

The same is true of *N'ilah*. We implore God to help us repent and to forgive us before the gates of mercy[7] close; but do the gates of mercy ever close? Isn't *t'shuvah* ("returning") a day-in, day-out, lifelong responsibility? What kind of God pronounces severe decrees, yet unfairly limits the appeals process? "Too late, it's been sealed!" It's we who look at our watches, turn our thoughts to the breaking of the fast, cut the liturgy short to sound *t'ki'ah g'dolah* "on time." Shouldn't God be beyond such pettiness?

Are You? And come to think of it, how could what we've done possibly compare with what You've not done?

Standoff.

The unique Jewish tradition of challenging God goes back to Abraham: Suppose there are fifty innocents in Sodom and Gomorrah—"Must not the judge of all the earth do justly?" (Genesis 18:24–25). It continues through Abraham's children and grandchildren,[8] and then through Moses (Numbers 14:11–23), and the prophets—like Jeremiah (12:1):

> You are always vindicated, God
> whenever I bring a case against You.
> Nevertheless, I will continue to challenge You:
> Why does the way of the wicked prosper;
> why do they live at ease, all those who are faithlessly
> faithless?[9]

Wiesel invoked the classic case: Job, the unrelenting challenger and ultimate protester. Jesus the Jew on the cross challenged God in the very words of the psalmist: "My God, my God, why have you forsaken me?" (Psalm 22:2). The Rabbis developed the tradition further, not the least in *Lamentations Rabbah*—a commentary on the destruction of the First Temple, but written in the shadow of the Second—where even the angels charge God with "succeeding in his youth but failing in old age."[10] The challenge is almost invariably brought as a lawsuit, questioning the justice and fairness of life itself.

And of God, life's author.

The tradition resurfaces regularly after that. Amidst the appalling savagery meted out to the Jews of Eastern Europe in the 1648–1649 Chmielnicki massacres, an anonymous protestor wrote:

> Dear God, why do you withhold your mercy?
> Witness our helplessness! . . .
> And if the old ones have sinned
> Why should the little children be the terrible victims?[11]

The late eighteenth-century Hasidic teacher Levi Yitzhak of Berditchev inserted an actual *din Torah* (a lawsuit) in his *Kaddish*:

> Good morning to You, Master of the Universe.
> I, Levi Yitzhak, son of Sarah of Berditchev,
> I come to you with a *Din Torah* from Your people
> Israel.
> What do You want of Your people Israel? . . .
> From my stand I will not waver,
> And from my place I shall not move
> Until there be an end to this Exile.
> *Yisgadal v'yiskadash shmei raboh*—
> Only Your Name is magnified and sanctified.[12]

It continued in popular song, sometimes explicit, sometimes enigmatic.

An Alte Kashe	**An Old Question**
Fregt di velt an alte kasha	The world asks an old question
Tra-la tra-di-ri-di rom?	Tra-la tra-di-ri-di rom?

Entfert men: Comes the reply:
Tra-di ri-di-rei-lom! Oy Oy!   Tra-di ri-di-rei-lom! Oy Oy!
Un az men vil, kon men oikh   And if you wish you may
zugen   say:
Tra-i-dim!   Tra-i-dim!
Blabt dokh vater di alte   But still the old question
kashe: remains:
Tra-la tra-di-ri-di-rom?   Tra-la tra-di-ri-di-rom?[13]

At the beginning of the twentieth century, Russian-born Alter Brody brought the tradition of challenge with him to New York and expressed it with sharpness honed by tragedy in a poem, "The Holy Ledger":

The Jew
Like a mad accountant
Trying to make sense out of a senseless ledger
Balancing the Holy Scriptures of his life
With double entry bookkeeping.
With good and with evil.
With reward and with punishment.
Juggling the accounts
To make debit and credit meet.
To cover up
The latest overdraft on his agony.
But sometimes
In a moment of revulsion
In a moment of insidious sanity
He flings down his pen,
Calling God Himself to account.
For the terrible, impossible, inexcusable
Entries in his book.[14]

There is, we say, a book of life sealed at the end of N'ilah. *But what part do we play in the sealing and who makes it irrevocable?*

It is we, not God, who are called to remember who we are during *Yizkor*. It is God whom we challenge for supposedly closing the gates of mercy at the end of *N'ilah*. On no account should we drift off into wristwatch inspection and relieved anticipation of *t'ki'ah g'dolah* but, instead, make a personal, unilateral decision to end the standoff. We must challenge God to resume the ancient dialogue and respond to the indictment for loss and suffering. Ours and God's.

☙❧

Sliding Doors and Closing Gates

Rabbi Lawrence A. Englander, CM, DHL, DD

As the film *Sliding Doors* opens, Helen (played by Gwyneth Paltrow) has just been fired from her job and is heading for the subway to make her way home. She reaches the platform just as the doors to the train begin sliding shut. Will she manage to get on board?

Well, that depends on your perspective. The movie traces two parallel lives: one in which Helen misses the train, and the other in which she manages to squeeze between the doors into the subway car. Each scenario will determine a different fate: whether she begins a new successful career, whether she finds her true love—and even whether she lives or dies. The meaning implicit in the story is that seemingly insignificant circumstances or decisions can determine whether opportunities are gained or lost.

This is also a message of *N'ilah*. Instead of sliding doors, we get closing gates. As the sun sinks toward the horizon, we each become Helen rushing to make it through the opening on time. *P'tach Lanu Sha'ar* ("Open a Gate for Us") captures our sense of desperation: "Open a gate for us when the gate is locked . . . for the day has passed." After

---

Rabbi Lawrence A. Englander, CM, DHL, DD, was ordained in 1975 and is rabbi emeritus of Solel Congregation, Mississauga (Ontario), which he founded. In 1984, he received his DHL in Jewish mysticism and rabbinics and has taught at York University (Toronto) and Leo Baeck College (London). Among his writings are articles on Jewish mysticism and a book, *The Mystical Study of Ruth*. He is former editor of the *CCAR Journal*. As a passionate advocate of Reform Zionism, Rabbi Englander coedited (with Rabbi Stanley Davids) *Fragile Dialogue: New Voices in Liberal Zionism*. In 2005 he was appointed as a member of the Order of Canada for his work in the community.

spending an entire day beseeching forgiveness from God and from our fellow human beings, we are still unsure if we have done enough, if there may yet be some misdeed, some oversight that we have missed. Will our prayers be acceptable to God? To our loved ones? To ourselves?

As we rush toward those closing gates, we may also be pondering the opportunities we failed to grasp during the past year. Is there someone to whom we should have apologized, yet still stubbornly refuse? Did a friend, associate, or neighbor reach out to us without our even responding? Harriet Beecher Stowe once wrote (in *Little Foxes*), "The bitterest tears shed over graves are for words left unsaid and deeds left undone." The image of closing gates reminds us that opportunities do have deadlines.

But *Sliding Doors* conveys yet another message. Throughout the movie, Helen faces other doors that open and close: to an office building, to an apartment, and to an elevator. Her decision whether or not to enter—or even to recognize that the door is opening—will also affect her fate. So, too, a highlight of *N'ilah* is *Tei'anu V'tei'atru* ("May You Be Answered and May Your Request Be Granted"), which gives us an alphabetical list of gates that we may someday encounter in our walk through life: gates of light, gates of blessing, gates of righteousness, gates of peace, and so on. Behind these gates lie enticing hopes for the coming year. But there is a catch: when a gate opens, we must still take the initiative to walk through it.

In reviewing past decisions, we frequently engage in an exercise of "what if" or "if only." For example:

"If only I had continued with those piano lessons."
"If only I had chosen a different career."
"If only I had kept my promise to a loved one."

For some of these "regrets," it is really not too late. For others, it may be, since we cannot always rewind our life and start afresh. Nevertheless, we need not be mired in the past, weighed down by despair. Even choices poorly made have futures that are as yet not fully determined. Instead of fatalism, Judaism counsels hope. The "gates of gladness," "of good council," and even "of assistance" may be open even for choices that cannot fully be undone. The gates that lie open at the end of *N'ilah* encourage us to replace "what if" and "if only" with "can do; it is not too late."

A midrash (*Avot D'rabbi Natan* 6) explains how Rabbi Akiva became a great scholar. As a forty-year-old illiterate shepherd, leading his flock to water, he chanced upon a rock with a hollow carved out in the middle. Drawing closer, he discovered that a tiny rivulet from an over-hanging cliff had caused a steady drip of water to fall upon that rock. He thought to himself, "At my age, I never thought I could begin an educa-tion. But if water can carve out stone, then surely Torah can engrave itself in my heart!" Even something as simple as a drop of water can open a gate and transform a life—if we are ready to take the chance.

Tei'anu V'tei'atru concludes, "May [God] seal you in the book of good life." The metaphor of gates has been replaced with the image of an open book. I imagine that the pages are blank, inviting us to pick up the pen and write our chapter for the coming year. As we write, we will catch up on chapters that came before, sometimes scratching out old sentences and starting again, sometimes writing paragraphs that go nowhere for the moment but lay open to possibility. But only by writing in the "book" will we have any idea of where the story goes. Only by making deci-sions and acting upon them will we find out what happens when we walk through the gates.

The Yom Kippur liturgy bids us to make an end to procrastina-tion and indecision, to walk with confidence into the coming year. Even though some gates of opportunity may close behind us, others will open up instead, inviting a new life's chapter replete with fresh decisions and novel results.

꧁꧂

Help Us Stay Open

Rabbi Shai Held, PhD

P'tach lanu sha'ar, b'eit n'ilat sha'ar . . . "Keep the gates open for us," we plead, "even as the time for them to close has come." The plain sense is clear: as Yom Kippur wanes, we implore God to hold the gates (of heaven? of repentance?) open just a little while longer.

Yet on another level, the gates in question are the ones we ourselves construct—and spend much of our lives locking. The prayer gives voice to the central challenge of the spiritual life: how do we open our hearts (and keep them open)? "God," we declare, "we are experts at closing. So, please, at this moment *and at all moments*, help us stay open."

So many forces conspire to lock our gates, to close us off—from ourselves, from one another, and from God. By dint of being human, we are experts at locking the gates of our hearts.

We are wounded, so we shut out others; the world overwhelms us, so we shut out its tears; the world frightens us, so we shut out its laughter. We are burdened by doubts and encumbered by disappointments, so we shut out God; we are busy, even frantic, so we shut out our spouses, our children, our parents, our friends. Vulnerability is risky, so we shut out intimacy; suffering is terrifying, so we shut out empathy.

Rabbi Shai Held, PhD, theologian, scholar, and educator, is president, dean, and chair in Jewish thought at Hadar, where he also directs the Center for Jewish Leadership and Ideas. He received the 2011 Covenant Award for excellence in Jewish education and teaches for synagogues and educational institutes across the United States and Israel. Rabbi Held holds a doctorate in religion from Harvard University and is an alumnus of the Wexner Graduate Fellowship and a faculty member of the Wexner Heritage Program. He has written *Abraham Joshua Heschel: The Call of Transcendence* and *The Heart of Torah*, a two-volume collection of essays on the Torah.

As Yom Kippur begins to fade, we stand *before* God and *with* each other, requesting the gift of openness. *P'tach lanu sha'ar, b'eit n'ilat sha'ar:* where before we locked the gates, help us now to keep them open.

Help us open our hearts: to each other, to people we know and to people we don't; to people we love and to people we decidedly don't. Help us apologize and forgive; help us open our hearts to ourselves—so that we can heal the wounds that keep us disconnected, that prod us to close our gates again and again. Help us open up to You—so that even when the world feels devoid of You, we hear Your voice and feel Your presence.

In one of his most stunning poems, Yehuda Amichai writes, "Open closed open. That's all we are." Before we come into the universe, everything is open. The minute we are born, we close it off within ourselves. Only after we die will it all be open again. The final words haunt me: "Open closed open—that is what we are." The dream and the demand of the spiritual life is precisely the opposite: open open open. That is the goal, the whole point of all spiritual striving: open open open.[1]

The reward of a *mitzvah* is the *mitzvah* itself, so the reward of living with an open heart is living with an open heart. Or, to put it differently: the reward of opening our hearts is that we are truly open—truly alive.

But opening our hearts can be enormously difficult. Addressing the Israelites as they are about to enter the land, Moses charges them to "circumcise the foreskin of your hearts and stiffen your necks no more" (Deuteronomy 10:16). As the verse makes clear, a circumcised heart is the antithesis of a stiffened neck. To circumcise the heart is to conquer stubbornness and become genuinely receptive to God. The image of a circumcised heart thus symbolizes "achieving a condition of responsive openness to God's word."[2]

Twenty chapters later, however, the people have yet to obey, for Moses announces that in the future "God will circumcise your hearts and the hearts of your offspring to love Adonai your God with all of your heart and being, in order that you may live" (Deuteronomy 30:6). Taking the two verses together, we learn that "it takes both strenuous human effort and profound divine blessing to transform the human heart . . . both will and grace are necessary."[3] As Yom Kippur ends, therefore, we stand before God and offer our entreaty: Let us, You and we, together open our hearts.

As the sun sets and Yom Kippur threatens to disappear, we realize that it is finally time: time to stop delaying and hiding; time to stop being clever and analytical and ironic and removed; time to ask for just one thing, therefore: God, help me open my heart, that I can truly serve You and the people and the world You created.

I revisit these words of *N'ilah* often during the year: *P'tach lanu sha'ar, b'eit n'ilat sha'ar.* Open my heart, God, whenever I am tempted to close it. Help me keep it open when I feel it closing despite my best intentions; help me keep it open when I don't even notice it closing.

At the end of every *Amidah*, we ask God: *P'tach libi b'toratekha*, "Open my heart to Your Torah." But in praying these words, I sometimes intend an alternative but equally plausible meaning: "Open my heart *with* [not *to*] Your Torah"—God, "use Your Torah to open my heart." I can think of no better aspiration for the religious life than this: may God's Torah help us live with our hearts wide open.

☙

The Shifting Presence of God[1]

Rabbi Elie Kaunfer, DHL

N'ilah means "locking." But what, exactly, is being locked?

As a child, I was terrified at the prospect of being locked out. "Open for us the gates," we would read, "even as they are closing," and I would think, "Only seconds remain before the gates of forgiveness clang shut without me inside." And then it would be too late, because "on Yom Kippur it is sealed."

But the Rabbis are clear: the gates of repentance actually never lock. "The gates of *prayer* are sometimes open and sometimes closed, but the gates of *repentance* are always open."[2]

So what gets locked at *N'ilah*'s end?

Although most people do not realize it, the liturgical climax of Yom Kippur is not the confessions and the accompanying poems for pardon (the *s'lichot*), but the *Avodah* (the liturgical unit in *Musaf*, which recollects the ancient sacrificial cult)—prayers that many congregations run through quickly or even omit altogether. It is there that the high priest encountered God directly in the Holy of Holies—so profound a moment that he prepared for the possibility of dying during it. Only then was God's ineffable name pronounced; all doors to God were open; God's presence was

---

Rabbi Elie Kaunfer, DHL, is the president and CEO of Hadar, an institute committed to Jewish learning and community building (www.hadar.org). He received rabbinic ordination and a doctorate in liturgy from the Jewish Theological Seminary. He is the author of *Empowered Judaism: What Independent Minyanim Can Teach Us about Building Vibrant Jewish Communities* (Jewish Lights). Rabbi Kaunfer lectures widely on prayer and building grassroots Jewish communities, is a Wexner Graduate Fellow and Dorot Fellow, and has served as faculty for Wexner Heritage and scholar-in-residence at the Federation's General Assembly.

patent. The doors that lock at *N'ilah* are those that had opened during the *Avodah*, the ones that afford us direct access to God.

This conclusion follows from the Talmud, where Rabbi Yochanan (in some versions Shmuel) claims it is merely the Temple's gates that lock, but Rav (whom tradition follows) says it is the gates to heaven[3]—an understanding that conjures up the loss of God's presence, far away and unattainable. These gates of heaven first appear in Jacob's dream, where Jacob concludes, "Surely this is none other than the House of God, and this is *the gate of heaven*" (Genesis 28:17).[4] At the *Avodah*, this gate of heaven reopens, and God is present. At *N'ilah*, in Rav's imagery, the gate swings shut and God retreats beyond it.

God's receding presence is what lies behind *N'ilah*'s final ritual moments: the sevenfold repetition of "Adonai is God" and the shofar blast. The custom of repeating the line seven times (which originated in medieval France) is said to accompany God's presence as it rises toward heaven after spending the last twenty-five hours with us.

> We say "Adonai is God" seven times in order to accompany the Presence God (the *Shekhinah*), as it rises and takes leave, climbing higher than the seven heavens—since Israel has finished its prayers. While [Israel] prays, the *Shekhinah* is present among us, but afterward it returns to its place.[5]

The original context of the declaration "Adonai is God" is Elijah's battle with the priests of Ba'al (1 Kings 18:39). As the Israelites experience God's presence descending to accept Elijah's sacrifice, they proclaim, "Adonai"—the Jewish God, and not Ba'al—"is God." As *N'ilah* ends, this shout is inverted from a greeting of God's presence to a farewell.

Finally, there is the *t'ki'ah g'dolah* of Yom Kippur, which (among other interpretations)[6] is considered a sign of the *Shekhinah* leaving the congregation.[7] Some congregations follow the custom of delaying the blast until after *Ma'ariv* (the evening service, following *N'ilah*), but even they say, "The *Shekhinah* waits" until *Ma'ariv* is over.[8] In either custom, the shofar blast heralds the departure of God's presence.

My teacher Dr. Raymond Scheindlin once taught that the whole point of Yom Kippur—the main event of the day, so to speak—is the intense encounter with God that lasts until *N'ilah*. In the day's best moments, we feel this presence strongly. We even act like angels (not eating, wearing white, singing praises all day), the beings closest to God's presence. Yom Kippur is not only about turning over a new leaf and repenting. It is also about rediscovering what it is to feel the reality of God in our lives. How might we behave if God were as deeply felt every day?

But what are we to do once the gates are locked? Must we wait an entire year for God to return?

One more *N'ilah* image comes to our rescue. The *N'ilah* shofar is said to mirror the blast that sounded when Moses returned with the second set of Ten Commandments.

> Moses our teacher went up to receive the second tablets . . . on the new of Elul, and came down on the tenth of Tishrei. He ordered [the shofar] to be blown when he went up *and when he came down*. Thus it was established that later generations should blow it on the night of the new moon of Elul and the night following Yom Kippur, as a remembrance of the blasts that marked the joyous acceptance of the second tablets. [9]

In this understanding, the final *t'ki'ah g'dolah* is a reminder of the covenant that was renewed after the sin of the golden calf and the process of forgiveness that followed—a process that occurred on the first Yom Kippur and that we rehearse every Yom Kippur thereafter. Taken together with the image of the shofar blast accompanying the departing presence of God, we have a powerful contrast. On the one hand, God's immanent presence is no longer available; on the other hand, God's covenant has been renewed and restored. While we lose the immediacy of the *Shekhinah*, we retain the relationship to it, as mediated through Torah.

N'ilah marks a shift in our relationship with God. To be sure, the immediacy of God that we feel on Yom Kippur now comes to an end. But an echo of it persists through Torah, the living testament to the eternal possibility of God's presence in our lives.

ᏩᎥᎳᎩ

The Guardians at the Gate

Rabbi Sandy Eisenberg Sasso, DMin

For an entire month leading up to the High Holy Days, the liturgy repeatedly invites us to mend our ways, atone, and seek pardon. All these pleas to enter the gates of forgiveness, reconciliation, and renewal, and yet we reach the final service of the Days of Awe, *N'ilah*—and the liturgy imagines us still standing outside those gates!

> Open a gate for us when the gate is locked on us, for the
> day has passed.
> The day will pass; the sun will set and pass; we will
> come before your gates.

N'ilah was the time for closing the gates of the ancient Temple. The divine gates of repentance, by contrast, are never closed—or so the Rabbis say. But the service seems to suggest otherwise: it issues a warning that our time is running out, that the gate is about to be locked and we still have not entered. Why has it taken us so long?

Rabbi Sandy Eisenberg Sasso, DMin, is rabbi emerita of Congregation Beth-El Zedeck in Indianapolis, where she served for thirty-six years, and director of the Religion, Spirituality, and the Arts Program in Indianapolis. Her award-winning children's books include *God's Paintbrush*, *Shema in the Mezuzah* (winner, National Jewish Book Award), *Creation's First Light* (National Jewish Book Award finalist), and *Anne Frank and the Remembering Tree*. For adults, she has written *Midrash: Reading the Bible with Question Marks* and *Jewish Stories of Love and Marriage: Folktales, Legends and Letters* (coauthor, Peninnah Schram). Her newest children's book is *Who Counts? 100 Sheep, 10 Coins, and 2 Sons* (coauthor, Amy-Jill Levine).

N'ilah evokes Franz Kafka's surreal parable "Before the Law," from *The Trial*. In Kafka's narrative, a man accused of wrongdoing seeks admittance to the law in order to clear himself. But a guard bars him from entering. Maybe he can enter later, the guard suggests, but it will not be easy: the law has many gates and guards, each more powerful than the other. So although the gate is open, the man remains outside, waiting for permission, which he never receives. At the end of his life, the man wonders why no one else has tried to enter the gate. The guard explains, "No one else could ever be admitted here, since this gate was made only for you. I am now going to shut it."

At *N'ilah*, each of us stands before our own personal gate, a gate made only for us. The gate is always open, but like Kafka's protagonist, we are waiting, held back by guards who keep us from entering. Their names are Doubt, Pride, and Fear.

Doubt is a pessimist. It tells us we are too old to change; we are not good enough to warrant forgiveness, not strong enough to ask for it. Doubt is agnostic. There is no proof that there is a God, so why even search for transcendence when we'll never achieve it anyway?

Pride is a cynic. It expands our ego and contracts our conscience. It says that we are above it all, that we needn't admit the truth; we can get away with lies, with hurting others. Nobody is all good, all the time. So take all you can while you can, before someone else takes it away first. If we don't take advantage of the situation, others will. Pride is an atheist. There is no God, so why waste our time seeking meaning where there is none?

Fear is a naysayer. It says, don't risk being truthful; it is not worth it. If we become vulnerable and admit wrongdoing, we will only open ourselves to criticism. Judgment by others is painful; our own, even more so. If we let down our guard, we can be hurt. Who wants a new way of being when change is so difficult? Fear is faithless. It believes that there might be a way to find transcendence, but it is too treacherous to try.

When Moses ascended Mount Sinai to receive the Torah, the Midrash says, he too was confronted by gatekeepers, angelic ones, who questioned God's decision to give the sacred Torah to a human being made of flesh and blood, lower in status than they were. Doubting his right even to be there, they sought to attack him physically (*Exodus Rabbah* 28:1). At first Moses listened to the pessimists, the cynics, and the naysayers. He was afraid. "Sovereign of the universe," he pleaded, "I fear, lest the angels consume me with the fiery breath of their mouths."

God instructed him to confront the gatekeepers. "Hold fast to the throne of glory," God advised, "and answer them back!"

So Moses grasped hold of the throne of glory and argued with angels. He claimed that only those—*precisely* those—who had been enslaved, lived among idol worshipers, worked, conducted business, had been jealous, and confronted evil should receive the Torah.

Moses won the argument, the Talmud says (Shabbat 88b). He passed through the gate, even after the people's sin of worshiping the golden calf, and received Torah for Israel.

It was then that "God passed before him and called: Adonai, Adonai, merciful and gracious God, endlessly patient, most kind and truthful, extending kindness to thousands, forgiving sins and transgressions and misdeeds, cleansing" (Exodus 34:6–7). Whenever the people of Israel would sin, the recitation of these words would bring compassion and forgiveness.

These same verses from Exodus, referred to as the Thirteen Attributes of God, mark the beginning of Yom Kippur and its end—they are part of the *Kol Nidre* service but also central to *N'ilah*, chanted immediately after we pray, "Open a gate for us." *N'ilah* closes out the long day of fasting and prayer with one last directive: Hold on to the awesome power of this day; hold on to the throne of glory, and confront doubt, pride, and fear, all the gatekeepers who would have us believe that we cannot change. Remind them who we are and that only we who have been uncertain, frightened, and self-righteous can enter the gate of repentance and walk on through it, however broken, to become whole again.

Openings at Closing Time

Rabbi Jan R. Uhrbach

"Open a gate for us when the gate is locked."

Although we no longer witness the physical gates of the Temple closing at the end of Yom Kippur, this fervent plea remains one of the most potent moments of our liturgy. Perhaps we've experienced a heightened connection with God or with our truest, purest selves. Perhaps instead we now feel a heightened sense of how much work we've yet to do, and we fear we've wasted a precious opportunity. Either way, it can be hard to let the gates close.

But shouldn't we be praying that the gates *remain* open, rather than pleading to "open a gate for us," as if the gates would be opening for the first time?

One possible understanding comes from Martin Buber:

> It is written: "Open to me the gates of righteousness."
> We are serving in the right way as long as we feel that we
> are still on the outside, and beg God to open the gate to
> true service for us.[1]

Rabbi Jan R. Uhrbach graduated from Yale University and Harvard Law School, received ordination from the Jewish Theological Seminary, and is now director of the Block/Kolker Center for Spiritual Arts at the Jewish Theological Seminary, where she teaches prayer and liturgy. She served on the editorial committee for the Rabbinical Assembly's *Machzor Lev Shalem* and was associate editor of its *Siddur Lev Shalem* (the Shabbat and festival siddur). Rabbi Uhrbach is also the founding rabbi of the Conservative Synagogue of the Hamptons in Bridgehampton and a distinguished teacher of Torah.

In this view, what matters is not the gates but ourselves. We must always
see them as closed, so that we remain in a mode of longing, knocking
on the gates, wanting to draw closer. The closer we get, the greater our
yearning. The moment we feel we've arrived inside, we're wrong.

Rav Soloveitchik takes a similar approach:

> It is not enough . . . to say, "I have sinned." God is not,
> so to say, compelled thereby to keep the gates open. . . . If
> we wish to repent of our ways we must cry out and beat
> incessantly at the gates so that they allow us and our con-
> fession to enter within. . . . Unless one knocks on the gates
> loudly and continuously, repentance and confession are
> impossible.[2]

Here too, it is our own longing that matters, a state of mind symbolized
by frantic knocking. Merely showing up or fulfilling the technicalities of
the laws of *t'shuvah* (repentance and return) is insufficient.

This emphasis on our internal longing focuses us on the very nature
of the gates in question. The Rabbinic tradition identified three gates to
God: gates of prayer, gates of repentance, and gates of tears:

> [Rabbi Samuel ben Nachman taught]: The gates of prayer
> are sometimes open and sometimes closed, but the gates
> of repentance always remain open. . . . As the *mikveh* is
> sometimes open and sometimes closed, so too the gates of
> prayer are sometimes open and sometimes closed; but as
> the sea ever remains open, so is the hand of God ever open
> to receive one turning in repentance.[3]

> Rabbi Eleazar said: Since the destruction of the Temple,
> the gates of prayer are locked. . . . Yet though the gates of
> prayer are locked, the gates of tears are not.[4]

We may include all of these texts—as well as the interpretations of Buber
and Soloveitchick—when we pray for the gates to open. But perhaps
the prayer is most powerfully directed to yet another "gate": the gate of
our own hearts. We are the ones who are closed. The urgency of *N'ilah*
comes from our realization that despite this forty-day period of repentance from the first of Elul to the end of Yom Kippur, we haven't even
really begun. We've said the words, but our hearts are still sealed shut.

We ask God to open the gates of heaven, but the help we need is in opening ourselves.

This interpretation helps explain the fact that the name of our service, *N'ilah* (from the Hebrew root *nun ayin lamed* = "to slam or be bolted shut"), is also a term used for one of the five prohibitions of Yom Kippur: wearing leather shoes, known as *n'ilat hasandal*.[5] What's the connection?

A Hasidic master, Menachem Mendl of Rimanov, connects the prohibition on shoes to God's command to Moses at the burning bush: "Remove your sandals . . . for the place on which you stand is holy ground" (Exodus 3:5). On Yom Kippur, he teaches, all of creation experiences an elevation, and the entire earth rises to the level of *admat kodesh*, "holy ground." We may not walk anywhere on it with leather shoes.

We remove our shoes for many reasons: to show respect and humility, to tread lightly and do less damage, and also to feel connected directly with the earth's holiness—to allow our soles (pun intended) to *feel* the soft caress of velvety grass, the pain of rocks and thorns, and everything in between. Metaphorically then, the prohibition against *n'ilat hasandal* connotes the need to be open to the fullness of life's experience and the potential for holiness everywhere; dulling our sensitivity is forbidden.

N'ilah is about opening our souls (not only our soles!) to the fullness of life's experience and the potential for holiness everywhere, and doing so specifically at a time when we focus on closing: the end of Yom Kippur. *N'ilah* is more than an ending to Yom Kippur. It offers its own challenge for the year ahead: when I encounter the things that usually make me shut down, when fear might make me close myself off, whenever I find myself at an emotional, spiritual, or intellectual point of closure, I am to insist on remaining open. *P'tach lanu sha'ar*, "Open a gate for us when the gate is locked on us, for the day has passed": not "*even though* the gate is locked on us," but "*specifically at* the time that the gate is locked"—that is, the gates of the heart.

At *N'ilah*, all references to being "inscribed" are changed to "sealed": not that we be sealed closed, but that we be sealed open.

Figure: Decorative flourish

The Sliding Doors of *N'ilah*

Dr. Wendy Zierler

The film *Sliding Doors* (1998) could have been about *N'ilah*. As the film opens, its chief character, Hannah—just fired from her job—barely misses her train. In a replay, however, we see her squeezing through the doors in time, and the rest of the film spins out two alternative narratives that follow. The sliding doors symbolize the minute factors that determine one's destiny.

N'ilah's gates (or doors) are evoked with *P'tach lanu sha'ar b'eit n'ilat sha'ar, ki fanah yom*, "Open a gate for us at the time of the locking of the gates, as the day is passing." But *fanah* ("passing") can also mean "turning"—as in expressions implying chance, like "the turn of events" or "as things turn out." It is as if the opening or locking of the gates—and our chances of passing through them—hinge not just on intent but on chance as well. Yom Kippur is a set of sliding doors that one hopes to enter by virtue of timing, intent, and spiritual openness. They close at *N'ilah*, at which time we hope we will not have been barred from passing through them, by circumstances beyond our control.

Dr. Wendy Zierler earned a PhD in comparative literature from Princeton University (1995) and an MFA in fiction writing from Sarah Lawrence College (2016) and is now the Sigmund Falk Professor of Modern Jewish Literature and Feminist Studies at Hebrew Union College–Jewish Institute of Religion (New York). She is author of *Movies and Midrash: Popular Film and Jewish Religious Conversation* and *And Rachel Stole the Idols: The Emergence of Modern Hebrew Women's Writing* and was coeditor, with Carole Balin, of *To Tread on New Ground: Selected Hebrew Writings of Hava Shapiro (1878–1943)*. She has contributed to all the books in the Prayers of Awe series.

Well before the film, poet Yehuda Amichai investigated the sliding-door imagery of *N'ilah* in his monumental novel *Lo me'akhshav, lo mikan* (*Not of This Time, Not of This Place*, 1963).[1] His protagonist, Joel, is a man of divided loyalties, torn between old and new, there and here, his Jewish religious past in Germany and his secular adult present in Israel. Middle-aged, married, and a successful archaeologist, he should have his life in order. But lately, like the doomsday prophet after whom he is named, he has been brooding over his end. He longs for a coherent sense of his own life—"that everything should be bound together, childhood, adolescence, man and beast, war time and peace time, memories of the past and prophecies of the future" (p. 374).

At a party, Joel's friend Mina suggests that he cure his midlife malaise by spending the summer in Jerusalem, falling in love. When Joel tells her, though, about his recent dream of returning to his native Weinberg—a fictionalization of Amichai's native Wurzburg—Mina advises him to do both at the same time: return to Germany but stay in Jerusalem simultaneously. She herself lives that way all the time. Joel tells Mina that she is mad—which she actually is. That very night, in fact, Joel accompanies Mina as she checks herself into a mental hospital. Its gateway and building with bars on the windows remind Joel of *N'ilah*'s gates that open or lock shut. Joel thus likens the heavenly halls of forgiveness to the sterile corridors of a psychiatric hospital, as if getting one's life in order is like atonement—the "at-onement" Joel seeks—but is impossible to achieve unless one is insane or dead. Joel must resign himself to a life of choices without ever finding the wholeness he seeks.

As illustration, the novel (like the movie) now branches off into two parallel tracks, corresponding to Mina's two options. Half of the novel describes Joel's return (*t'shuvah*) to Weinberg for the purpose of meting out revenge against those who murdered his childhood and his childhood friend Ruth. In this narrative strand, Joel believes that taking vengeance will provide him a metaphorical *N'ilah*, a sense of closure and release. "I'm coming just to close the door that hasn't been properly closed in my life. A door that's swinging on its hinge and disturbing my sleep in Jerusalem" (p. 64). The other track describes Joel's love affair in Jerusalem, a kind of anti–Yom Kippur, in which he withdraws from his past, his family, and his people and falls madly in love with a Christian American doctor named Patricia. In the Weinberg section, Joel seeks closure through revenge; in the Jerusalem section, he attempts to forget his past through love and sex.

Throughout the Weinberg section, Amichai struggles with the glaring absence of justice and order by juxtaposing the Holocaust with the Yom Kippur service. Comparing and contrasting the tragic end of his friend Ruth in a concentration camp to *N'ilah*, Joel laments, "At the time of Ruth's death, they did not say *Adonai hu ha'elohim* seven times and not *Sh'ma yisrael*" (p. 126). Her death was senseless and random; it questioned the very existence of a just God who hears the prayers of Israel.

If Joel must now give up his idea of a God who makes life ultimately come out well, he is also incapable of exorcising the memories that fracture his life's journey in the first place. His trip to Weinberg convinces him that the memories will not evaporate, but that memory and commemoration matter, and that he will not, therefore, be able to neatly organize and seal the chapters of his life, as one hopes to seal the Jewish penitential moment with *N'ilah*. He settles for reducing the nostalgic fantasy of his childhood and his adult guilt to their proper size.

In contrast with the Joel who travels to Weinberg, the Joel who stays in Jerusalem makes no effort whatsoever to revisit his German Jewish past—an extreme example of *sh'lilat hagolah*, the Zionist concept of "negating the diaspora." This Joel dismisses his painful past by rewriting his life story purely from the perspective of his newfound relationship with Patricia, "in the same way that historians rewrite the story of a nation after a revolution" (p. 349). To complete this process of detachment, Joel secludes himself for two weeks on the Mount Scopus campus of Hebrew University—this is pre-1967, when Mount Scopus was in Arab hands and cut off from the rest of Jewish Jerusalem. He hopes to return, completely divorced from his past (p. 540).

But Joel never returns—a metaphor for the act of *t'shuvah* that never takes place. Up on Mount Scopus he steps on a hidden land mine from a previous war—"not of this time, not of this place"—and is killed.

In unequivocal terms, Amichai dramatizes the sliding-doors consequences of choices. The "Jerusalem" track pronounces a liturgically resonant death sentence upon the Joel who chose a path that precluded the idea of return, in more than one sense of the term. The Joel who returns first to Weinberg and then back to Jerusalem lives, but without accomplishing what he sought to do there—to resolve life's conflicts into a simple seamless narrative of vengeance or justice. A total Yom Kippur atonement (at-onement) of the spirit turns out to be impossible in this human time and place, and yet there are partial attainments, and these remain worth the effort. He learns what we, the readers—we, the worshipers—need to know: "He who never sets out can never return. What is never begun can never be finished. To live is to begin and to end" (p. 618), but hopefully with moments and reckoning and insight along the way.

Commentaries on "God Whose Deeds Are Awesome"

(*El Nora Alilah*)

Chazak (Be Strong)

A LIGHT AT THE END OF THE TUNNEL

Rabbi Jonathan Blake

Everything about *N'ilah* points to the darkening day, the end of the "grace period" when repentance and prayer can reach God's throne. We spend all Yom Kippur afternoon entering that darkness. It begins with Jonah, fast asleep in the dismal hold of the ship, then cowering in the belly of the fish and in the roiling black waters off the Jaffa coast. The *Avodah* service following takes us inside the dim innermost sanctum of the ancient Temple; and *Eleh ezk'rah*, the following martyrology, presents the darkest extremes of human cruelty. Then comes *Yizkor*, the memorial service: a direct confrontation with grief, death, mortality, loss.

So we have spent all afternoon walking through the Valley of the Shadow only to get to *N'ilah*, and the actual setting of the sun—when, however, we get a glimpse of liturgical sunlight.

I do not minimize *N'ilah*'s continuing darkness, mind you. The very word means "closing, locking." Indeed, in Temple times, *N'ilah*

Rabbi Jonathan Blake is senior rabbi of Westchester Reform Temple in Scarsdale, New York. A graduate summa cum laude of Amherst College (1995) and ordained from Hebrew Union College–Jewish Institute of Religion, Cincinnati (2000), Rabbi Blake is a noted speaker, singer, and commentator on Jewish text and Jewish life—appearing on CNN, in *GQ* magazine, and in the HBO/Cinemax documentary films *51 Birch Street* and *112 Weddings*. He has contributed to several books, including *Encountering God: El Rachum V'chanun—God Merciful and Gracious* and *Text Messages: A Torah Commentary for Teens* (both Jewish Lights). This fall, he launched a podcast, *Everything Is Connected*. He and his wife, performing artist Kelly McCormick, reside in Westchester County, New York.

was offered at the end of every day, as *n'ilat sh'arim*, "the closing of the gates"—literally, the locking of the Temple at sunset. Nowadays, the gates close literally as well. (When *N'ilah* begins, I sometimes spot our synagogue custodians standing in the back of the room, reverent but ready to begin the great post-holidays cleanup, so they can lock up the building and go home to their families even as we go home to break-fast with ours.)

But despite this closing and closure, *N'ilah* pleads primarily for opening and openness—from God and worshiper alike—thus, the change in mood from gathering shadows to the glimpse of sunlight even in the darkness. Musically, the old weeping Eastern European *nusach* gives way to melodies in major keys. The tempo picks up. We shift our attention from our mortality to that which is eternal. We realize that we may escape the "harsh decree" after all, that the promise of spiritual renewal, of a year of life and blessing, is at hand.

It all comes together in the gorgeous Sephardi *piyyut* (liturgical poem) with which *N'ilah* opens: *El Nora Alilah* ("God Whose Deeds Are Awesome," p. 98–100). Its hopeful theme comes through in the acrostic encoded as the first letter of every line—not just the author's name, "MoSHeH" ("Moses" [ibn Ezra, c. 1055–1138])—but then, *Chazak!*, the affirmation that he can "be strong" with hope for tomorrow. As a Sephardi poem, but now recited by many Ashkenazim as well, it is a lovely, and fitting, demonstration of *k'lal yisrael*, Jewish unity. At the most spiritually critical moment of the Jewish calendar, with our very lives hanging in the balance, the two great Jewish civilizations come together to remind us we can "be strong" because even in the gathering darkness, the light of hope and unity is dawning.

I, for one, have found that *El Nora Alilah* gives me the strength I need to make it to the end of the day—largely because of its music: the bright major keys associated with the Jewish music of Thessaloniki, Baghdad, Istanbul.

Some communities sing it as a sprightly jig; others, as a graceful waltz, in 3/4 or 6/8 time. In our synagogue, we sing it as a hushed hymn. Each time we get to the repetitive line *el nora alilah*, our voices swell at the opening words, the direct address and praise of the Most High ("God whose deeds are awesome"); but then slow down to a near-standstill and quiet down to a barely audible hush at its ending, *bish'at han'ilah* ("as the gates close").

So much music resides even in the lyrics: the long, open *ahhh* sounds with which each stanza opens and closes; the internal rhymes; the cascade of steady pleading—as the Reform *machzor*, *Mishkan HaNefesh*, renders it, "Free us of falsehood . . . rid us of sin . . . embrace us in grief . . . console us in pain . . . judge those who hurt us . . . be near to us . . . restore the remnant of Your flock . . . increase our offspring . . . bless us with joy."

The poem is a densely woven tapestry of assonance, framed around the opening phrase *el nora alilah* and the closing rhyme *bish'at han'ilah*. The verses repeat, mantra-like, as if to induce a meditative state and, with it, spiritual transformation.

El Nora Alilah says everything that need be said on Yom Kippur. It summarizes it all. The chorus swells with the journey from tears to hope; we see, clearly now, bright as a new day, a light at the end of the tunnel.

The musical arrangement here at Westchester Reform Temple was introduced by Cantor Stephen Merkel, of blessed memory. Cantor Merkel was a Juillard-trained operatic baritone before training for the cantorate. *El Nora Alilah* was a moment to demonstrate both the power and the subtlety of his God-given voice. It seemed only right that after twenty-four hours of the cantorial strength displayed at *Kol Nidre*, *Un'taneh Tokef*, and *Sh'ma Koleinu*, *El Nora Alilah* would be less a thunderous coda and more a gentle note of grace. To this day, whenever we sing it, I hear Stephen's voice singing through me and my colleagues. I remember his *N'ilah* smile saying, in effect, "We've almost made it to *Havdalah* . . . Can you smell the bagels and lox and kugel?" When, in 2007, Cantor Merkel died at age fifty-seven after a long battle with lymphoma, a great heart ceased to beat and a great voice fell silent. Somehow through the mystery of melody at *El Nora Alilah*, he comes alive for those of us who knew and cherished him.

El Nora Alilah tells us the gates are closing, the sun is setting; but prayer, memory, unity, and hope can open them wide and let the light in.

⊙〜〜〜〜〜⊙

I Am Pleased to Report That the World Did Not End—Although Awe Is in Order

Rabbi Paul Freedman

The Large Hadron Collider is an enormous physics experiment at CERN, on the Swiss-French border. As its construction was nearing completion, the newspapers featured exotic stories that it might unintentionally create miniature black holes that could swallow up the universe before breakfast; I even received an urgent email from a congregant asking if I thought the world was going to end at half past eight that morning when it was due to be switched on. "So yeah . . . reply please," he wrote, "before 8:31 would be helpful."

I am pleased to report that the universe did not end. (I even had the confidence to send him my reply at 8:20 a.m.) And I was left wondering if he asked me because he couldn't think of anyone else to email on matters of particle physics at such short notice or because he felt the End of the World was a matter for his rabbi. Whether the question was scientific or religious, there were soon loads of protons (they're the hadrons) whizzing round a twenty-seven-kilometer circular underground

---

Rabbi Paul Freedman is senior rabbi of Radlett Reform Synagogue, one of the largest and fastest-growing synagogues in the United Kingdom. He was final editor of *Haggadateinu*, the first British Reform Movement Haggadah and is coeditor of its next *machzor*. He contributed to a prior volume in this series (Prayers of Awe), *Naming God:* Avinu Malkeinu—*Our Father, Our King* (Jewish Lights).

tunnel, though the real fun of making some of them smash into each other hadn't yet begun.

When I say "whizzing," I mean going very fast, almost at the speed of light—which is top speed for anything. So when one proton hits another proton coming the other way, there's a lot of energy involved. In fact, it's enough energy to investigate the sort of thing that was going on just a fraction of a second after the big bang. One particle that physicists were hoping to see coming out of these high-energy collisions was the long-awaited Higgs boson, sometimes called the God particle. The Higgs boson would complete the Standard Model of particle physics and explain how some of the tiny particles that make up you and me and everything else in the universe have any mass so that gravity can work (on you and me and everything else in the universe, as well).

Something did go wrong, though it didn't bring about the end of the universe; it just ended up taking an extra year to get those protons whizzing around and then smashing into each other. The collisions have been getting faster and faster since. Sifting through the statistical debris of these collisions, it took another four years of this phenomenal cutting-edge science and international collaboration to see evidence of the elusive God particle.

At the beginning of the Ten Days of Awe, at Rosh Hashanah, we say, *Hayom harat olam*, "On this day the world was conceived." To me, that doesn't mean literally that the big bang was on Sunday, the twenty-fifth of Elul, just under fifty-eight centuries ago, but it is still a unifying, universal idea, that Rosh Hashanah (six days later) is when Judaism marks humanity's coming into being. So during the *Yamim Nora'im*, the Days of Awe, it is quite fitting to contemplate the mystery of the universe, to marvel at its vastness, to feel awe and reverence at the sheer improbability of quarks and leptons and bosons and all the fundamental constants being just what they needed to be for the universe, and our solar system, and life, and you and me, even to be possible.

Still, we are here—not just the unimaginably vast universe in which we find ourselves, but also the inconceivably small particles from which we are built. And perhaps most miraculous of all is our ability to marvel at it all and to want to understand it better. In our awe, we can think from the enormous scale of cosmology and astrophysics down to the minute scale of particle and quantum physics. But somewhere between the two is the human scale, the scale on which we live our lives, and that of course is the other aspect of these Days of Awe, when we consider and seek forgiveness for our own actions. "On Rosh Hashanah it is written, and on Yom Kippur it is sealed."

There comes a time, late on Yom Kippur afternoon, especially if you have been fasting, perhaps after many hours in services, perhaps after many confessions—some personal and heartfelt, others merely recitations, somebody else's words in a book—after all that, there comes a moment as daylight starts to fade, when time is running out. We have said all we were able to say, or pray, or admit to each other or to ourselves or to God, and Yom Kippur will soon be over. Soon it, whatever "it" is, will be sealed.

There is something wonderful, uplifting, and satisfying about those concluding minutes of Yom Kippur, at *N'ilah*, "as the gates close." It ought to be terrifying. Will the gates close too soon, before we are through to a new year, before we have been granted atonement, before we are reconciled with ourselves? Will *our* world end? And yet, our having traveled the journey through Yom Kippur, when we have come so far, there is a sense in which we are carried through together as a community. Even before that final *t'ki'ah g'dolah* from the shofar, we feel the new year, the year ahead, and the world outside awaiting us. Our work, our atonement, is done. "It" is sealed. The world, we trust, will not end.

El nora alilah, hamtzei lanu m'chilah, b'sha'at han'ilah. I am pleased to report that God, whose deeds are awesome—indeed, whose very *universe* is awesome—once again grants pardon, as our prayers and the gates close.

࿙࿚

A Poem Worth Praying and a Song Worth Singing Our Way to the End

Rabbi Andrew Goldstein, PhD

For over fifty years, since I first began staying all day in synagogue on Yom Kippur, my favorite prayer has been *El Nora Alilah*. I loved it as a tired young teenager because it announced that soon the Day would be over; and I loved it later as a rabbi leading services, for the same reason. But this latter-day love arrived with mixed feelings: relief that I had survived another grueling performance, but regret that my favorite day was ending. All along I (like most worshipers) have cherished this prayer because of its cheerful tune, so uplifting after all of the deliberately serious and mournful melodies for the rest of the Day. I have also reveled in the rhyming sounds of the Hebrew without bothering to take in their meaning: *p'liLAH* and *aliLAH*, for example, rhyming with better-known Yom Kippur vocabulary like *m'chiLAH* and *n'iLAH*.

But lately I have begun to see the poem as even more: it is a neat encapsulation of the High Holy Day liturgy and that liturgy's overall assurance of divine pardon.

Rabbi Andrew Goldstein, PhD, is president of Liberal Judaism, UK, a vice president of the European Union for Progressive Judaism, and emeritus rabbi of Northwood & Pinner Liberal Synagogue. He was coeditor of *Machzor Ruach Chadashah* and chairman of the editorial committee that produced *Siddur Lev Chadash*. He coedited two liturgical anthologies, *High and Holy Days* and *A Book of Jewish Comfort*, and has contributed to all eight volumes of the Prayers of Awe series.

Discovery came when honored with the task of coediting our latest Liberal High Holy Day *Machzor Ruach Chadashah*—time to look beyond the melody and the rhyming words, and to discover

- the author was most probably the Spanish poet Moses ibn Ezra (c. 1055–1135);
- his poem introduced the concluding Yom Kippur service only in Sephardi liturgy, not Ashkenazi;
- but the early Reform *Hamburg Gebetbuch* (of 1819) had Sephardi influences, and
- previous British Liberal prayer books, even though of Ashkenazi bent, adopted it also but omitted at least one verse and changed two intriguing words in another.

First, the author: From a course I had once taught on Spanish Jewish poets, I remembered Moses ibn Ezra as a writer of rather daring secular poems, often with explicit sexual meanings. But he wrote many other poems of deep spiritual and religious depth.

He suffered greatly in his life, first exiled from his native home in Muslim Spain, then abandoned by family as an older man, and becoming a wanderer again at the end of his life because he found his new home in Christian Spain so contrary to his liking. These trials are reflected in many of his poems, despite others that express a firmer faith, and in *El Nora Alilah* we have a fine example of the latter.

It is a perfect introduction to our final service of the Day of Atonement; the thoughts of a genuine human being, a man of many sides, not just a saint. For isn't this the character of us all—human beings with failures, not just merits, alternating between lows and highs, depression and inspiration? These extremes certainly describe the life of Moses ibn Ezra. But *El Nora Alilah* transcends all that. And the more I looked at it, the more I discovered why. The closing phrase of each verse (*bish'at han'ilah*, literally "at the hour of the closing") reminds us that time is short: there is but one last chance to repent before the Day of Atonement ends. But the succeeding verses add depth to the message by summing up the themes of the Day. As we list them in our Liberal liturgy:

- "Grant that we find ourselves forgiven at the closing of the Gates."
- "Blot out our sins, our dishonest ways."

- "Be our refuge, bring judgement on our oppressors, deliver us from danger, grant us joy and honour, renew as in ancient days, restore to the remnant of your flock their honour and glory."

There you have it, a concluding poem that encapsulates our thoughts: the need to seek forgiveness, to hope God will blot out our sins, and to hope also that we can anticipate a year of joy and safety for ourselves and our people. A simple and brilliant poem. Then I discovered how prior Liberal Jewish liturgy had altered the poem. First, we changed two words in line 7. We have (as did our preceding prayer books and the *Union Prayer Book* on which ours was based), "Restore to the remnant of Your flock their *honour and glory"—tiferet ut'hilah*. The original has *oholivah v'oholah*—two personal names used by Ezekiel 23:4–5 to allude to Jerusalem and Samaria, the capitals of the two political divisions in ancient times, the Southern Kingdom of Judah and the Northern Kingdom of Israel. A nice thought—that in the future, divisions in the Jewish community come together in unity.

Why was a substitution made? The original is surely more striking than our bowdlerized version, but the strange words leave modern worshipers puzzled, and at the end of Yom Kippur one wants clarity, not confusion. Also, if you look up Ezekiel 23, you will see that Oholivah and Oholah are accused of being whores—and that is not even the least offensive image in what is quite a shocking chapter. I wonder if this appealed to the "other side" of Ibn Ezra's nature!

A number of non-Orthodox prayer books stick by the original words, but all omit the final verse (line 8): "Michael, prince of Israel, and Elijah and Gabriel: Announce our redemption, as our prayers and the gates close."

Editors of progressive liturgies frequently shortened prayers by omitting additions that had somehow crept into the original, and line 8 is almost certainly not by Ibn Ezra, as it comes as something of an afterthought. It follows the acrostic of Ibn Ezra's name (MoSHeH CHaZaK, "Moses be strong"), formed by the opening letters of the verses prior. In addition, these editors were attracted to the Germanic tradition of philosophical rationalism; no wonder they omitted a verse that invokes angels. Given today's revived interest in mysticism, however, who knows what future prayer books will decide?

Why is *El Nora Alilah* a favorite of so many? Not so much its words, actually, but its melody and rhythm, so upbeat and jaunty, just the mood we need as we approach the end of the long Day. Yom Kippur begins with *Kol Nidre*, where the music is more important than the meaning of the words. And it ends the same way—albeit with words that are perfect for *N'ilah*. And though I am a lifetime rational Liberal Jew, I confess that I will leave the synagogue this Yom Kippur hoping that Elijah and his angelic companions, Michael and Gabriel, are waiting for me outside, singing this happy song.

Between Urgency and Hope

Rabbi Lisa D. Grant, PhD

Yom Kippur is an awesome day, in the full meaning of the word. It can take us to a deep place of contemplation about and connection to our innermost questions, our community past and present, and—the most elusive subject of all—God. It asks us to reflect on our deeds, our thoughts and intentions, and to seek forgiveness for all our many missteps and imperfections. At its heart is a plea to be inscribed for good—to find the strength and courage and comfort and resilience to be our best selves no matter what comes our way in the year ahead. Nowhere are these themes more resonant, more compelling, than in the final service of the day, *N'ilah*.

Traditional texts tell us that *N'ilah* is to begin when the "sun hits the top of the trees" or about thirty minutes before it sets. It is a liminal time, a time of endings and beginnings, a time between day and night, a time of crossing over to a new year. It is then that we are at our most vulnerable: tired, drained, hungry, and filled with trepidation—but also promise. With the sun setting upon us, we picture heavenly gates closing before us, leaving us face-to-face with a moment of truth. We have

Rabbi Lisa D. Grant, PhD, is Director of the Rabbinical Program and professor of Jewish education at Hebrew Union College–Jewish Institute of Religion (New York). Her research and teaching focus on adult Jewish learning, Jewish leadership, and Israel in American Jewish life. She has coauthored and edited three books and authored numerous articles, book chapters, and curriculum guides. Before coming to HUC–JIR (in 2000), Dr. Grant received her BA from the University of Michigan, an MBA from the University of Massachusetts, Amherst, and a PhD from the Jewish Theological Seminary. She studied for the rabbinate while continuing her full-time responsibilities of teaching and scholarship and was ordained in May 2017.

one last chance to pour out our hearts in prayer before the gates of forgiveness close.

In most communities, *N'ilah* opens with the *piyyut* (poem) *El Nora Alilah*, "God whose deeds are awesome," a line drawn from Psalm 66:5. With the exception of the final two couplets (line 8 in the liturgy here, p. 100), which were added later, this liturgical poem is attributed to Rabbi Moses ibn Ezra, a late eleventh- to early twelfth-century Spanish commentator and poet. Originally Sephardi, therefore, it is nonetheless part of many Ashkenazi services nowadays as well. Perhaps in tribute to its Spanish roots, however, even these Ashkenazi synagogues are likely to sing it with a Sephardi melody, upbeat, joyful, and inviting. Indeed, traditional texts instruct us to sing the *piyyut* with joyful enthusiasm to awaken a sense of holiness as the day draws to a close.

I find this to be one of the most powerful moments of the day.

El Nora Alilah introduces us to this final hour. It is fraught with urgency but open to possibility. Familiar themes evoked throughout the High Holy Days are packed into a few short lines. Like most *piyyutim*, it is redolent with biblical references, but grammatically altered for poetic affect. Biblical verses in first-person singular, for example, are subtly changed to the third-person plural. In the second stanza (line 2), the poet draws on Psalm 123:1, "To You, I lift my eyes," but changes the voice so that it reads, "To You, *they* lift *their* eyes." In the Rosh Hashanah haftarah, Hannah cries out, "*I* have been pouring out *my* soul to God" (1 Samuel 1:15). The third stanza (line 3) reframes it as "To You, *they* pour out *their* souls." Traditional translations generally preserve the third person, but more contemporary translations (such as the Conservative Movement's *Lev Shalem* and the North American Reform Movement's *Mishkan HaNefesh*) have taken further poetic license to put them in the first-person plural, perhaps aspiring for a more intimate connection to God. Placing our personal pleas for forgiveness, mercy, protection, and salvation in the collective voice reminds us we are not alone. We are all in need of God's grace, God's comfort, and God's mercy.

As the *piyyut* draws to a close, it turns from the personal to the national, first (line 6) asking God to remember the righteousness of our ancestors and renew *their* days "as of old"; and then (line 7) to restore *us*, "the remnants of the flock," to grant us length of days, and finally (in the added couplet, line 8) to bring tidings of redemption now, at the hour of the closing of the gates.

The most resonant and most powerful part of the poem is the chorus, "God whose deeds are awesome, grant us pardon" (line 1). This rhythmic refrain fills us with hopeful anticipation mixed with an urgent pleading. How fitting that these emotions—hope and urgency—are in tension at this in-between hour. It is that very tension that makes us most open to hearing God's voice, feeling God's presence, finding God's comfort. God is all-powerful, after all, but will God hear us? We plead with God to wipe away our sins, to protect us, show us compassion, and renew us. "Grant us pardon," we keep pleading. *We* are human, not fully worthy, but *You* are God, the all-compassionate One. This is the moment. If not now, when?

At first, the upbeat, joyful melody to which the *piyyut* is generally sung may seem dissonant to the message of the text. But perhaps that is the point. The lively chorus builds momentum for this final service of a very long day, momentum that might even sustain us in the year to come. To be sure, like all years, this one too will be filled with challenges and sorrows, missing the mark, and moments of despair. But there is also hope: hope in God's forgiveness, in our own strength to resolve and reflect, to return and repair. The lively melody doesn't mask the awesomeness of the task. Rather, it qualifies that task, by reminding us to find joy in the challenges of being human, of being awake to the world, of living in the uncertainty of whatever may come, and in affirming that God's grace and mercy are always open to us.

The gates never completely close. They remain ajar, inviting us to find the crack where God's light comes in.

☙❧

El Nora Alilah and the Two Faces of the Day of Atonement

Rabbi Dalia Marx, PhD

The Day of Atonement has two faces: one is saturated with awe, grandeur, and somber thoughts about human fragility and fate; the other is filled with joy that comes from feeling the heavy weight of wrongdoing being lifted from one's heart and anticipating the promise of turning a new page in the book of life.[1] "There were no happier days for Israel," says Rabban Shimeon ben Gamaliel, "than the fifteenth of Av and the Day of Atonement" (Mishnah Ta'anit 4:8).

In many synagogues, however, we encounter mostly the fearsome side of the day. The atmosphere is stern and solemn, the music is lofty and somber, the *Yizkor* service and the liturgical poems (*piyyutim*) that recall Jewish martyrology and suffering predominate. Arguably, the best-known High Holy Day addition is *Un'taneh Tokef,* the terrifying hymn that ponders life's fragility and is said to derive from a persecuted Jewish martyr in medieval Germany.[2] Knowing that Yom Kippur is the holiest

---

Rabbi Dalia Marx, PhD, is a tenth-generation Jerusalemite who earned her doctorate at the Hebrew University and her rabbinic ordination at Hebrew Union College–Jewish Institute of Religion (Jerusalem and Cincinnati). She is a professor of liturgy and midrash at the Jerusalem campus of HUC–JIR and teaches also in various academic and nonacademic institutions. Marx writes for academic and popular publications and is active in promoting liberal Judaism in Israel. Aside from several books that she has coedited, she has herself authored *When I Sleep and When I Wake: On Prayers between Dusk and Dawn* (in Hebrew) and *A Feminist Commentary of the Babylonian Talmud.*

and most awesome day in the Jewish year, we imagine it must also be stern and serious. But is it precisely so everywhere?

The vast majority of American Jews are Ashkenazi; they have roots in Europe—more exactly, Eastern Europe. Their ancestors were overwhelmingly affected by czarist pogroms and rabid hostility in Poland, Romania, and the other states in the region that once housed Jews in large numbers but which often turned on them, especially in the nationalist frenzy following World War I. It is no wonder, then, that their liturgical atmosphere is heavily suffused with the morose fog of suffering.

The same holds true in many ways for many Ashkenazi synagogues in Israel. But Israel is so much more ethnically diverse: almost half the Jewish population there is Sephardi or Mizrahi—Jews who came from the Mediterranean and North African countries, primarily. This diversity in population produces a parallel diversity in the experience of holy days, Yom Kippur included.

To be sure, the basic liturgy of Ashkenazim and Sephardim is similar, in that both are constructed from identical building blocks: *Kol Nidre*, an altered *Amidah*, confessions, the symbolic recollection of the sacrificial cult of old (*Seder Ha'avodah*), readings from Torah and the prophets, and the unique concluding service, *N'ilah*. But they differ in detail, and these details add up to quite a different experience, not just in the wording of the prayers, but in the sound. "It is the tone that makes the music," they say, and here, the tone, the music, the feeling—indeed, the very atmosphere of the liturgy as whole—is different.

Sephardi prayers for Yom Kippur also have "two faces," but, generally speaking, Sephardi or Mizrahi Jews, who call the Day "the white fast" (as opposed to the ninth of Av, "the black fast"), tend to emphasize the joyous aspects of spiritual purification and beginning anew. The *Yizkor* service that arose in the aftermath of the Crusaders' massacres of Rhineland Jews does not appear at all in most Sephardi prayer books; nor does the hair-raising poem *Un'taneh Tokef*, with its opening image of even the angels "gripped by shaking and trembling" for fear of "the day of judgment" when God determines "who will live and who will die, . . . who by fire and who by water," and so on.

This Sephardi emphasis on the positive is especially evident at *N'ilah*, the concluding service whose tone is set in Sephardi tradition by Rabbi Moses ibn Ezra's liturgical hymn *El Nora Alilah* ("God Whose Deeds Are Awesome"). Nobody wants to miss it; even young children playing outside rush into the synagogue to join the singing. And indeed, one of the poem's verses, one that is sung with special passion (although it is a later addition to the text[3]), is dedicated to them:

May you merit living many years, parents and children With joy and happiness at the time of *n'ilah*.	תִּזְכּוּ לְשָׁנִים רַבּוֹת, הַבָּנִים וְהָאָבוֹת בְּדִיצָה וּבְצָהֳלָה בְּשָׁעַת הַנְּעִילָה.

This statement is based upon the blessing *Tizku l'shanim rabbot* ("May you merit many years [of life]"), which Sephardi Jews wish each other at the end of the Day of Atonement (and other times as well).[4]

The process of atonement, which began with the start of Elul, a whole month prior to the new year, is finally, after forty days and forty nights, coming to an end. People arrive at *N'ilah* ready to pour their collective emotion into a fierce and vigorous congregational singing of *El Nora Alilah*—"God whose deeds are awesome, grant us pardon, as our prayers and the gates close."

Moses ibn Ezra (c. 1055–after 1135, Spain), who embedded his name in an acrostic of the first letters of each strophe—"*MoSHeH CHaZaK*" ("Moses be strong" or "strength for Moses")—took the phrase *El Nora Alilah* from Psalm 66:5: "Come and see the works of God who is held in awe for his deeds [*nora alilah*]." In content, the poem portrays people trembling in fear of punishment ("Those who are called 'few in number' lift their eyes to You and worship in trepidation"), not altogether unlike the Ashkenazi *Un'taneh Tokef*; but the melody and performance of *El Nora Alilah* are festive and joyous, a wonderful example of the way the overt aspects of the liturgy (the text and its literal meaning) can be utterly transformed by symbolic and latent ones (its performative aspects).

However, the text of *El Nora Alilah* too has contributed to its popularity, because it vividly encapsulates the complexity of emotions at this moment of the day—the desire, that is, to take advantage of the "last-chance" moment for atonement and assure renewal for the year just dawning. "Announce a year of favor," the poem concludes, "as our prayers and the gates close." The exuberant elation one may feel after taking part in the intense and demanding day of prayer and fasting—these are vividly expressed in *El Nora Alilah*.

In a few minutes the gates will close and the day will be over, but now there is still time . . . the hungry and thirsty people gather strength through a powerful singing of *El Nora Alilah*, the anthem that concludes the twenty-four-hour day of fasting. For many, its lively melody so encapsulates the flavor of the day that they hum it on their way back from the synagogue and throughout the days that follow. My mother would chant it absentmindedly whenever she thought of Yom Kippur. These two bookends for *N'ilah*, *El Nora Alilah* at the beginning and the shofar and singing of "Next Year in Jerusalem Rebuilt"[5] at the end, punctuate the climactic ending to the day.

Classical Ashkenazi prayer knows many hymns for *N'ilah* but not *El Nora Alilah*, which was exclusively Sephardi and Mizrahi. For well over a century, however, the poem has made steady inroads into non-Orthodox Ashkenazi liturgies as well.[6] The process works both ways, of course—some Sephardi and Mizrahi synagogues now include a *Yizkor* service and won't miss *Un'taneh Tokef*. Such borrowings on both sides are essential manifestations of inclusion, not mere "exotic" flourishes but integral ways of rounding out High Holy Day worship with the best that Jewish tradition has to offer.

The inclusion of *El Nora Alilah* (and the special atmosphere it creates) is, therefore, an affirmation of rich and multifaceted Judaism for our time. It is a symbol of a contemporary Jewish culture that strives to represent the many voices of our past and present and to include the experiences and sentiments of Jews of all origins, east and west. Such a diverse and multivocal Judaism is essential to the rich and sustainable Jewish future for which we aspire.

⁂

An Awesome Sense
of Mischief

Rabbi Charles H. Middleburgh, PhD

The luminous twelfth-century Jewish poet Moses ibn Ezra was a man of many parts, but it is for his poetry that he is best remembered. His presence is felt in the *N'ilah* service through his poem *El Nora Alilah*. Although Sephardi originally, it was borrowed by nineteenth-century Reformers in Hamburg, so that it now can be encountered in many Ashkenazi prayer books as well.

As a child I always looked forward to its uplifting and dynamic melody, which struck such a contrast to the typical High Holy Day heaviness. Ever since then, for over four decades of leading High Holy Day services, a single bar of the music is enough to catapult me back in time to those early experiences.

As an adult, having studied medieval Hebrew poetry with Professor Raphael Loewe, *z"l*, at University College London, my engagement with the poem has only deepened.

Two things in this *piyyut* stand out for me. In its original version the penultimate verse contains two feminine names (Oholivah and Oholah); the last, three masculine ones (Michael, Gabriel, and Elijah).

Rabbi Charles H. Middleburgh, PhD, is dean and director of Jewish studies at Leo Baeck College, London, where he has taught for thirty-four years. Together with Rabbi Andrew Goldstein, PhD, he has edited the UK Liberal Movement's *Machzor Ruach Chadashah* and two anthologies, *High and Holy Days* and *A Jewish Book of Comfort*. A lifelong conservationist, he has published two collections of poetry inspired by the natural world and has had poems included in two wildlife books and the forthcoming Reform Judaism (UK) *machzor*. He is a regular contributor of *divrei Torah* to the CCAR "Voices of Torah" commentaries.

These final three are relatively well-known to Jews: the archangels Gabriel and Michael and the prophet Elijah are invoked to announce the dawn of redemption. The former two are relative strangers to Jewish lore. They occur as metaphoric characters in Ezekiel 23 within the context of a return to Zion, but their identity remains a mystery and their presence there something of a puzzle.

The final verse is usually omitted from progressive liturgies because progressive Judaism does not subscribe to angelology or to the idea of a biblical prophet physically returning to announce the coming of the messiah (even though we pay lip service to it at our Passover tables with Elijah's cup and opening the door for Elijah).

The same editors tend to replace the enigmatic Oholah and Oholivah with *tiferet* and *t'hilah*, "glory" and "praise"—a substitution that fits neatly with the rhythm of Ibn Ezra's poem. But why is the substitution made in the first place?

The answer lies in Ezekiel's original usage. He issues a towering denunciation of the cities of Samaria and Jerusalem, personifying them as Oholah and Oholivah, two women who are luridly objectified with explicit detail of their sexual degradation. Just a sense of the much longer passage can be conveyed by the chapter's opening lines:

> There were two women, daughters of one mother. They played the whore in Egypt . . . while still young. There, their breasts were squeezed and their virgin nipples were handled. . . . As for their names, Oholah is Samaria, and Oholivah is Jerusalem. (Ezekiel 23:2–4)

As a poet, Ibn Ezra realized that Shomron and Yerushalayim (Samaria and Jerusalem) did not fit with his poetic meter, while Oholivah and Oholah did. Their overwhelmingly negative connotation as whoring sinners, moreover, struck him as apt for a poem designed to promise redemption, even for the sinners whom we too know ourselves to be, on Yom Kippur. Editors of progressive liturgies, however, have felt that whatever its poetic virtues, any allusion to such a text would be wholly inimical to worship.

The other object of intrigue is the key word in the refrain, *alilah* (from the verbal root *ayin lamed lamed*), and its several possible meanings. In *Machzor Ruach Chadashah* we translated the refrain as "O God, whose deeds are awesome" and the Sephardi *machzor* produced by the UK Spanish and Portuguese Jewish community renders it as "Lord Almighty, girt with might." The Hebrew root has clear implications that these renditions echo, but they miss something important.

The Dictionary of Classical Hebrew cites no fewer than six verbs with these letters, and although the meaning of one, "to do," clearly underlies the word—*alilah* does mean "deed"—there is a rather delicious nuance in the reflexive form (*hitalal*), which means "to make fun of" or "to pretend." The most famous use of this reflexive is in Exodus 10:2, where God speaks to Moses of having "made fun of" or "toyed with" the Egyptians: "You may recount in the hearing of your children and your children's children how I toyed with [*hitalalti*] the Egyptians, by displaying my signs among them."

Theologically speaking, this is a most uncomfortable choice of words in the context of the plagues—we can hardly believe that God sent plagues merely to "toy with" the Egyptians—like an almighty cat playing with a country of puny mice! But in the context of Ibn Ezra's great *N'ilah* poem, it provides something very special. To get at what I mean, consider the book of Jonah, which we also read on Yom Kippur as part of the afternoon service that traditionally comes immediately before *N'ilah*. The standout moment there is when God upbraids Jonah for feeling so angry at the fact that the Ninevites, whose death he had prophesied, are actually saved in the end.

"Are you so deeply grieved about the plant?" God asks, referring to a shade-giving plant that God provided for Jonah but then killed, leaving Jonah open to the sun.

"Yes," he replied, "so deeply that I want to die."

Then Adonai said, "You cared about the plant that you did not work for and which you did not grow. . . . Should I not care about Nineveh, that great city of more than 120,000 persons who do not yet know their right hand from their left, and many beasts as well?"

Read correctly, I believe that God is teasing Jonah, toying with him as a loving and indulgent parent. If you listen hard enough, you can hear God smile.

We don't have too many indications in the Bible that God has a sense of humor, so it is striking that on Yom Kippur (of all times) we read a book where it is definitely on display. At the solemn moment when Yom Kippur is coming to a close, with a year of opportunity and danger opening up before us, it may help to be reminded that God is not above a sense of humor. The closer we feel to God, the more loving, and gently teasing, God may become.

The image of closing gates suggests being locked outside of a space into which we may not venture for a full twelve months. Yet the God of awe, but also of love and humor, is never shut off from us, never so removed that we cannot hear divine encouragement and feel a divine smile.

☙

Endings and Beginnings

N'ILAH'S "COMMENCEMENT ADDRESS"

Rabbi Sonja K. Pilz, PhD

In our culture, we love to celebrate beginnings for their inherent joy and optimism. "New" seems to be an equivalent of "good." The only endings we like are those that look forward to new beginnings thereafter: the awarding of degrees, for example, where American universities, anyway, invite speakers to give "commencement" addresses.

By contrast, we deplore what is uncomfortable or depressing. With regard to most endings, therefore, we are, at best, ambivalent: leaving our childhood home, a long-standing job, and certainly a marriage. These are all moments at which we have to part, to close a door, to say goodbye. To be sure, there is always the promise of a new home of our own, a better job, and another marriage, but with the future still cloudy, we see only the ending, not the beginning thereafter. Similarly, we have trouble recognizing that most beginnings, even the best ones, have to be paid for with an end—and that some endings are indeed a blessing.

The overall atmosphere of *N'ilah* combines aspects of both ending and beginning. *N'ilah* marks the end of a difficult day, after all, so its

Rabbi Sonja K. Pilz, PhD, teaches liturgy, worship, and ritual at Hebrew Union College–Jewish Institute of Religion (New York). She received rabbinic ordination from Abraham Geiger College in Berlin (2015) and a doctorate from Potsdam University, also Berlin (2015), where she served as junior professor of Jewish ritual and practice at the School of Jewish Theology before coming to HUC–JIR. She is the author of "The Earth Is the Eternal's and the Fullness Thereof: Jewish Food Culture and the Blessings before Eating" and *Food and Fear: Metaphors of Food in the Stories of Destruction*.

liturgical structure transmits messages of relief, gratitude, and overflowing joy. For example, compared to the High Holy Days elsewhere, the pattern of its *s'lichot* (petitions for pardon) changes in order to emphasize mercy and forgiveness over sinfulness and guilt. But this newfound message of relief is not reflected in traditional Ashkenazi music, which, until the very end of Yom Kippur, still sounds rather gloomy. Despite the structure of prayers that provides the hope of a new beginning, the music still reminds us of our decree about to be sealed and the weight of our possible punishment. The music fills the air with solemnity and gravitas. Only at the end of *N'ilah*, when it is already dark outside, will we be allowed to look ahead and imagine all the good that might await us there.

This contrast between the penitential music and the hopeful structure of the liturgy is typical of the traditional Ashkenazi services, however. Sephardi tunes differ; they subscribe less thoroughly to the sounds of suffering and sin. In many *contemporary* Ashkenazi synagogues, too, more and more hopeful and confident tunes can be heard—including the assertive beat[1] of *El Nora Alilah*, a Sephardi *piyyut*[2] that has found its way into these services. It is sung between the silent *Amidah* and its repetition, while the last sunbeams of the day still color the tops of the trees. Looking at the sky alone, one realizes that the *piyyut* indeed introduces the end of the day, "closing" Yom Kippur while God is "closing the gates of heaven," thereby sealing our destiny for the new year. It is a moment of an ending, but at the same time, it is a moment of pure joy and relief: Yom Kippur is about to be over! God will forgive! We are almost done! We have prayed (well) enough! Yes, our destiny is about to be sealed—but for good! What a relief!

The service continues to call upon God's mercy and forgiveness, but it includes much more. *El Nora Alilah* itself moves on from the themes of mercy and forgiveness (stanzas 1–3), to those of joy and pride (stanza 4), defeat of our enemies (stanza 5), renewal of the wonderful days that we imagine our ancestors enjoying (stanza 6), a good year to re-gather us in the Land of Israel (stanza 7), and redemption (stanza 8). *El Nora Alilah* does not speak only of forgiveness; instead, it is a messianic text[3] full of hopes for the future, with its musical tones and beat full of energy and passion for the year to come.

The Ashkenazi adoption of *El Nora Alilah* testifies to a broader phenomenon: our overwhelming desire nowadays to feel happy and hopeful during our prayer experiences. *El Nora Alilah* provides just this sense of the end of Yom Kippur as a hopeful beginning. The fourth stanza, for instance, requests that we be sealed "for honor and joy" (*l'hod ul'gilah*), not just for forgiveness. We want joy and happiness, dignity and pride in our land(s), and a covenantal relationship with our God. We do not wish only to be forgiven as sinners; we wish also to enjoy our life renewed.

Indeed, the ubiquity of our wish for joy can, at times, disguise the very reason for the joy we seek. It is important to acknowledge that some joyful beginnings are not easy. Some homes are dangerous. Some working environments are abusive. Some marriages are harmful. Some prayer experiences are challenging. Some periods of our lives are hard. *El Nora Alilah* celebrates a God who knows all this and whose message sometimes simply is: Enough already. Enough. Close this door. Close this chapter of your life. Move on. Yom Kippur is over. Take a deep breath and begin the New Year. By including *El Nora Alilah* in our *N'ilah* services, we include a moment that liberates us from the focus on our pain, our failures, and the mistakes we made during the last year, reminding us of the joy that really can be ours. Judaism today is not about the constant fear of failure. It is about joy and pride and promise. It is about embracing the fact that in order for something new to begin, the old chapter has to end.

☙

Childhood Memories and Life's Gates

Rabbi Dennis C. Sasso, DMin

Growing up in Panama, at Kol Shearith Israel, a Spanish-Portuguese congregation whose founders stemmed primarily from the Caribbean islands of Curaçao and Saint Thomas, I loved the sweet melodies of the Dutch Sephardi heritage. My fondest childhood memories of the High Holy Days resonate with the lyrical and plaintiff, yet hopeful cadences of *El Nora Alilah*. Soon after moving to Indianapolis in 1977, I asked our *chazzan* to include *El Nora* as part of our *N'ilah* there—even before the song had found broad acceptance in the Ashkenazi liturgy.

I consider *El Nora* a mirror into the soul of its author, Moses ibn Ezra (c. 1055–1135), one of the most prolific, versatile, and accomplished poets of the Spanish-Hebrew Golden Age of Al Andaluz (present day Andalusia, in southern Spain). His secular poetry is among the most sensual of his circle, and his religious and liturgical creations among the most inspiring and beautiful. So impressive is the body of his penitential prayers (*s'lichot*) that he is often referred to as Hasalach, "the master of *s'lichot*."

Interestingly, in this best known of his *s'lichot*, the term *s'lichah* ("pardon") does not appear. Instead, Ibn Ezra appeals to *m'chilah*—a

---

Rabbi Dennis C. Sasso, DMin, has been senior rabbi of Congregation Beth-El Zedeck since 1977 and is active in interfaith and civic causes. A past president of the Reconstructionist Rabbinical Association, he serves on the Board of the Lake Institute for Faith and Giving, IUPUI Center on Philanthropy. He is the recipient of several doctorate of divinity degrees, honoris causa. He is also affiliate professor of Jewish studies at Christian Theological Seminary. A native of Panama, he writes and lectures on Sephardi and Caribbean Jewry. Rabbi Sasso and his wife, Rabbi Sandy Eisenberg Sasso, were designated "Hoosier Jewish Legends" by the Indiana Jewish Historical Society.

higher level of forgiveness. In *s'lichah*, we repent of our offense and appeal to God for forgiveness. In *m'chilah*, we go beyond forgiveness to request absolution, a term from the vocabulary of jurisprudence that denotes God's gracious annulment of any debt or obligation that we might owe on account of the sin in question.

El Nora Alilah seems to point to a period in Ibn Ezra's life when, having been exiled from his beloved Granada, distanced from his kin, and living now in Christian Spain, the poet feels dejected and stripped of human companionship and support. In his loneliness, he appeals to the God whose mercy and love are inexhaustible and ever present. On his mind, then, is not just Yom Kippur, but life itself. The poem is certainly a litany for the ending hours of the sacred day of Yom Kippur, but it evokes also the ending stages of a person's life, a theme to which Ibn Ezra returns often. Elsewhere, Ibn Ezra reflects:

> Let man remember throughout his life
> He's on his way toward death:
> Each day he travels only a little
> So he thinks he's always at rest.[1]

The image of "the closing gates" in *El Nora Alilah* is a reminder not only that the Day of Atonement comes to a close, but that our lives too will end at the inexorable reality of the grave that opens and then closes over us. We are urged to seek reconciliation and atonement with God and neighbor before approaching these final gates as well.

In another short verse, Ibn Ezra laments, "Let man wail whose years are consumed. . . . For his life is like a dream."[2] One wonders if his later Spanish compatriot, playwright Calderón de la Barca (1600–1681), who authored the well-known Spanish drama *La Vida Es Sueño* (*Life Is a Dream*), ever came across these lines.

As subtle and powerful as is the versification of *El Nora Alilah*, so too is its melody, which, with slight variations, is heard throughout the Spanish-Portuguese Sephardi world, from Amsterdam and London, to New York, the Caribbean, and Panama. "The ascending and descending lines of this music mirror the range of emotions in [the] final hours," says Abraham Lopes Cardozo, *chazzan* of New York's famous Spanish Portuguese Synagogue from 1946 to 1986.[3] In some communities the melody is martial, even regal, in tempo; in other communities it is sung in a romantic, nearly sensuous mode. The first appeals to the majestic, sovereign nature of God; the second, to the God of love and forgiveness.

I have a recording of my grandfather, toward the end of his life, singing this hymn and the Sephardi table song *Bendigamos al Altisimo* ("Let us bless the Most High"), with the typical Spanish-Portuguese pronunciation of the *ayin* as an "ng" sound: *El nora Ngalilah El nora Ngalilah; hamtzi lanu m'chilah; b'sha'ngat han'ngilah.*

This is also how I learned to recite the *Sh'ma* as a child: *Shemang Israel . . . Barukh shem k'vod malkhuto l'ngolam va'nged.* There is something lovely about that "ng" pronunciation of the *ayin*. It is neither mute nor deeply guttural, but rather a flowiNG and healiNG sound, even as the prayer is intended to be.

The *pizmon* (as it is called in the Sephardi tradition) *El Nora Alilah* has a refrain and six verses built on the acrostic allusion to the author's name: MoSHeH CHaZaK. Some traditions add two verses, one wishing *Tizku l'shanim rabbot . . .* ("May you merit abundant years . . ."), which is the standard Sephardi greeting for the Days of Awe, and the other invoking the blessings of the archangels Michael, Gabriel, and the prophet Elijah. In the first one, the wish is for *banim* ("sons") and then either *avot* ("fathers" or "ancestors") or, in some versions, *banot* ("daughters"). It is likely that the *avot* is the older version and the *banot* a nod to contemporary egalitarianism. The reference to the angelic and messianic images in the second added verse links the personal redemption of this year's Yom Kippur to a future messianic consummation of *g'ulah*, "redemption" for all, thus positioning the opening prayer, *El Nora Alilah*, to anticipate the service's closing refrain, *L'shanah haba'ah birushalayim*, "Next year in Jerusalem."

El Nora Alilah embodies the hope that we may find forgiveness, acceptance, and fulfillment at three critical moments: at each year's beginning, at our personal life's ending, and at the consummation of Israel's redemptive history, at the very end of time.

The Grand Conclusion
Shofar and *Sh'mot*

Editor's Introduction

Rabbi Lawrence A. Hoffman, PhD

The "Grand Conclusion" of *N'ilah* (as we have called it) is especially memorable. A detailed account of its history and message can be found as appendix B, "The Climactic End to *N'ilah*: The Making of a Tradition." We provide a brief summary of that account here.

The proper name for this concluding ritual is *Sh'mot*, "Names," usually a reference to "names of God," but here denoting specifically the names of God that are embedded in three acclamations that the congregation shouts aloud as its closing affirmation of faith:

1. *Sh'ma yisrael, Adonai eloheinu, Adonai echad* ("Hear, O Israel, Adonai is our God; Adonai is One").
2. *Barukh shem k'vod malkhuto l'olam va'ed* ("Blessed is the One the glory of whose kingdom is renowned forever").
3. *Adonai hu ha'elohim* ("Adonai is God").

The first two are well-known, part and parcel of every morning and evening service. The third is reserved for *N'ilah*. It recalls the biblical tale of Elijah's contest with the prophets of Ba'al (1 Kings 18:20–40). When God miraculously sets fire to the sacrifice offered by Elijah, while Ba'al fails to ignite the one offered by his own prophets, the onlookers exclaim (v. 39), "Adonai is God; Adonai is God."

Custom differs, but the general Ashkenazi practice is to say *Sh'ma yisrael* once; *Barukh shem* three times, and *Adonai hu* seven times. These verses are followed by the blowing of the shofar (just one blast in Ashkenazi practice, a *t'ki'ah g'dolah*—a "great" or "long" sustained blast called *t'ki'ah*)—and a fourth verse:

4. *L'shanah haba'ah birushalayim*[1] ("Next year in Jerusalem")—borrowed from the end line of the Passover seder.

In Sephardi practice, *Barukh shem* is said just once (like the preceding *Sh'ma*), and *L'shanah haba'ah* is lacking. In addition, the shofar is blown four times—an opening and closing *t'ki'ah* and, in between, the other two sounds specified by the Talmud: *sh'varim* (a wailing sound repeated three times) and *t'ru'ah* (a staccato set of at least nine short blasts).

Of all these units, the shofar was earliest—part of our first extant prayer book, *Seder Rav Amram* (c. 860 CE). Over time, custom has varied as to whether to blow it once or four times.

Since the shofar is normally associated with Rosh Hashanah alone, a variety of reasons are given for including it at *N'ilah* of Yom Kippur also: to recall Leviticus 25:9, which mandates the shofar on Yom Kippur to announce the Jubilee year; to confuse Satan, who is prohibited on Yom Kippur from playing out his role as prosecuting attorney before God, but who returns to that task when *N'ilah* ends; or just to announce the end of the fast so that householders can go home to prepare dinner.

None of the *N'ilah* verses go back as far as the shofar. *Sh'ma*, *Barukh shem*, and *Adonai hu* were added by French Jews in the eleventh or twelfth century. As time went on, some communities said all three verses, while others said *Adonai hu* alone—the practice that Joseph Caro (sixteenth century) recorded in his influential law code, the *Shulchan Arukh*. But Caro was Sephardi, writing in the Land of Israel. The Polish authority from the same century, Moses Isserles, knew of several German rabbis who said *Sh'ma* and *Barukh shem* as well, so he "corrected" Caro's Sephardi practice to make it accord with Ashkenazi custom. Eventually, all three verses characterized not just Ashkenazi but Sephardi ritual as well.

By the sixteenth century, several traditions—some older, some newer—came to be associated with the verses. *Sh'ma* had to be said just once—because there is but one God; *Barukh shem* was said three times, a reference to God's reign over us—past, present, and future. The seven-fold *Adonai hu* was linked to the belief in not just one but seven heavens; it marked the passage of God's earthly presence, the *Shekhinah* (which had come to rest among us on Yom Kippur), back home to the last of the heavenly layers. Alternatively, it had kabbalistic implications because of the number seven, which denoted the lower seven *sefirot* through which the *Shekhinah* passed on its way upward.

L'shanah haba'ah birushalayim ("Next year in Jerusalem") is a much later addition. In the High Middle Ages, following the Crusades, it had become a conclusion to the Passover Haggadah. It was added to *N'ilah* only in the late eighteenth or early nineteenth century—popularized by the enormously influential Hafetz Hayim (Israel Meir Hakohen Kagan; 1838–1933). Its messianic implications are evident from another giant in Jewish law, Yechiel Michal Epstein (1829–1908), who says it heralds "the good news that God has heard our prayers." The prayers in question are Yom Kippur's petitions for forgiveness, but also, given the technical term "good news" (*b'sorot tovot*), an oblique reference to the ultimate "good news" (as in Christianity, as well) of a possible messianic coming.

It is usually recited once only, but some congregations say it three times, and in Israel, the word *b'nuyah* is often added, giving us *L'shanah haba'ah birushalayim b'nuyah*, "Next year in Jerusalem, rebuilt."

Annotated Translation

Dr. Joel M. Hoffman

The Final Verses

[1]Hear, O Israel, Adonai is our
God; Adonai is One.
[2]Blessed is the One the glory
of whose kingdom is renowned
forever.
[3]Adonai is God!

[1]שְׁמַע יִשְׂרָאֵל, יְיָ אֱלֹהֵינוּ,
יְיָ אֶחָד.
[2]בָּרוּךְ שֵׁם כְּבוֹד מַלְכוּתוֹ
לְעוֹלָם וָעֶד.
[3]יְיָ הוּא הָאֱלֹהִים!

Shofar Blowing

[Ashkenazi practice: *t'ki'ah g'dolah.*]
[Sephardi practice: *t'ki'ah, sh'varim, t'ru'ah, t'ki'ah.*]
[Traditional custom in Land of Israel: *t'ki'ah, sh'varim, t'ru'ah, t'ki'ah.*]

[4]Next year in Jerusalem!

[1]לַשָּׁנָה הַבָּאָה בִּירוּשָׁלָיִם!

[Sephardi congregations conclude with *Tei'anu V'tei'atru.*
See pp. 106–108.]

174

Commentaries on the Shofar and *Sh'mot*

(Not) Last Words

Dr. Annette M. Boeckler

The end of Yom Kippur cannot fail to make an impression: its doors of Yom Kippur need to close before we die of hunger and thirst; a whole day in synagogue without sunlight, relationships, and even chance encounters; a livelihood and ordinary affairs on hold.[1] Quite properly, we cannot wait for Yom Kippur to be over.

Unsurprisingly, the liturgy itself outfits the occasion with special insight. But most of us miss it. Not so Yom Kippur's celebrated beginning, where we even arrive early to hear *Kol Nidre*, especially in Ashkenazi services, where cantors treat it as so specially sacrosanct. Only few of us, however, devote equal attention to Yom Kippur's conclusion. Service leaders, too, come to *N'ilah* hungry, thirsty, and tired, anxious just to finish the day's spiritual marathon. The exact time of the end of *N'ilah* has been checked in advance, and the shofar blowing has been arranged, but the last phrases of *N'ilah* are rarely given the attention they deserve. Properly understood, however, these lines can prove as emotionally impactful as *Kol Nidre* the night before. *Kol Nidre* on the one hand and *N'ilah* on the other: two bookends to frame this most sacred day of the Jewish year—*Kol Nidre* to lead us into Yom Kippur, and the last lines of *N'ilah* to lead us back into life renewed. These last few lines present nothing less than the cultic drama of death and resurrection.

Dr. Annette M. Boeckler lives in Switzerland, where she is Jewish subject leader ("Fachleiterin Judentum") at ZIID (Zurich Institute for Interreligious Dialogue, formerly Zurich Lehrhaus, www.ziid.ch), and active member of Or Chadasch Zurich. Until 2017, she was lecturer for Jewish liturgy and Jewish biblical interpretation at Leo Baeck College in London and manager of the college's library. Her research field is the theology of Jewish prayer, especially the development of German liberal liturgy after the Shoah. She loves traditional *chazzanut* and has led services in Germany, the United Kingdom, and Portugal. She is currently helping to build Progressive Judaism in Lisbon and Porto.

The verses in question are these, numbered in order of their appearance:

1. *Sh'ma yisrael, Adonai eloheinu, Adonai echad.*
    "Hear, O Israel, Adonai is our God; Adonai is One."
2. *Barukh shem k'vod malkhuto l'olam va'ed.*
    "Blessed is the One the glory of whose kingdom is renowned forever."
3. *Adonai hu ha'elohim.*
    "Adonai is God!"

The first verse (*Sh'ma . . .*) is said once, the second (*Barukh . . .*) three times, and the last (*Adonai . . .*) seven times.[2] The ark doors are then closed, and the shofar is sounded.[3]

This closing ritual is known as *Sh'mot* ("[Sacred] Names")[4] or *P'sukei Hayichud* ("Statements [or Verses] of Unity"). It stems from the thirteenth century[5] and was influenced by medieval German mystics who thought that invoking God's various names could grant personal protection.[6]

Barukh shem k'vod—initially the response to hearing the Temple priests pronouncing God's ineffable name aloud (Mishnah Yoma 3:8)—is repeated three times corresponding to God's reign (*malkhut*), past, present, and future: *Adonai melekh, Adonai malakh, Adonai yimlokh l'olam va'ed*, "Adonai is king, Adonai reigned, Adonai will reign forever and ever."[7] The last statement, *Adonai hu ha'elohim*, is what our biblical ancestors are said to have proclaimed after the prophet Elijah demonstrated God as the only true and powerful deity (1 Kings 18:39). Medieval authorities saw its sevenfold repetition alluding to the seven heavenly spheres below God's actual presence (*Shekhinah*).[8]

What is striking is the parallelism between this ritual at the end of Yom Kippur and the ritual at the end of life: the deathbed confession itself (*Vidui*). It can be found in some prayer books,[9] but more commonly it turns up in Jewish guides on death and dying or in manuals for cantors and rabbis. Details vary, but typically, when the end is approaching, those present (or the dying person him- or herself) say the following verses "distinctly and solemnly" (numbered to correspond to the *N'ilah* verses, above; the "extra" verse, not found in the *N'ilah* ritual, is labeled with a zero):

(0.) *Adonai melekh, Adonai malakh, Adonai yimlokh l'olam va'ed.*[10]
(2.) *Barukh shem k'vod malkhuto l'olam va'ed* [three times].
(3.) *Adonai hu ha'elohim* [seven times].
(1.) *Sh'ma yisrael, Adonai eloheinu, Adonai echad.*[11]

Some manuals advise, "The words *Adonai echad . . .* should be said at the very moment when the sufferer expires";[12] sometimes it is suggested that the *Sh'ma* be repeated as often as necessary so that the person dies at the word *echad* ("one").[13] Immediately after the person has died, those present say the *Barukh atah . . . dayan emet* ("Blessed are You . . . the true judge"). In *N'ilah*, this would be the moment of the shofar.

The deathbed ritual dates to seventeenth-century Italy and was in fact an adaptation from the Yom Kippur liturgy.[14] In 1619, the Venice burial society (*chevra kaddisha*) told Rabbi Leon da Modena (1571–1648):

> When it comes time for one of our members to go and watch over the sick person, and to stand by him as is our custom, we have no ritual for what to recite and say in order to escort the soul of this person as he dies and returns his soul to God who gave it.[15]

Leon da Modena therefore prepared an eighteen-page leaflet[16] with biblical verses, prayers, and confessions, mostly from the Yom Kippur liturgy. The last verses to be said are as follows:

(3.) *Adonai hu ha'elohim* [three times].
(1.) *Sh'ma yisrael, Adonai eloheinu, Adonai echad.*
(2.) *Barukh shem k'vod malkhuto l'olam va'ed.*

These words are to be recited in the presence of a *minyan* (a prayer quorum of ten male Jews), including a scholar, all of them having arrived after someone has been ill for at least five days. This makes dying into a social event and a guarantee that all is done properly for the dying person's soul to depart. The last line (*Barukh shem*) is considered by the Midrash to be the final words of Jacob/Israel as he was dying (*Genesis Rabbah* 98:4). But the order changes from manual to manual.

The most important manual is *Ma'avar Yabok* (Mantua, 1626)[17] by the Italian kabbalist Aaron Berechiah ben Moses ben Nehemiah of

Modena, at the request of his *chevra kaddisha* in Mantua.[18] Although he had to contend with the extra verse (labeled zero), he did what he could to reorder the other verses to fit the *N'ilah* liturgy:

(1.) *Sh'ma yisrael, Adonai eloheinu, Adonai echad.*
(2.) *Barukh shem k'vod malkhuto l'olam va'ed.*
(0.) *Adonai melekh, Adonai malakh, Adonai yimlokh l'olam va'ed.*
(3.) *Adonai hu ha'elohim.*

Then follow various names of God, each carefully chosen:

1. *m'yuchad* ("the Unified One," a kabbalistic reference to the masculine and feminine sides of God that come together in harmony);
2. *ehyeh asher ehyeh* ("I am who I am," God's name from the story of the burning bush, Exodus 3:14);
3. *hu hayah hu hoveh v'hu yihyeh* ("He is, He was, He will be," a statement of God's eternality, known also to us from the familiar prayer *Adon Olam*);
4. *hu memit um'chayeh* ("He brings on death and gives [renewed] life [after death]," an obvious reference for the context.)

The ritual is supposed to continue even after the exact moment of death, but it remains unclear at what point the soul departs and what words remain to be recited afterward.

Ma'avar Yabok became especially famous as the paradigmatic Jewish book of death and dying and was reprinted, abridged, and translated endlessly, to the point of becoming the model for similar Jewish manuals worldwide.[19] This is how liturgy imagines the end of life: a moment completely dominated by the presence of God's name.

The deathbed ritual is, therefore, a mirror of *N'ilah*—with this all-important difference: at the end of Yom Kippur we don't die. Just the opposite, actually.

Traditionally speaking, dying is imagined as the movement of the soul through the gates that separate life from death, this-worldly existence (the *olam hazeh*) from the other-world of the divine, the "world to come" (the *olam haba*). The gates of the ark that close with *N'ilah's* end symbolize these gates of death, and the point is, at *N'ilah*, they mercifully close without taking our soul through them. We are granted another year. Therefore the last thing heard in *N'ilah* is not the sacred names, but the shofar that follows, the call to change, to move ahead. In ancient times the shofar called the Israelite camp to move on. In future times it will announce the messianic times. And in our present it is the sound of change and hope—the shortest definition of life after all, for life ceases when all change and hope are gone.

Instead of a passage into death, the *N'ilah* doors close after we have said our last statements but know our souls will not depart, not this time, anyway; instead, we get the shofar's resurrection into life renewed.

〇〜〜〇

The Passion of Praying Large, Not Small

Dr. Erica Brown

With the last breath of Yom Kippur, a hush descends on synagogues, allowing worshipers to focus entirely on *N'ilah*'s dramatic conclusion: the three Hebrew words *A-donai hu ha'elohim*, repeated seven times as a drumbeat of fidelity. "A-donai is God; A-donai is God; A-donai is God!" A day devoted to changing ourselves, our relationship with others, and our relationship with God ends with one word, "God," enveloping us in a final embrace of holiness. A final *Kaddish* sends us into the new year as new beings in relationship with the sacred.

For all its drama, however, this annual Yom Kippur ritual pales in comparison to the occasion from which these words are taken. Travel back with me some twenty-eight hundred years in time to Mount Carmel, where, high atop the mountain, we look down upon a large swath of the biblical Land of Israel. In front of us, Israel's king, Ahab himself, has assembled 450 prophets of Ba'al to fight with the lone Elijah, the zealous prophet, to see who is the mightier, Ba'al or God.

Ahab was the least of Elijah's problems. More troubling to him were the Israelites and their ambivalent religious commitments. "How long will you straddle the fence?" Elijah demands of the crowd that has gathered for the contest. "If the Lord is God, follow Him; but if Ba'al, follow him." Tellingly, "the people answered him not a word" (1 Kings

---

Dr. Erica Brown is an associate professor at George Washington University and director of its Mayberg Center for Jewish Education and Leadership. She is the author of eleven books on leadership, the Hebrew Bible, and spirituality. Her latest book is *Jonah: The Reluctant Prophet*. She was a Jerusalem Fellow and is a faculty member of the Wexner Foundation, an Avi Chai Fellow, and the recipient of the 2009 Covenant Award for her work in education. Her blog is at ericabrown.com.

18:21). Looking for commitment, Elijah gets mere silence: the tepid, fickle faith of supposed adherents preferring to hedge their bets.

"I am the only prophet of the Lord left," Elijah concludes (1 Kings 18:22). But knowing he has God on his side, Elijah proceeds anyway. He dares his opponents to prepare their sacrifice while he prepares his own. "The one who responds with fire—that one is God." Only now does the gathered crowd speak up, as if the whole thing is one big sporting event, a heavyweight wrestling match between would-be gods: "Very good!" they shout in unison (v. 24). Returning to Mount Carmel—you and me—we too can seat ourselves down for a good show. Elijah does not disappoint.

For hours the followers of Ba'al shout and dance around their altar.

> But there was no response; no one answered. . . . Elijah taunted them, saying, "Shout louder. After all, he is a god! Perhaps he is deep in thought, or busy, or traveling. Maybe he is sleeping and must be awakened." So they shouted louder and gashed themselves with knives and spears, as was their custom, until their blood flowed. Midday passed, and they continued their frantic prophesying until the time for the evening sacrifice. But there was no response, no one answered, no one paid attention. (1 Kings 18:26–29)

The drama mounts as all eyes turn to Elijah, whose turn has come. "Lord, the God of Abraham, Isaac, and Israel!" Elijah prays. "Let it be known today that You are God in Israel. . . . Answer me, Lord, answer me, so these people will know that You, Lord, are God and that You are turning their hearts back again" (1 Kings 18:36–37).

With that, God's fire hurtles toward the earth, scorching and destroying in order to rebuild the faith that was tested and tried. And then, we hear these famous words, not seven times but twice: "When all the people saw this, they fell prostrate on the ground and cried, 'The Lord is God! The Lord is God!'" (1 Kings 18:39).

Dozens of biblical verses pronounce the reality and unity of God. In Deuteronomy we read, "Unto you it was shown so that you might know, the Lord is God; there is none beside Him" (4:35). Later, the very spine of our *Sh'ma* insists, "The Lord is our God; the Lord is One" (6:4). The pronouncement is universalized in 1 Kings: "That all the people of the earth may know that the Lord is God and that there is none else" (8:60). "You alone are God," says the psalmist (Psalm 86:10). And

1 Chronicles, one of the last two books of our Bible, reiterates: "O God, there is none like You, neither is there any God beside You, according to all that we have heard with our ears" (17:20).

In Chronicles, we heard it, but at Mount Carmel, we saw it. Our eyes convinced us of a truth we knew but were too emotionally feeble to affirm. Satisfied with a mediocre faith, our biblical ancestors traveled a religious path that demanded little, and therefore they contributed little as well. Only when Elijah invited them into the drama of a decision did they see the value of throwing themselves all in.

Nelson Mandela once wrote, "There is no passion to be found playing small—in settling for a life that is less than the one you are capable of living." Elijah did not play small; and as *N'ilah* ends, we do not pray small either. When we close our holiest day with the very same words uttered by the ancient Israelites, we recapture the passion that true commitment entails. *N'ilah*'s conclusion articulates that commitment loud enough to carry us through the year ahead. As darkness falls upon us, we step down from Mount Carmel, step out of fasting and prayer, and step forward into our collective futures, guided by a powerful affirmation of commitment.

෬෩෩ඖ

The Final Moments of *N'ilah*

MEETING ELIJAH, ONCE AGAIN

Rabbi Jeffrey K. Salkin

No Jew in his or her right mind would willingly miss the *Kol Nidre* declaration that establishes the beginning of Yom Kippur.

But, when it comes to the other end of the holiest day of the year, many sanctuaries are comparatively empty—this despite the heartfelt pleas of rabbis and lay leaders, urging congregants to stay.

And that is a pity. Because Jews who stay to the very end of *N'ilah* are in for a rare liturgical treat—that is, if they know what is "really" going on.

Rabbi Jeffrey K. Salkin serves as the senior rabbi of Temple Solel in Hollywood, Florida. He was ordained as a rabbi at Hebrew Union College–Jewish Institute of Religion in New York. He was one of the first Jews to earn the Doctor of Ministry degree from the Princeton Theological Seminary. He is the author of ten books—the most recent of which is *The JPS B'nai Mitzvah Torah Commentary*. He has written books about bar and bat mitzvah, Jewish versions of masculinity, interreligious affairs, Jewish thought, and Zionism. Several of his books have won national awards. Rabbi Salkin is a columnist on Judaism for *Religion News Service,* which features his award-winning blog, *Martini Judaism: For Those Who Want to Be Shaken and Stirred.* Hundreds of his essays have appeared in the *Washington Post, The Huffington Post, Tablet, Mosaic, Forward,* and *JTA.* He has discussed the American political scene on CNN and the BBC, and he has contributed numerous articles to scholarly journals.

What is really going on is "death"! Death is the unspoken theme of Yom Kippur (see p. 9).

Before *Kol Nidre*, we take the scrolls out of the ark, and we stare into its empty space, as if staring into an open coffin.

We fast on Yom Kippur to imitate death. Traditional Jews wear the white linen *kittel* as a reminder of the burial shroud that they will some-day wear. Woody Allen once quipped, "It is impossible to experience one's own death and still carry a tune." He was wrong; on Yom Kippur, Jews experience their own death and spend the entire day carrying a multitude of tunes.

This focus on death comes through also in the Yom Kippur scriptural readings. The traditional Torah reading for morning describes Aaron's casting of lots "after the death of the two sons of Aaron" (Leviticus 16:1)—to determine which goat will live, cast out into the wilderness, laden with people's sins, and which will die, laden with the people's sins.

The parallel reading in Reform synagogues is Deuteronomy 29 and 30, reminding us that the covenant is made with those who are not yet born, and with those who have died, and that God places choices of life and death before us.

Later in the day, the liturgy itself adds stories of ancient martyrs and a memorial service we call *Yizkor*. The afternoon haftarah provides the book of Jonah, who descends into the bottom of the ship and then is swallowed by a large fish—twin symbols of death. A frustrated Jonah prays for his own death. The fish ultimately vomits Jonah up on dry land—a symbol of rebirth.

At the end of *N'ilah*, the Jew in the pew experiences his or her death; that is why we pronounce the *Sh'ma* (as if it were the deathbed *Sh'ma*) and the sevenfold *Barukh shem k'vod*.[1]

But in the middle of this dramatic moment, the liturgy inserts a reference to a biblical story—the prophet Elijah's confrontation with the prophets of Ba'al (1 Kings 18:16ff).

Under King Ahab and Queen Jezebel, the Northern Kingdom of Israel had introduced the worship of the Canaanite god Ba'al. Elijah therefore summoned the prophets of Ba'al to a "theological showdown" on Mount Carmel, near modern-day Haifa. Since the country was suffering a terrible drought, each party would prepare a sacrifice intended to convince their respective deity to send rain. Which god would respond—Ba'al or Adonai?

Adonai, not Ba'al, consumes the sacrifice, with the implicit promise of imminent rainfall. God wins! Then, the people cry out, "Adonai alone is God, Adonai alone is God!" (*Adonai hu ha'elohim*; 1 Kings 18:39).

The confrontation at Mount Carmel was an all-day event, stretching from morning "until the hour of presenting the grain offering" (the afternoon sacrifice of *minchah*; Deuteronomy 18:29). Bible scholar Alex Israel writes, "In that twilight hour—the *N'ilah* hour at the end of the day—Israel proclaims its undivided religious allegiance."[2]

Our own *N'ilah* too falls late in the afternoon—just when the confrontation on Mount Carmel would have reached its exciting climax. It is as if the entire day of Yom Kippur is a replay of the day on Mount Carmel. We are all standing at Mount Carmel again. Who is the true god—Adonai, the god of sacred relationships, or the false god, Ba'al, the god of power and control?

At the end of Yom Kippur, Adonai has triumphed once again. We proclaim the same words that the people of Israel proclaimed back on Mount Carmel: "Adonai alone is God, Adonai alone is God."

After Ba'al fails to consume the sacrifice, we read that Elijah "repaired [actually, *vayirapei*, "healed"] the damaged altar of Adonai" (1 Kings 18:30).

Why does he "heal" the altar, rather than build a new one?

Because he wants to demonstrate that when our relationship with God becomes disrupted, we can repair it.

We say the *Sh'ma*, rehearsing our own death. We remind ourselves of God's victory over idolatry at Mount Carmel.

The shofar is blown, its blasts resembling the cries of a newborn infant.

That newborn infant is you, me, all of us—reborn, reimagined, and ready to heal the altar of God.

One more detail. For reasons that are not given in the Bible, but possibly as his own penitential exercise intended to influence Ba'al to accept the sacrifice and end the drought, Ahab had spent the day fasting. With the confrontation over, Elijah tells Ahab, "Go up, eat and drink, for there is a rumbling of approaching rain" (1 Kings 18:41). And just as Ahab broke his fast as the rain approached, so too do we. Because the rain of the Sukkot season is approaching for us, as well.

☙

PART V
Concluding Meditations
As *N'ilah* Ends

"Go Forth Joyfully, Eat Your Meal, and Drink Your Wine"

Rabbi Edward Feld

N'ilah: Yom Kippur is almost at its end. We are past exhaustion. Our fasting has moved us through headache, hunger, and light-headedness. At times, we wondered if we could sustain the fast, but as we start *N'ilah*, we know that we will make it to the end, for the day's end is only an hour away.

And we ask ourselves: What has this day meant for us? Why have we gone through this suffering? What has it added up to?

This we know. We have done our part. We have fasted. We have prayed. We have confessed—over and over again. The extensive liturgy has made us wonder if there is anything more to say. We have recited more prayers than we do on any other day, yet for all the prayers, the confessions, the gnawing hunger, something feels incomplete.

What we find in *N'ilah* are hints of the day gone by—particularly in the confessions. We omit the double acrostic of the Long Confession (*Al Chet*) altogether and settle for just the brief alphabetical list of the Short

Rabbi Edward Feld has served as rabbi-in-residence at the Jewish Theological Seminary of America, rabbi of the Society for the Advancement of Judaism, and Hillel director of Princeton University. He is a noted teacher and lecturer throughout North America and has published widely on halakhic and ethical issues, Jewish theology, and biblical themes. He is the author of *The Spirit of Renewal: Faith After the Holocaust* and *Joy, Despair, and Hope: Reading Psalms*; and is senior editor of the Rabbinical Assembly's *Siddur Lev Shalem* and *Mahzor Lev Shalem*, for which he was listed as one of the Forward 50—the fifty outstanding American Jews.

Confession *(Ashamnu)*. But the brevity brings no relief; instead, with its staccato form there creeps in an element of desperation, a gnawing feeling of incompleteness. The fast has demonstrated just how weak we are, how vulnerable, how fragile. No matter what we do, we will inevitably come up short—for at the end of the day, it turns out we are all too human.

Fortunately, *N'ilah* provides *one* aspect of the liturgy in all its fullness—the Thirteen Attributes of God, emphasizing God's kindness, God's compassion, God's forgiveness (*Adonai, Adonai, el rachum v'chanun,* "Adonai, Adonai, merciful and gracious God"; see p. 106). According to some customs, the Thirteen Attributes are recited only on *Kol Nidre* evening and at *N'ilah*; in others, it is recited only once at each service during the day, but multiple times at *Kol Nidre* and *N'ilah*. Either way, it is as if without the assurance that forgiveness is possible altogether, we could neither have begun the day nor have dared to end it. Only the knowledge that forgiveness is possible can justify our plumbing the depths of our own inadequacies and then declaring the day a success and moving on to another year of hope and promise.

The physical weakness we feel from fasting is a metaphor for the larger spiritual weakness. We are so driven by our appetites, our everyday desires, our self-concern, our feelings of hurt, our jealousy of others— all conspiring to overcome our best selves. The liturgical insistence on God's forgiveness allows us to make peace with who we are. We leave the day with less ego, more genuinely open to relations with others. We can reassess what is important in our lives and recognize that those who have offended us are also weak, vulnerable, and in need of forgiveness. We are renewed precisely through this acknowledgment of mutual vulnerability: we seek forgiveness and we grant it. Having conceded the illusion of our own mastery, we settle back into the common human condition of striving and failing, with the sense that God wants nothing more; God welcomes us for who we are—weak though we may be, striving to do good. A forgiving God recognizes our humanity.

With this insight dawning over the course of *N'ilah*, the mood of the service changes. Instead of experiencing the gravity of the day, the sense of being judged, we become joyful at having made it through. A nineteenth-century cantorial tradition captures the change in mood by changing tunes during the course of *N'ilah*—beginning with sad and plaintive Yom Kippur melodies but moving on to joyous and communal singing. What began with great solemnity ends with rising spirits.

That sense of renewal, and even celebration, is captured in the *piyyut* written for *N'ilah* by the eleventh- to twelfth-century Spanish poet Moses ibn Ezra. To this day, it is included in the Italian rite and now also in the new North American Conservative *Mahzor Lev Shalem* (p. 418).[1] The refrain captures this sentiment perfectly: "Go forth joyfully, and with a full heart partake of your meal and drink your wine."

At the end of the day, we have reason to be joyful. We can go home and celebrate the very fact that we are human beings with physical needs and almost unlimited yearning. We are frail and we will fail, but in that very admission there is redemption. The day began with that sense of failing, and now, having experienced God's forgiveness of our shortcomings and acceptance of our humanity, we can rejoice in the most basic human pastime: eating and drinking in company with others.

Halakhic authorities recommend that at the conclusion of Yom Kippur we immediately begin building the sukkah. Sukkot is the holiday of joy, but curiously, that festive joy is experienced in a fragile hut, a recollection of how Yom Kippur has allowed us to confront our own weakness and vulnerability and allowed us to celebrate who we truly are.

N'ilah forces the acknowledgment of just how imperfect and fragile we are. Living with that realization, we have asked for forgiveness and forgiven others. Now, in the hut that mirrors our own fragile condition, but feeling forgiven and loved, we can be forgiving, and loving, and invite our guests to join us.

⌇⌇⌇

A Love Affair at *N'ilah*

Rabbi Aaron Goldstein

Sometimes we get lucky: a ritual manages somehow to become a "tradition" that no one wants to miss. The concluding *Havdalah* of Yom Kippur is such a phenomenon in my congregation—to the extent that a third of the community present on Yom Kippur morning wait around or come back, so as to experience it.

There are, first, your "professional" Jews—the clergy and *shamashim*, the choir, the stewards, and even the security detail. Some remain at shul all day long—in the sanctuary or, sometimes, outside it! Others return for mid-afternoon learning or, certainly, for *Yizkor*. It would be churlish to leave at *N'ilah*, however, so even if they have come specifically for *Yizkor*, they have become used to remaining through the final shofar call and the flickering, mingled flames of the *Havdalah* candle. By now they don't want to miss it.

Even as we begin, the candle's primitive luminescence casts its ethereal glow on a singular sight: radiant faces resplendent with warm smiles and gleaming, reflecting eyes—unified and full of love. At this moment of light within darkness we sing, "My beloved is mine and I am his" (Song of Songs 2:16).

These words are normally recited, read, or sung at the time of the year directly opposite to the High Holy Days, Song of Songs being the *megillah* (scroll for liturgical reading) associated with Pesach. For my ancestors in the biblical Land of Israel (where Song of Songs was written), Pesach was the most erotic time, when all nature bursts with fertility.

Rabbi Aaron Goldstein is the senior rabbi of Northwood and Pinner Liberal Synagogue, London, chair of the Conference of Liberal Rabbis and Cantors UK, and lecturer in practical rabbinics at Leo Baeck College, London. His rabbinical studies at Leo Baeck College and Hebrew Union College–Jewish Institute of Religion in New York fostered a love for applying meaningful liturgy to the congregational setting.

Even in my colder British climate, I can at least imagine that natural awakening of love, enhanced by the spring's abundant warmth, refreshing rains, and cooling breezes. The arriving summer, by contrast, is so hot that tempers fray and we easily lose ourselves in personal irritations and fleeting pettiness. Love becomes harder to sustain.

But then comes the fall, with *N'ilah*'s reigniting of the eternal love affair between God and Israel. We have completed the process of *t'shuvah*, our return: On Rosh Hashanah we emptied ourselves, ritually took the lint from our pockets—all the accumulated grime from the year—and let it be borne away on cleansing waters. On Yom Kippur we fill ourselves up again, not with material food for the belly, but with spiritual nourishment for the soul. We join in the exuberant, even raucous, singing of *El Nora Alilah*, but then call out to God, in quiet confidence:

> Open a gate for us [*p'tach lanu sha'ar*]. . . . [For] You extend your hand to sinners [*ki atah noten yad l'foshim*]. . . . You set humans apart from the outset, considering them worthy to stand before You. . . . You, Adonai our God, lovingly gave us this Day of Atonement, an end to, and complete forgiveness and pardon for, all our sins, so that we cease to oppress with our hands, and return to You and observe your gracious laws wholeheartedly. . . . [For] You are a God of forgiveness, gracious and merciful, endlessly patient, most kind and truthful.

We conclude by repeating the exclusivity of our love for the one God, *Adonai hu ha'elohim*, "Adonai is God"—our religious equivalent of, "I love You." God's response is heard in the final *t'ki'ah g'dolah*, the primal call of breath transformed through the length of horn that evokes the still, small voice of Elijah; loud to our mortal ear but whispered from a mighty mouth, "Israel, I love you too."

Now, filled to the brim with the best new-year intentions to repair the world with our rehabilitated heart, soul, and might, we experience *Havdalah*, the final pause before returning through the night's darkness into the secular world. As the candle is extinguished, we look around with an element of ecstasy that rivals that of the Israelite prophets who met God in deserts, plains, or hilltops, their faces radiant from the experience.

Here we stand (we say), "surrounded by members of our community. With them we share our happiness, and it becomes greater; our troubles, and they become smaller."[1] A sacred congregation of souls, all unique and individual, yet alike and bound by the common threads of humanity and the particularity of Israel. Here stand Jews of all shades and hues: Jews by birth or by choice, Jews by halakhic definition, Jews who fall outside that category but whom our British Liberal Movement fully accepts as well, and non-Jews too—our mixed multitude who once more comprehend why they are members of this Jewish Community.

There we stand as one, all together, bathed in the love of God, with the sizzle of flame being extinguished in wine still echoing in our eardrums; and as one, we turn to walk, hand in hand, through the open gates before they close for another year.

The love of God demands the association, the care, the love of and for our sisters and brothers of the House of Israel—for even as we pursue our spiritual life in union with God, we pass our earthly lives alongside the people gathered there that day. We leave, then, in the fading holiness of the departing day, sanctified by a love reignited with God, and with prayers that our renewed relationships with others may last until once more we call *P'tach lanu sha'ar*, "Open a gate for us."

"My beloved is mine and I am his" (Song of Songs 2:16).

☙ ❧

Denouement or Entwinement?

Rabbi Delphine Horvilleur

At the conclusion of a play, as in the final pages of a book, the spectator or reader anxiously awaits the story's denouement: literally, the "unknotting" or "untying" of the interwoven threads that constitute the plot.

How strange, then, that the sacred drama of Yom Kippur concludes with just the opposite: a service called *N'ilah*, meaning not just "locking" of the gates, but "knotting" or "tying" of a shoe.

How should we understand this paradox? What threads are unraveled during this solemn day only to need retying at its end? Why should we leave from a day of introspection "entwined" rather than "disentwined"—tied up in knots, so to speak, rather than satisfied by a proper resolution?

To understand this, we need to look at "knots" in Jewish ritual—in particular, the knotted tassels called *tzitzit* that we attach to the four corners of the *tallit*. As a verse in the *Sh'ma* reminds us (Numbers 15:39), we "look at them" to "remember" all of God's commandments.

Rabbi Delphine Horvilleur, the granddaughter of Holocaust survivors, is committed to retaining their memory and establishing a positive liberal and dynamic Judaism for future generations in Europe. After her ordination (Hebrew Union College–Jewish Institute of Religion, New York, 2008), she became rabbi of Congregation MJLF (Mouvement Juif Liberal de France) in Paris—the third woman rabbi in French history. She is chief editor of *Tenou'a*, a magazine of Jewish thought, has authored three books, and has contributed to all volumes in this Prayers of Awe series. Rabbi Horvilleur is particularly involved in Jewish-Muslim dialogue and in 2016 was granted the title of "Knight in the French National Order of Merit."

The knots of the *tallit* are mnemonic, therefore, a memory tool to prevent our "losing sight" of our obligations. An everyday parallel is the custom of tying a knot in our handkerchief to remember what we might otherwise forget.

Other civilizations use knots similarly. Take Andean writing, for example, the product of pre-Columbian culture:

> It was not written on clay tablets or pieces of paper. Rather, it was written by tying knots on colourful cords called *quipus*. Each *quipu* consisted of many cords of different colours, made of wool or cotton. On each cord, several knots were tied in different places. A single *quipu* could contain hundreds of cords and thousands of knots. By combining different knots on different cords with different colours, it was possible to record large amounts of mathematical data relating to, for example, tax collection and property ownership.[1]

For both Andeans and the Rabbis, knots were reminders of what is due, a visual witnessing of a contracted debt. In the Jewish case, the knots (the *tzitzit*) are reminders of the primary relationship that Jews call "being commanded" (*m'tzuveh/m'tzuvah*) by another, whether human or divine. Throughout the year, the *tallit*'s knots invite the faithful to look at them, to kiss them during prayer, and to cherish what they stand for: responsibility as living creatures toward God and the world.

When we die, we are relieved of responsibility and duty; and appropriately, the knots are then removed. As part of the ritual called *tohorah* and *halbashah* (purification and dressing of the dead before burial), the knots of the *tzitzit* are cut off; only then is the body enveloped in the *tallit*, there to rest for eternity.

In Judaism, then, the denouement—the resolution, the untying of knots—belongs only to the dead. The living wear knots to be reminded of their obligations and their debts. The dead need no such reminders, as they are freed of such responsibilities. Of the dead, we say, *Nishmatam tz'rurah bitzror hachayim*, usually translated as "Their soul is woven into the threads of the eternal life"; but it can also mean "the threads of those who are alive"—of us, that is, of those still living. The dead need no knots of their own; they are free from the obligation to remember. But we, the living, remember them because they become woven, or tied, into the fabric of who we are. They become knots in our lives and, as such, cannot fade from memory.

No wonder Yom Kippur ends with "re-knotting." Throughout Yom Kippur day, dressed in our white shrouds and without food or drink, we pretend that the knots are untied as on the day of final departure. We play dead, cut off from the world of the living, as if our debts to the living are effaced by the ritual. On Yom Kippur we do not need *quipus* . . .

On that day, our debts are forgiven, we say, discharged in full. That is the point of *Kol Nidre*, the prayer with which the day begins, and the actual meaning of the word *kippur* itself. Its Hebrew root *k.p.r.* gives us the verb "to cover"; the related noun *kaporet* denotes the cover of the ark, for example. On Yom Kippur, God "covers for us." Temporarily released from contracts of the year gone by, we are "covered"! Until *N'ilah* . . .

At the *N'ilah* moment of reconnecting to real life, the knots must reappear. We are back in the realm of debt, needing to remember our obligations.

Jacques Derrida liked to recall that the etymology of the word "analysis" is the Greek *analuein*, which means "to loosen links" or "to *dis*solve" them, but which could also be translated by the Latin *solvere* (to detach, to deliver, to acquit, or to *ab*solve). "*Solutio* and *resolutio* too have several meanings: *dis*solution, a broken link, release, disengagement, discharge (of a debt) *and* the *sol*ution of a problem."[2] During the twenty-four hours of Yom Kippur, we believe we have the *sol*ution, convinced that *dis*solution has brought *re*solution.

At *N'ilah*, however, we see that resolution has escaped us and that soon the ties that constrain and bind us will reappear. We will be re-entangled by the realization that we have not yet finished analyzing. Knots will always remain . . . as long as we live, as long as the gates of heaven remain closed to us.

૭ᴚᴚᴚᴖ

Ending with a Bang or a Whimper?

WHAT DO WE TAKE HOME WITH US?

Rabbi Jonathan Magonet, PhD

While working with Rabbi Lionel Blue *z'l* on the new edition of the High Holy Day prayer book of the Reform Synagogues of Great Britain (now Movement for Reform Judaism) back in the 1980s, we constantly asked ourselves certain questions.[1] For Yom Kippur, with its five full services, what was the theme, or themes, of each of them? How might they be distinguished from one another so that we could experience their changing nature as part of our individual and collective journey through the day? Common to each service are the *s'lichot* (petitionary prayers) and *vidui* (confession), but by working around these staples, we could blend new material with the old and allow the thematic progression to stand out.

When it came to *N'ilah*, I attended services using the previous prayer book, a reprint of the original version from the nineteenth century.

Rabbi Jonathan Magonet, PhD, is emeritus professor of Bible at Leo Baeck College in London, where he was principal (president) from 1985 to 2005. He is coeditor of three volumes of *Forms of Prayer* (the prayer books of the British Movement for Reform Judaism), editor of the eighth edition of *Daily, Sabbath and Occasional Prayers*, and currently coeditor of the forthcoming ninth edition of the *High Holyday Machzor*. He has contributed to all the volumes in the Prayers of Awe series. He is editor of the journal *European Judaism* and a research professor at Seinan Gakuin University, Fukuoka, Japan.

Many of the traditional *piyyutim* had been removed and replaced with a selection of psalms. The service seemed structure-less, in that the same psalms were endlessly repeated but for no particular reason other than to pad out the time. Rather than summing up all that we had experienced as worshipers for the past twenty-four hours, it was merely mind-numbing.

Lionel and I have very different temperaments, so each of us found our own way to express what we felt needed to be said at this closing stage of the day.

Lionel composed an opening prayer that sets the scene for the service, following *El Nora Alilah*:

> *N'ilah* has come and soon the gates of mercy will close. That which is done is done, and can never be recalled. For time alone does not heal the wounds we bear and the wounds we cause. We have prayed a little, we have grieved a little, asked for much forgiveness, and done much less to earn it. Our sins are not cast into the depths of the sea and no scapegoat has borne them into the desert. They are still with us, our familiar and unwelcome companions, riveted to our souls.
>
> Therefore, we turn aside from our cleverness, our self-reliance and our pride, and come to You as poor people who receive, as homeless folk who seek Your shelter, as failures who can at least admit their failure. The day is ending and we can no longer rely on our own good deeds, but on Your goodwill. Our minds no longer run about to seek You, but wait in patience for You to find us. As the gates of mercy close, we know each of us is precious in Your sight. You are our hope.[2]

I assembled a kind of dialogue made up of biblical verses tracing a lifetime in conversation with God. But I wanted to note that the relationship with God can be uncomfortable, even something we wish to escape at times; Psalm 139:7–8 nicely expresses that ambivalence. But God is also the tragic hero of the biblical narratives, waiting, often in vain, to be loved by human beings. And that, too, needed to be expressed in these closing moments. So here is the text, providing both perspectives, located shortly before the final *Avinu Malkeinu*, and I wonder how far it has been read or skipped over during the thirty or so years it has been available:

The word of the Lord came to me, saying:
Before I formed you in the womb I knew you,
Before you were born I set you apart. (*Jeremiah 1:4–5*)

> *You have taken me from the womb,*
> *carried me safely on my mother's breast . . .*
> *Do not be far from me. (Psalm 22:10, 12)*

As a mother comforts her child
so will I myself comfort you. (*Isaiah 66:13*)

> *Do not remember the sins of my youth and my wrongdoing*
> *but remember me in love. (Psalm 25:7)*

I remember the devotion of your youth,
the love of your bridal days,
when you went after Me into the desert
to a land unsown. (*Jeremiah 2:2*)

> *Whom have I in heaven but You?*
> *Beside You, I have nothing on earth.*
> *My flesh and my heart may fail*
> *but God is the rock of my heart*
> *and my portion forever. (Psalm 73:25–26)*

I betroth you to Me forever.
I betroth you to Me with integrity and justice,
with tenderness and love.
I betroth you to Me with faithfulness,
and you will know the Lord. (*Hosea 2:21–22*)

> *Where could I go from Your spirit,*
> *or where could I flee from Your presence?*
> *If I climb to heaven, You are there,*
> *there too, if I lie in the depths. (Psalm 139:7–8)*

I was ready to be sought by those who did not ask.
I was ready to be found by those who did not seek.
I said: "Here am I," "Here am I,"
to a nation that did not call on My name. (*Isaiah 65:1*)

> *So I looked for You in the holy place,*
> *to see Your power and glory.*
> *My soul is thirsty for You,*
> *my flesh is pining for You. (Psalm 63:3, 2)*

When you call Me and come and pray to Me,
I will hear you.

When you seek Me, you will find Me,
if you search for Me with all your heart.
I shall let you find Me. (*Jeremiah 29:12–14*)
> *Do not reject me in old age;*
> *when my strength is feeble, do not abandon me. (Psalm 71:9)*
When you are old, I am still the same,
and when your hair turns grey, I will support you;
I have made and I will bear,
I will support and I will save. (*Isaiah 46:4*)
> *Yet I am always with You.*
> *You have grasped me by the hand.*
> *You will guide me with Your counsel*
> *and afterwards receive me in glory. (Psalm 73:23–24)*[3]

Thirty years on, I am involved with a new editorial board as we seek to revise and reimagine the *machzor*, reevaluating the validity of our earlier intuitions as to what we might need as the day closes and we prepare to return to "real life."

My own compilation is a reminder that every year Yom Kippur challenges us to reassess our relationship with God as our lives change and evolve. We cannot know in advance what prayers we might need or what answering response we might hope for. This "dialogue" from our tradition may be of help, but I have changed my mind about where the passage belongs. I would move it to earlier in the day to give more time to reflect on what it offers. Now that the "gates" are closing, the traditional texts, so often repeated during the day and now so familiar that they are almost bereft of meaning, will have to carry us through them.

Lionel's prayer, I think, still belongs as an introduction to *N'ilah*. It puts into final perspective the heroic task we have undertaken, singly and collectively, on this day. We have tried to use the complex and demanding liturgical apparatus to help us let go, if only for a moment, of our ultimate conviction that we are the center of the universe. Perhaps it is precisely the abandonment of that self-centered illusion that opens us to the experience of awe, both terrifying and liberating, that these Days of Awe provide. We take home the knowledge that we have sought and possibly found God on this day; we can only "wait in patience for You to find us."

Closing Time

Rabbi Janet Marder and
Rabbi Sheldon Marder

At my back I always hear
Time's winged chariot hurrying near.
— Andrew Marvell (1621–1678), "To His Coy Mistress"

Open closed open . . . That's all we are.
— Yehuda Amichai (1924–2000), *Open Closed Open*

I get the willies when I see closed doors.
— Joseph Heller (1923–1999), *Something Happened*

N'ilah is a sustained wrestling with impermanence, loss, and the finality of death. The very title bespeaks the problem. In days of old, at *z'man han'ilah* ("the time the gates close"), the priest would lock

---

Rabbi Janet Marder was ordained by Hebrew Union College–Jewish Institute of Religion (New York, 1979) and serves as the senior rabbi of Congregation Beth Am in Los Altos Hills, California. From 2003 to 2005 she served as president of the Central Conference of American Rabbis, the first woman in that role. She is coeditor, translator, and commentator for two liturgical projects: *Mishkan HaNefesh: Machzor for the Days of Awe* and *Mishkan HaLev: Prayers for S'lichot and the Month of Elul*. She became a Senior Rabbinic Fellow at the Shalom Hartman Institute, Jerusalem, in 2007.

Rabbi Sheldon Marder was ordained by Hebrew Union College–Jewish Institute of Religion (New York, 1978) and serves as rabbi of the San Francisco Campus for Jewish Living in San Francisco, California. His recent articles include "Doorways of Hope: Adapting to Alzheimer's" and "What Happens When We Use Poetry in Our Prayer Books—And Why?" He is coeditor, translator, and commentator for two liturgical projects: *Mishkan HaNefesh: Machzor for the Days of Awe* and *Mishkan HaLev: Prayers for S'lichot and the Month of Elul*. He became a Senior Rabbinic Fellow at the Shalom Hartman Institute, Jerusalem, in 2007.

the Temple gates from within (Mishnah Midot 1:9), a sign of the passing of a day that would never come again. "Time's arrow" goes in one direction only, so that each passing day moves us ever closer to death. The modern "translation" for *n'ilah* might, therefore, be the title of Joseph Heller's sequel to *Catch-22*, a novel about a sixty-eight-year-old Yossarian facing old age and mortality: *Closing Time*.

The urgency associated with this inevitable closing upon the past comes through in the twelfth-century Sephardic poem with which *N'ilah* opens: *El Nora Alilah*. Its rhythmic refrain *bish'at han'ilah* ("as the gates close"; see p. 98–100) is a repetitive drumbeat reminder that this is "closing time"—for Yom Kippur, now; for our very lives, some day.

Another *N'ilah* poem, *Ad Yom Moto* ("Until the day we die"), echoes the reminder of mortality: "Until the day we die, You await our repentance, to turn us toward true life. . . ."[1] The message of human frailty and finitude appears also in *Yizkor* and *Eleh ezk'rah*, our personal and historical remembrance of the dead; and in the *kittel*, the traditional garb for Yom Kippur, evoking burial shrouds. *N'ilah* is meant to overwhelm us with the truth that, every day of every year, death is closer. We feel, with Archibald MacLeish, "How swift how secretly / the shadow of the night comes on."[2]

But as much as *N'ilah* signifies inevitable endings (of Yom Kippur day and life itself), it also pleads—and even protests: "*P'tach lanu sha'ar* . . . Open a gate for us when the gates are being closed, for the day is about to fade. The day shall end, the sun shall set. Let us enter Your gates!"[3]

As the iron gates swing shut, as the shadow of night comes on, signaling time's implacable advance, the liturgy dares to push back. We prisoners of time seek reprieve. As if we can stop the setting sun with words alone, we shout out, half imploringly, half demandingly: "Open a gate for us."

These words are read, traditionally, as simple pleading. But the phrase is ambiguous, evocative and haunting enough to suggest the power of the human voice to resist its own impermanence. Maybe the gates don't have to close—not all of them, anyway!

"Before we are born," wrote Yehuda Amichai, "everything is open. . . . As long as we live, everything is closed within us. And when we die, everything is open again. Open closed open. That's all we are."[4] To be alive is to be "closed," constrained by time, locked into mortality.

Consigned to the consciousness that time is running out, we long to slow it down. With doors closing daily, we lament our vanished youth, cling to possessions we do not need, hurt others and ourselves—all because we do not want to accept the inevitable. *N'ilah*'s plaintive depiction of the passing of the day and its call to "open a gate" articulate the human struggle against our fate.

Theoretical physicist Alan Lightman writes:

> I don't know why we long so for permanence, why the fleeting nature of things so disturbs. . . . In our churches and synagogues and mosques, we pray to the everlasting and eternal. Yet, in every nook and cranny, nature screams at the top of her lungs that nothing lasts, that it is all passing away. All that we see around us, including our own bodies, is shifting and evaporating and one day will be gone. . . . Daylilies bloom and then wilt, leaving dead, papery stalks. Forests burn down, replenish themselves, then disappear again. Ancient stone temples and spires flake in the salty air . . . and eventually dissolve into nothing. Coastlines erode and crumble. Glaciers slowly but surely grind down the land. . . . Eyesight fades, hearing diminishes, bones shrink and turn brittle.[5]

The liturgy of *N'ilah* knows all this: that everything we cherish will someday be gone; that we ourselves are fleeting phenomena, disappearing like daylilies; that "the gates are closing." And we protest: not just yet! "Open a gate for us."

Yet Yom Kippur's insistence on human finitude concludes not with lament nor even with protest, but in a burst of exultation. Precisely because life is brief, it has infinite value. Precisely because the good things of life do not last, they are all the more precious and beautiful.

Andrew Marvell's poem "To His Coy Mistress," bemoaning "time's winged chariot," concludes with a passionate charge to enjoy life while we can: "Let us roll all our strength and all / Our sweetness up into one ball, / And tear our pleasures with rough strife / Through the iron gates of life."

At first glance, the concluding mood of Yom Kippur conveys the same sense of *carpe diem*. A medieval poem for *N'ilah*, based on Ecclesiastes 9:7, declares, "*Lekh b'simchah*—Go forth in gladness, your heart filled with joy: eat your bread and drink your wine!"[6] The Sephardic staple *El Nora Alilah* ends similarly: "Daughters and sons, be worthy of your years—may they be many, and filled with joy!"[7]

But the joy of *N'ilah* is more than a call to seize the day and burst through "the iron gates of life." Though we are mortal, we are endowed with a spark of divinity; our lives matter. Blessed with God's most sacred gift, we are charged to cherish that gift as long as we live and to trust in a love that will outlive us all.

So just before the final blast of the shofar, we call out, *Adonai hu ha'elohim*, "Adonai is God!"—proclaiming our faith in a transcendent source of goodness and truth, though we ourselves are fallible and frail. No, we do not live forever, but through goodness and truth we are linked to the One who does. Even as the gates are closing and the darkness falls, we rejoice in the ultimate triumph of light and life.

What's in a Building?

IF STONE COULD SPEAK

Rabbi Julia Neuberger, DBE

The *N'ilah* service at West London Synagogue is always full to bursting and quite short in length. For we have to end at 7:00 p.m. on the dot, whatever time the fast actually finishes! That requirement is not quite Torah *min hashamayim* ("going back to Sinai"), but the custom does date back to the synagogue's founding in 1840 as a breakaway from the two Orthodox communities of London, Ashkenazi and Sephardi. It is always adhered to. The rabbis look at their watches surreptitiously. If need be, we skip a section here, a section there. But we cannot miss *N'ilah*'s finale, so skilled timing is everything.

The synagogue fills up during *Minchah*. *Yizkor* follows, precisely at 5:15—beautiful, solemn, and slow-paced. The end of the day still seems far away. We hear a suppressed sob or two. The tension is palpable. Then comes the short *N'ilah* sermon, preparing us for the end of the day. After that, only forty-five minutes remain. The tension mounts. People sing their hearts out in *El Nora Alilah*. We read in unison. We skip a bit. We

---

Rabbi Julia Neuberger, DBE, has an MA (Cambridge University) and rabbinic ordination (Leo Baeck College) and is an independent member of the House of Lords, UK, and senior rabbi of West London Synagogue, where she particularly loves her role as pastor and the synagogue's vibrant social action program. She formerly served as chief executive of King's Fund, London, and as government-appointed chair of the review of the Liverpool Care Pathway (end of life) and of diversity in the judiciary. Her honorary doctorates include Cambridge and University of London, and she was Bloomberg Professor at Harvard Divinity School in 2006. Rabbi Neuberger's most recent book, *Is That All There Is? Thoughts on the Meaning of Life and Leaving a Legacy*, is being followed up by a book (in process) on the nature of care.

reach the last prayer in English: "The day is closing. . . ." And the mood shifts, from somber to expectant, from deep reflection to an anticipation of the end.

And then we reach the final sung *Kaddish*, *Avinu Malkeinu*, and the last three lines, culminating in *Adonai hu ha'elohim* read once, sung six times. Then a massive *t'ki'ah g'dolah* with a whole family of shofar blowers, from the father whose blast lasts an astonishing four minutes to his children in ever-decreasing height blowing for less.

At that point, both joy and relief pervade the congregation. The air, foul smelling and thick with the day's prayers and efforts, seems miraculously to clear. The rabbis rush for the entrance to greet the congregation before they leave. And by 7:30 the building is deserted, waiting for tomorrow and the start of sukkah building.

And yet the building, now empty, shadowy, holds its Yom Kippur memories. You can almost feel the presence of previous generations in the pews. From descriptions of the pillars in Amy Levy's novel *Reuben Sachs* (1888) to the stained glass windows in memory of Leslie Holt, who perished in World War I, our forebears are there. The building's memories stretch back to 1870, when it was built, and even to the 1840s, when the congregation was first formed. Today's worshipers finish their *N'ilah* and take their leave, but my mind's eye recollects the men of long ago arriving in evening dress for the morning service, for they would have stayed up to pray all night, and having dressed for Yom Kippur eve dinner the night before, they necessarily appeared the same way the next morning, a *tallit* wrapped around the splendid velvet jackets. For the same reason, the women, upstairs in those days, but always present, as much as the men, would arrive in evening dress the next morning, splendid in silks and satins, many of them in the traditional white of mourning that befits the Yom Kippur penitential spirit.

And our forebears stayed all day. Like us, it was full to bursting for *N'ilah*. Like us, they finished at 7:00 p.m. The music they sang at *N'ilah* is the same as we sing—the same *Avinu Malkeinu*, the same *Adonai hu ha'elohim*. Many of the tunes we sing today go back to the 1840s, though more are mid- to late nineteenth century: Lewandowski, Mombach, Naumbourg. They too heard the organ played till their hearts broke at *N'ilah*; they too celebrated the choir for keeping going all those hours. This organ has been there since 1870. The cramped choir stalls are unaltered. The choir has always been crowded in there, singing their hearts out, getting hotter and hotter as the day goes on, until at *N'ilah* the temperature is almost unbearable.

What would these pews, walls, and pillars tell us of *N'ilah* if they could speak? That generations of the same families have stood and sat where we stand and sit, sharing with us the same highs and lows, the same joy and relief at the opening of the gates of prayer, the gates of atonement? That they too shuffled impatiently until very near the end, when a sense of awe and relief overcame them at *N'ilah*'s final note of hope and triumph? That they too prayed and atoned, but—unlike us—did so as the bombs dropped on London in the 1940s, for the synagogue never closed? That they too heard the shofar blasts at the end and wondered if the glorious stained glass windows, weakened by wartime bombing, would withstand the blast?

All this and more colors *N'ilah* at West London, a service few will miss, a service, they tell us, that gives them resolution of spirit and conscience to face the year ahead. And as the rabbis sink exhausted into our own fast-breaking, we feel a sense of awe at how the building, with all its memories, shapes the solemnity of the day.

The gates close, and the shadows deepen into darkness. *N'ilah* is over for another year. The congregation is released, with a sense of relief that is almost cathartic.

And they begin the New Year properly, ready to celebrate their plenitude at Sukkot and to give to those who do not share so abundantly. They do so with joy in their hearts. For the gates have closed, and they rejoice in life renewed.

☙✦❧

Yom Kippur Is Almost Over

WHAT WILL HAPPEN TO THE WINE?

Rabbi Jacob J. Schacter, PhD

It has been a long day, a very long day, intense and draining. Dusk is beginning to settle and we look at our watches. An hour to go. A half hour to go. Only five more minutes. Yom Kippur is ending, but so what, really? Has all this effort mattered, really? What insights or experiences are we taking with us? Are we taking *any* insights or experiences with us?

Among those who inherit a share in the world to come, Rabbi Yochanan (Talmud, Pesachim 113a) lists those who dwell in the Land of Israel, those who raise children to study Torah, and those who recite *Havdalah* (the prayer over wine that concludes the Sabbath and separates it from the workweek following).

This is a strange list. It evokes memories of a song I heard countless times while watching *Sesame Street* with my children (many years ago): "One of these things is not like the others." I understand the centrality of

---

Rabbi Jacob J. Schacter, PhD, is University Professor of Jewish History and Jewish Thought and senior scholar at the Center for the Jewish Future at Yeshiva University. He coauthored the award-winning *A Modern Heretic and a Traditional Community: Mordecai M. Kaplan, Orthodoxy, and American Judaism* and is sole author of *The Lord Is Righteous in All His Ways: Reflections on the Tish'ah be-Av Kinot by Rabbi Joseph B. Soloveitchik* and close to one hundred articles and reviews in Hebrew and English. He is the founding editor of the *Torah u-Madda Journal*.

Israel and the importance of Torah, but *Havdalah*? Why should I merit a share in the world to come just for reciting *Havdalah*?

The Talmud itself wonders about this and explains that Rabbi Yochanan meant not just those who recite the prayer but those "who leave over wine from *Kiddush* [Friday night] for *Havdalah* [Saturday night] [*d'meshayer mekidusha l'avdalta*]." But what kind of explanation is that? So what? Why does this matter so much? Who cares?

We should all care, actually, because of the implied lesson presented here for life's important moments generally—including Yom Kippur. It is not enough to acknowledge the arrival of Shabbat as a day of meaning and holiness; we must also appreciate it as it ends, so as to take that meaning and holiness into the mundane world of work that follows. Metaphorically speaking, we save some of the wine that ushers in the Sabbath and use it as the wine to usher in the week that now begins.

So too Yom Kippur. Unless we extend its lessons into the days, weeks, and months that follow, we have not fully benefited from the wisdom of the day. We are to take the "wine" (as it were) of Yom Kippur and sip it, savor it, throughout the year. But what is the "wine" of Yom Kippur?

When we return the Torah to the ark after it has been read, we chant a well-known verse from Lamentations (5:21), *Hashiveinu*, we say, "Return us, O Lord, to Yourself, and let us return; renew our days as of old [*chadeish yameinu k'kedem*]." What are these "days of old" that we want renewed? The Midrash (*Lamentations Rabbah* 5:21) associates this "of old" (*k'kedem*) with Adam, about whom the Bible writes: God "drove out Adam [from Eden], and stationed cherubim to the east [*mikedem*] of the Garden of Eden" (Genesis 3:24). The *k'kedem* here is reminiscent of the *mikedem* there. But still, what actual lesson is the Midrash trying to teach?

To arrive at the lesson, we need to recognize that the word *kedem* appears earlier, at the very beginning of Adam's story, where God "planted a garden in Eden, to the east [*mikedem*], and placed there Adam" (Genesis 2:8). Why is only the second, much later, reference to *kedem* reminiscent of the *kedem* in the verse "Renew our days as of old [*k'kedem*]"? What's wrong with the first one?

At stake is the realization that the first *mikedem* (when Adam is planted in Eden) refers to the "good old days" of long ago to which we nostalgically wish, sometimes, to return. But we can't! The Midrash warns us against the romantic delusion that we can ever re-create the days of Eden. They are an anomaly, unrealistic and unsustainable in the world of history, time, and circumstance. In a way they are the Yom Kippur of life—time we block off annually to do without life's normalcies: not just work, but even eating, drinking, and serving our bodies in any way whatever. The only return possible is to the days *after* Adam left the Garden, when he put behind him the ideal world of miraculous holiness and entered the mundane space of everyday existence, where, although barred from reentry to Eden by the cherubic guards, he was still in close proximity to God.

We do not live our lives in the Garden of Eden of Yom Kippur, deeply immersed in prayer and in the spirit of Judaism. We live our lives *after* Yom Kippur, in the hustle, bustle, and tussle of the "real world."

At the moment of *N'ilah*, forced to reconsider our own return to everyday life, let us try to take Yom Kippur's message with us: the constant refrain of *Hashiveinu*, "Return us . . . renew our days as of old [*k'kedem*]." What we need as Yom Kippur ends is the assurance that even the days outside of Eden can be renewed for good.

In his thoughtful account of saying *Kaddish* for his father, Leon Wieseltier remarks, "I have read of people whose lives are transfigured in an instant. I do not believe that such a transfiguration can happen to me. For what changed these people was not only the instant, but also their subsequent fidelity to the instant."[1]

As the *Kaddish*, so Shabbat and Yom Kippur. Each has its own wine that we should try to carry with us into the "real world," the ordinary days of life that follow.

☙

Don't Let the Gates Slam Shut behind You

Rabbi David A. Teutsch, PhD

The High Holy Day season is full of powerful symbols—the shofar on Rosh Hashanah, the Torah scrolls held before the open ark as a court on *Kol Nidre*, and the crumbs we sprinkle at *tashlich*, to name but a few. For as long as I can remember, though, the most powerful symbol for me has been the image of *N'ilah*'s closing gates.

These gates are said to be *sha'arei t'shuvah*, "the gates of repentance," or, more accurately, "the gates of return"—our return to a path of meaning. What I love most is that the very fact of their closing implies how wide open they were beforehand. I particularly associate those open gates with *Kol Nidre*, but we can walk through them any time on Yom Kippur.

What does it mean that they suddenly swing shut as that day ends? If it means the hard work of the day is done, that is one thing. But it seems to imply that the opportunity to return has actually ended—and that strikes me as awful. Returning to greater awareness of the Divine, to ethical action, and to spiritual living should be an opportunity that is always available.

Perhaps that explains the alternative tradition that says the gates stay open until Sh'mini Atzeret, the eighth and final day of Sukkot. It is

Rabbi David A. Teutsch, PhD, is professor emeritus at the Reconstructionist Rabbinical College, where he served as president for a decade. He has authored or edited dozens of books and articles and is the editor in chief of the groundbreaking *Kol Haneshamah* prayer-book series and a three-volume *Guide to Jewish Practice*, the first of which won a National Jewish Book Award. He earned his PhD at the Wharton School, where his dissertation was on organizational ethics. A past president of the Society of Jewish Ethics and of the Academic Coalition of Jewish Ethics, he is also an avid biker.

easy to see why our ancestors extended the time of *t'shuvah* until then. On Sh'mini Atzeret they said the prayer for rain, believing their *t'shuvah* affected the amount of rain their crops would receive. A late Hasidic tradition goes even further: it delays the closing of the gates until Hanukkah. But that would still leave the gates closed for eight months of the year. So my problem remains. Perhaps the insistence on having the gates close reflects the experience of people whose prayer practice is limited to the High Holy Days—but that seems wrong to me.

The day before each Rosh Chodesh ("the new moon") is called Yom Kippur Katan, "the little Yom Kippur." Some traditional Jews treat it as a minor fast day to consider the past month and do *t'shuvah* to the extent needed—as if the gates of our annual Yom Kippur reopen for one short day at the close of every month. But even that is not frequent enough. The weekday *Amidah*, which is recited morning, afternoon, and evening, includes the following blessing: "Blessed are You who rejoices in our return" (*harotzeh bit'shuvah*). In our tradition, the process of wrestling with our inner demons and moving ourselves toward right living is ongoing each and every day. Why, then, do we talk about the gates closing at *N'ilah*?

Perhaps the answer lies in human psychology. For most of us, constant moral and spiritual striving is prohibitively difficult. Our other commitments—to family, work, and so on—take time and effort and drain us of mental energy. It is rare indeed to have a whole day given over to spiritual engagement with none of the usual distractions. Maybe the gates don't actually close at *N'ilah*, but on Yom Kippur we feel them to be especially open.

Yom Kippur starts at *Kol Nidre* with considerable anticipation. People feel charged by the atmosphere of celebration and anticipation, resistance and nervousness. A sense of communal unity dominates the entire day. Its liturgical redundancy—the *Amidah* and confessions recited no fewer than ten times, traditionally—wears us down and opens us up. Engagement with each succeeding cycle of readings drives us deeper into ourselves, opens us to further personal insight, and lowers our resistance. The absence of food and drink eliminates distraction, helps us focus on the spirit rather than the body, and lowers resistance further.

The saying "*N'ilah* comes early" reflects the profound challenge of doing complete *t'shuvah*. It is more than a one-day task, and the end of Yom Kippur comes too swiftly if we are fully engaged in it. Fully doing *t'shuvah* has no shortcuts. For that reason I begin the task at the beginning of Elul and work myself up to devoting the whole day of Yom Kippur to it. Like most people, though, I need all the help I can get, especially at *N'ilah*, when I usually find myself in a reverie, transported by the liturgy and challenged by exhaustion as the day starts slipping away.

El Nora Alilah, the *piyyut* written by the eleventh- to twelfth-century Spanish poet Moses ibn Ezra, sets the tone with its insistent request for God "whose deeds are awesome" to pardon us now, "as the gates are closing" (*bish'at han'ilah*). In singing this *piyyut*, I feel viscerally the gates moving on their hinges, closing bit by bit.

The time from there to the end of the service goes by in a blur. Before I know it, I am on my feet along with the whole community chanting the *Sh'ma* and affirming the unity of the Divine—and, by extension, the unity of the shared communal experience of doing so together, in one voice. *Havdalah* follows, ending this most intense day and returning us to our individual everyday lives.

How well we sustain the *N'ilah* turning of mind throughout the rest of the year depends on many factors. Do we retain our connectedness to the community that so powerfully uplifted us and moved us toward goodness as we affirmed the final *Sh'ma* together? Do we build into our lives daily spiritual disciplines that sustain the high resolve of *N'ilah*? Do we surround ourselves with people who demand high ethical standards and a serious effort to better the world? Are we reinforced in our roles as loving family members? These are the real-life variables that can determine how lasting the effect of Yom Kippur will be.

So I work each year, after *N'ilah* ends, to enhance my chances of answering these questions more positively, hoping for a greater sense of comfort when the gates start swinging shut next *N'ilah*. We often talk about the year as if it were a circle or cycle. Much better is the image of a spiral carrying us ever upward.

◎

Appendices
Going Deeper

Appendix A

The Boldest Claim: God Reaches Out a Hand

Rabbi Lawrence A. Hoffman, PhD

When my oldest son was still a child, he took ill while we were at camp together, and the only family doctor within miles was a rather questionable gentleman sporting an honorary discharge from the army on his wall but no certificate of graduation from medical school. Still, he was licensed to prescribe the antibiotic we thought our son would need, so we visited his office and waited our turn. The waiting room featured a book with stories to read to the sick children while they sat there.

The book opened naturally at a story that, fortunately, I reviewed to myself first. I say "fortunately" because it turned out to be a compilation of tales with a Christian evangelical message. I never did read it to my son, but I surely remember it.

The story featured two little boys in a hospital, Tommy (who had been there for several weeks) and Joey (newly admitted after a horrible car accident). One look convinces Tommy that his new roommate will never last the night. Tommy therefore tells Joey not to fear death, because even though he is a sinner, Christ will forgive him. He need only hold out his hand and he will find Jesus reaching out a hand in return, to pull him safely into heaven. Tommy awakens the next morning to find Joey dead, as expected, but lying stiffly with his right arm outstretched. Tommy rejoices, knowing that Joey has followed his advice and been welcomed by the similarly outstretched hand of God.

As I sat there, making up my own story in place of this one, I meditated on the difference in cultures between the editors who had supplied the tale of Tommy and Joey and what my Jewish waiting-room story would have been. To begin with, it would have highlighted healing, not dying; life, not death. I thought also that I would never have come up with the image of God's outstretched hand.

I know now that I was only partly right. God's outstretched hand is actually a central Jewish metaphor, the very heart of the *N'ilah* service.

To understand it fully, we need to go back to a third-century debate on the meaning of *N'ilah*, carried in the Babylonian Talmud (and discussed more fully above, pp. 3–4): "What is *n'ilat sh'arim* [the closing of the gates]," the Talmud asks (Yoma 87b). Rav identifies it as an extra *Amidah*. His opponent Samuel, however, says it is the prayer "What are we, what are our lives?" By the ninth century (at the latest), Rav's *Amidah* was included, but so was Samuel's prayer, along with a preface, "You extend your hand"—precisely the image of the waiting-room story, with, however, this difference: God does not extend a hand to welcome us into life after death. Rather, God reaches to us at the end of Yom Kippur to pull us out of our fasting with the promise of life renewed here upon this earth.

The prayer is cited in this book's liturgy section ("'You Extend Your Hand' [*Atah Noten Yad*]," p. 67–69), but for purposes of more thorough discussion, we can conveniently repeat it here, dividing it into the two parts involved. Samuel seems to have been quoting the first words of part B (below), a set of rhetorical questions that emphasize human failing. Part A (below) is the later addition—a preamble to B, on the comforting theme of God's extending a hand. Part A was added, perhaps, because of the felt need, as the day comes to its end, to emphasize the "solution" of Yom Kippur (God's reaching out to us), not just the "problem" (human fallibility).

Part A: Preamble to B as B's solution (God comes to our aid): added later by Amram (c. 860) and used in Ashkenazi rite

> ¹You extend your hand to sinners, and your arm reaches out to accept those who repent. ²Teach us, Adonai our God, to confess all of our sins before You, so that we cease to oppress with our hands, and You accept us before You in perfect repentance like fires and fragrances, as You promised. ³Our obligatory fires are

endless, and our guilt-offering fragrances countless, but
You know that our end is the maggot and the worm, so
You offer us increased forgiveness.

Part B: Original prayer from Talmud providing the problem (human frailty)

[4]What are we? [5]What are our lives? [6]What is our love?
[7]What is our righteousness? [8]What is our salvation?
[9]What is our strength? [10]What is our might? [11]What can
we say before You, [12]Adonai our God and our ancestors' God? [13]Are not all mighty ones as though they
were nothing before You, men of fame as though they
never existed, the educated as though without knowledge, and the wise as though without insight, for most
of their acts are without value and the days of their life
worthless before You? [14]Man barely rises above beast,
for everything is worthless.

Interestingly enough, Sephardi tradition does not have part A, although probably not as a matter of principle. Rather, the two traditions (Ashkenazi and Sephardi) hark back to different medieval prototypes. Our first comprehensive prayer book is *Seder Rav Amram* (c. 860 CE); our second is *Siddur Saadiah* (c. 920 CE)—*seder* and *siddur* were equivalent words back then, both of them meaning "order," as in "order of prayer." Both Amram and Saadiah were authorities in Babylonia (modern-day Iraq), and both wrote "orders" of prayer. Amram's went to Spain but was copied by scribes everywhere, including northern Europe (France and Germany), the lands of Ashkenaz. Saadiah's went to Spain as well but never infiltrated Ashkenazi practice, for the simple reason that Saadiah wrote his book in Arabic, a language that was not understood north of the Pyrenees, whereas Amram used Rabbinic Aramaic, the language of the Babylonian Talmud and the scholarly language for Rabbinic Jews everywhere. Amram (whose book reached Ashkenaz) is our source of part A ("You extend your hand"). Saadiah (whose book influenced Sephardi Spain) does not have it.

What Saadiah has instead is an alternative introduction to part B that we can call A[1], also on the theme of God's power to forgive, but without the imagery of the divine hand reaching out to us. Ashkenazi tradition follows Amram; Sephardi tradition follows Saadiah.

Part A¹: Alternative preamble to B as B's solution (God comes to our aid): added later by Saadiah (c. 920) and used in Sephardi rite

> What can we say before You, You who dwell on high?
> And what can we relate before You, You who dwell in
> the heavens? For our sins are too many to count; our
> misdeeds are too mighty. But You, Adonai, are good,
> and pardoning, and greatly merciful to those who call out
> to You.

There is one more piece to this puzzle. Part B, the rhetorical rehearsal of human frailty ("What are we," etc.) that Samuel calls the essence of *N'ilah*, is also found within the daily morning service, along with these instructions: "You should always fear God inwardly and outwardly and gratefully acknowledge the truth and speak truth in your hearts, and rise early and say. . . ." These instructions lead into B, exactly as we have it in *N'ilah*, but with yet a third introduction—neither A ("You extend your hand"), nor A¹ ("What can we say before You"), but a third statement of God's mercy despite our sinfulness (call it A²).

Part A²: Yet a third preamble to B as B's solution (God is merciful); appears in daily morning service, not at *N'ilah*.

> Master of all worlds, we do not offer our supplications
> before You based on our righteousness, but, rather,
> based on your great mercy.

We do not know exactly what Samuel was citing. The Talmud provides only Part B's opening words. He might have been referring to all of part B as we now have it. Alternatively, readers of the Talmud, generations later, borrowed Samuel's opening words and then expanded them on their own to get the prayer that we now use. Either way, B was well enough known by the ninth and tenth centuries for Amram and then Saadiah to include it, each with his own introduction: "You extend your hand" (A) for Amram; "What can we say before You" (A¹) for Saadiah. Part B ("What are we") was similarly used by them in the daily morning service (not just in *N'ilah*, that is) as a meditation of human mortality.

In any event, part B did become standard fare for *N'ilah* as well (our subject here) along with an introduction (either A or A[1], but not A[2], which was reserved for everyday morning worship).

Now, on Yom Kippur, every single service has two confessions, both of them alphabetic acrostics: a short one, *Ashamnu* ("We have been guilty") and a long one, *Al Chet*, ("For the sin we have committed against You"). Every service but one, that is: *N'ilah. N'ilah* has only the first confession: the short one, *Ashamnu.* If we look at the placement of the entire prayer (A or A[1] plus B, depending on whether you are Ashkenazi or Sephardi), we see that it occurs where, normally, the lengthy second confession *Al Chet* would be found.

In sum, the Rabbis who formulated our liturgy decided that for *N'ilah*, a single confession, the short one, would suffice. Instead of the long one (*Al Chet*), they prescribed Samuel's prayer—a short statement of human failings (B), with an introduction on God's certain mercy (A or A[1]). The introduction differed for Amram (A) and for Saadiah (A[1]); and yet another introduction served when the prayer was said on regular weekday mornings (A[2]). But the message was clear. God does pardon us. And, according to Amram's prototype (A), God extends a hand in doing so.

Indeed, despite its placement in the service—where the long confession ought to be—Samuel's prayer (B) is not a confession at all. It does not list a variety of evils of which humans are capable; and it is not an acrostic, the normal style in which rabbinic confessions are couched. It is a reminder to God of human mortality, as if to say: God, You made us this way; we are really just human, You know. But You are forgiving. "You extend your hand to us" (A) or "You, Adonai, are good, and pardoning" (A[1]). We have reason to hope.

But there is more. Samuel's prayer B is followed by another prayer (C) that is its logical extension.

Part C:

> [1]You set humans apart from the outset, considering them worthy to stand before You. [2]For who can ask You, What are You doing? [3]And though they be righteous, what can they give You? [4]But You, Adonai our God, lovingly gave us this Day of Atonement, an end to, and complete forgiveness and pardon for, all our sins, so that we cease to oppress with our hands, and return

> to You and observe your gracious laws wholeheartedly.
> [5]In your great mercy, have mercy upon us, for You don't
> want the world's destruction. . . . [8]You are a God of for-
> giveness, gracious and merciful, endlessly patient, most
> kind and truthful, extending beneficence. [9]You want the
> wicked to repent, and You do not desire their death. . . .
> [14]For You are Israel's forgiver, and pardoner to the tribes
> of Jeshurun in every generation, and we have no king
> who pardons and forgives other than You.

The burden of the message so far is that (B) we are only human and unable to rise to the level of perfection. God, therefore (to cite the Ashkenazi version, A), holds out a hand, understands our nature, and wants to forgive us.

Part C explains how we know that God understands and forgives us, namely "You set humans apart from the outset" (verse 1). God fashioned us to be what we are: different from other animals. Implicit is the biblical understanding of Adam and Eve as the sole creatures to have eaten from the tree of knowledge—the tree that gave them "knowledge of good and evil" (Genesis 3:5). Humans alone have a conscience, making us "worthy to stand before You" (verse 1). This indeed is the human condition: to know there is such a thing as righteousness, yet not always to be able to choose it. But God made us that way, so understands our dilemma. God (who created the world, after all) surely does not "want the world's destruction" (verse 5)—does not even want the death of the wicked (line 9)—and so will pardon us.

Part C is inseparable from B. The version in *Siddur Saadiah*, especially, shows us that it was meant as a logical continuation. To begin with, as Saadiah cites it, it begins no new paragraph. In addition, he prefixes the first word, *hivdalta* ("You set [humans] apart"), with a *vav*, which in context translates as the disjunction "but." Sure, we "barely rise above beast" (last line of B), "but" (first line of C) God "set humans apart . . . worthy to stand before You." Taken as a whole, the prayer is a grand statement about God (theology), humanity (anthropology), and the relationship between them:

> A. About God, we say: You reach out for us, for You will pardon us, no matter what we are.

B. About humanity, we concede: For indeed, we are nothing; we are mortal, after all—mere nothings in the grand scheme of things.

C. About the relationship that unites us, we say: *But* even in our mortality, you made us different, granting us the capacity to stand before You as we do now on Yom Kippur—because the whole point is, both You and we want pardon and reconciliation as the gates close.

Now, some forty years after sitting in the country doctor's waiting room, I think again about the image of God's extended hand. It is apparently both Christian and Jewish. To be sure, the Tommy and Joey story is not indicative of Christianity universally. But it does represent a certain classical, and mainstream, view of Christian consciousness—the view that emphasizes salvation from sin as a way to escape the finality of death. Classically speaking, Jews too have insisted on life after death, but *N'ilah* prefers the image of being sealed in the book of life, this life, not the next one. And when God "extends a hand" in the context of *N'ilah*, it is to welcome us back to life as we know it, but cleansed and ready for a new start.

One more thing. What should not go unnoticed is the Hebrew word for those who have been "set apart" as unique and to whom, therefore, "God reaches out." It is none of the words or phrases used for Jews alone. Instead, it is *enosh*, the Hebrew for "human being." This central *N'ilah* prayer is a bold statement of Judaism's universal promise that *everyone* is made in the image of God, able to seize God's outstretched hand and receive pardon for wrongdoing. This universal theme is set at the beginning of the High Holy Days, at Rosh Hashanah, when, the Mishnah (the first Rabbinic law code, c. 200 CE) says, "All who come into the world" (*kol ba'ei olam*) appear before God. As the High Holy Days end, we see again that all who come into the world—described now as *enosh*, humanity itself—can know God's outstretched hand of deliverance.

 formerlyformerly

Appendix B

The Climactic End to N'ilah: The Making of a Tradition

Rabbi Lawrence A. Hoffman, PhD

Exactly how are Jewish traditions born, nurtured, and brought to maturity in the prayer books that contain them? Books on Jewish prayer rarely pay attention to that question; the detail necessary to answer it is assumed to be too taxing for general readers.

But a series of books on High Holy Day liturgy ought somewhere to introduce the reality of Jewish tradition in all of its daunting specificity, and the concluding ritual for *N'ilah* lends itself perfectly to just that task. To begin with, it is inherently interesting: the long Yom Kippur fast is finally ending; darkness envelops the congregation as the ark doors—open throughout the service—are finally closed; worshipers actually shout their final set of lines, not just once, but three or seven times, and then listen to the final blast of the shofar. Also, the unit in question is relatively small—so it is manageable. And because it was not inherited full-blown from Talmudic times, later authorities had plenty of opportunity to approach it afresh and to weigh in on it. The result is an ongoing set of debates from the ninth to the nineteenth centuries, a fascinating look at the way Jewish tradition comes into being.

Fair warning: Like any good story worth telling, the plotline for this concluding *N'ilah* ritual is peopled with a dizzying plethora of protagonists—enough to make even classical Russian novels look simple. Like the characters in those novels also, the rabbinic personae of our tale often have more than a single name. They go sometimes by the titles of their major books, and by acronyms too—Rabbi Meir of Rothenberg, for instance, is also the *MaHaRaM* (*M*oreinu ["our teacher"] *H*arav ["the rabbi"] *R*abbi *M*eir). And because they read each other's works, often across great distances, the story line transcends simple geographic boundaries.

Our tale begins in ninth- to eleventh-century Babylonia (present-day Iraq), with precedent-setting remarks by rabbis called *geonim* (pronounced g'oh-NEEM; singular: *gaon*, pronounced gah-OHN), an honorific meaning something like "Your Excellency." Their words (generally sent as responsa, answers to questions on Jewish law) reached rabbis in western Europe, whose works are the next chapter in the tale. From Ashkenaz (northern and central Europe), we will sample authors from eleventh- to twelfth-century France and nearby Germany, primarily along the Rhine (cities like Worms, Mainz, and Cologne). From the thirteenth century on, we will watch this Ashkenazi Jewish community spread westward to places like Bonn and Rothenberg and then to what became the Austro-Hungary empire—mostly Vienna, but also Bohemia (the Czech Republic today) and Hungary. By the sixteenth century, our focus shifts to the great Ashkenazi migrations that founded Jewish centers in present-day Poland, Belarus, and Lithuania.

We have fewer sources for early Sephardi (Spanish) Jews—prior to the expulsion in 1492, that is—but we will look at what we have. In addition, we will see Jews who are neither strictly Ashkenazi nor Sephardi or who are a mixture of both: Jews in Provence, on the one hand, and Italy, on the other. Then, returning to the Sephardi story, we will trace Jewish exiles moving east across the Mediterranean into the rising empire of the Ottoman Turks, especially to the town of Safed, the Ottoman administrative center in the Land of Israel, where Kabbalah flourished in altogether novel ways. We will also catch up with a stream of "secret" Jews (conversos) moving north to the Netherlands. When Holland declared its Protestant independence from Catholic Spain (Treaty of Utrecht, 1588), the conversos abandoned their surface identity as Catholics and came out as Jews—thus heralding a northern Sephardi renaissance, quite different from the Sephardim who fell under kabbalistic influence in Safed. From Holland, they repopulated England, where Jews had been expelled in 1290, and traveled also to the New World, opening up a new chapter of Sephardi history there.

The geographic scope of the story can take your breath away: France, Germany, Spain, Poland, Italy, and more. But most of our tale antedates the geographic entities as we know them nowadays; individual towns, surrounding districts, and natural river basins matter more than arbitrary national borders that did not yet even exist. The terms "Ashkenazi" and "Sephardi" are themselves just generalizations that do not do justice to the widespread diversity of custom that characterized people's lives when travel was rare, life was pursued locally, and there was still no printing press to homogenize diversity across the miles.

My goal here is to illustrate the wonder of Jewish creativity that underlies Jewish worship, but to do so without sacrificing insight that comes only through detail. As I say, for readers unfamiliar with Judaism's most famous rabbis and their works, the cast of characters may prove intimidating, but I hope I have included enough contextual knowledge to make the whole thing manageable. What follows, then, is, more or less, "the whole story," summarized sufficiently for comprehensive understanding, but outfitted with enough particularity to leave the reader awestruck by the poetic complexity of Jewish tradition in the making.

The Ritual In Short

N'ilah is most memorable for its stunning conclusion: a set of one-line acclamations (sometimes called *Sh'mot*, "Names," shorthand for "Names of God") that are shouted aloud, and the blowing of the shofar. All in all, we can distinguish five discrete units that constitute the ritual as we now have it.

1. *Sh'ma yisrael, Adonai eloheinu, Adonai echad* ("Hear, O Israel, Adonai is our God; Adonai is One").
2. *Barukh shem k'vod malkhuto l'olam va'ed* ("Blessed is the One the glory of whose kingdom is renowned forever").
3. *Adonai hu ha'elohim* ("Adonai is God").

These verses are recited in different ways—in some places, once; in others, more—and are followed by the following:

4. The final sounding of the shofar (either one blast [*t'ki'ah*] or four [*t'ki'ah, sh'varim, t'ru'ah, t'ki'ah*]). *T'ki'ah* is the single long sustained blast; *sh'varim* is a trifold wailing sound; *t'ru'ah* is a staccato sound of nine short blasts; when *t'ki'ah* is extended at least

three times as long as usual, but, generally, for as long as the person blowing the shofar can sustain the sound, it is called *t'ki'ah g'dolah*, a "great *t'ki'ah*."

5. Although less frequent, we also find a further exclamation: *L'shanah haba'ah birushalayim* ("Next year in Jerusalem!").

At the outset, one must recall that Jewish time counts days from sunset to sunset. *N'ilah*, the concluding service of Yom Kippur, is, therefore, followed immediately by *Ma'ariv*, the evening service for the day after. To be sure, in some congregations, worshipers tend not to stay for *Ma'ariv*, so anxious are they to break their fast immediately; in fact, many non-Orthodox synagogues have settled for the reality of the situation and do not even have the *Ma'ariv* service in their High Holy Day prayer books. But the traditional sources we will survey assume it.

Given the desire to move directly from *N'ilah* into *Ma'ariv*, rabbinic opinion differed on such questions as when to blow the shofar (before or after *Ma'ariv*) and when to say *Havdalah*, the ceremony of separation for the end of Shabbat, but for holy days (including Yom Kippur) as well. I have largely overlooked these issues of timing, however. I merely name them here, preferring to concentrate on the substance of the ritual as it evolved.

These issues of "substance" revolve about which of the above five elements to include, what order they should follow, and whether to repeat any of them (and if so, how often). In addition, we find a *Kaddish*—a prayer reserved sometimes for mourners, but used traditionally as oral punctuation at various points in the service: a smaller version (the "Half *Kaddish*") is a semicolon, dividing discrete elements within a service; the larger "Full *Kaddish*" is a period at a service's conclusion. It is the Full *Kaddish* that appears here.

In most Ashkenazi congregations, nowadays, we find:

1. *Sh'ma yisrael* . . . (recited once)
2. *Barukh shem* . . . (recited three times)
3. *Adonai hu* . . . (recited seven times)
   Kaddish
4. One shofar blast (*t'ki'ah*)
5. *L'shanah haba'ah* . . . (recited once)[1]

As I indicated above, the Ashkenazi tradition began in tenth- to eleventh-century France and Germany (especially the German Rhineland) and then spread east and south throughout the rest of present-day Germany. In the sixteenth century, many Ashkenazi Jews settled in Eastern Europe, especially what was then the Kingdom of Poland, where their German rituals changed somewhat. We now differentiate the customs of Ashkenazi Jews who remained in Germany (*Minhag Rinus*, "the Rhineland Rite") from those who altered it in Poland (*Minhag Polin*, "the Polish Rite").

The order listed above is, technically, just for *Minhag Polin*, the Ashkenazi tradition that prevails in most places nowadays because of the vast number of Eastern European Jews who fled czarist rule in the late nineteenth and early twentieth centuries and settled elsewhere. The smaller percentage of Ashkenazi Jews who still follow *Minhag Rinus* say the *Kaddish* before the *Sh'mot* (items 1–3).

That order characterizes also the Spanish-Portuguese Sephardi practice nowadays. But the second line is recited only once, not three times, as in Ashkenaz, and the shofar is blown four times, not just once:

Kaddish
1. *Sh'ma yisra'el . . .* (recited once)
2. *Barukh shem . . .* (recited once)
3. *Adonai hu . . .* (recited seven times)
4. Four shofar blasts (*t'ki'ah, sh'varim, t'ru'ah, t'kiyah*)
5. *L'shanah haba'ah . . .* (recited once)[2]

Sephardi Jews add other material too, most notably the poem *Tei'anu V'tei'atru*, included in this volume (see pp. 106–108).

Each of these practices varies widely and has its own history.

⁂

We can begin our summary with the Bible, which assumes the practice of sacrifice, not communal prayer, so knows nothing about any of our services, including *N'ilah*. Even in the post-biblical era (after, roughly, the fifth century BCE) and as long as the Second Temple stood (until 70 CE), *N'ilah* meant the closing of the Temple gates, not a liturgical service like our own.

Worship as we know it came slowly into being only in the first two centuries CE, especially after 70, and attracted discussion thereafter in the two massive compendia of Rabbinic thought that we call the Palestinian (or Jerusalem) Talmud (the Yerushalmi, codified c. 400 CE) and the Babylonian Talmud (the Babli, codified c. sixth to seventh centuries CE). The term "*the* Talmud" refers to the latter.

We hear nothing about *N'ilah*'s concluding ritual, however, until *after* the Talmudic era, the period known as "geonic," after the title of the chief rabbinic authorities in Babylonia (mentioned above). These self-appointed "chief rabbis" claimed the right to determine policy for all Jews worldwide. Dating the geonic era is somewhat arbitrary, but for our purposes, we can consider it as, roughly, from 757 CE, the accession date of the first great *gaon*, Yehudai, to 1038, the death of the last great *gaon*, Hai. Our first two comprehensive prayer books emerge from this period: *Seder Rav Amram Gaon* ("The Order [of Prayer] according to Rav Amram Gaon, c. 860) and *Siddur Saadiah Gaon* ("The Order [of Prayer] according to Saadiah Gaon, c. 920). Further evidence is available from Hai, who is said to have composed a prayer book (no longer extant) but whose responsa on prayer were widely carried by later authorities.

The parts of this final *N'ilah* ritual—blowing the shofar and reciting the verses—are so intertwined that it is hard to extricate them from one another. But to the extent possible, we can begin with the shofar, which antedates the verses, and then move on to the verses.

From Bible to Middle Ages: The Shofar Blast

The geonic writings just mentioned already assume the shofar, but not the verses. After *N'ilah*, Amram moves directly into *Ma'ariv* and says, "After *Oseh Shalom* [the end of the *Ma'ariv Amidah*], we sound the shofar *t'ki'ah, sh'varim, t'ru'ah, t'ki'ah*, once, and the people go home in peace."[3] The shofar remained optional, however, as we see from Hai Gaon (about a century and a half later), who admits that he sees no reason to demand it and isn't quite certain why it is done altogether. From the Talmud itself (Rosh Hashanah 13b; Yoma 20a), he draws the idea that it might be a way to confuse Satan, who is rendered powerless on Yom Kippur but regains strength as soon as Yom Kippur is over. (Satan appears in the book of Job as Job's accuser. Rabbinic tradition sees him as a heavenly presence who tracks Israel's sins and accuses Israel of them before God.) But Hai's preferred possibility goes back to an arcane issue regarding the biblical calendar and its Jubilee year.[4]

The Bible mandates a Sabbatical year (every seventh year) and a Jubilee year (the *Yovel*, the year following every seven sabbatical cycles = every fiftieth year).[5] In the former, the land was given a rest from new sowing and reaping; old crops that came up anyway were left for anyone who wanted them, even animals passing by. In the latter, the land actually changed hands. It was to revert to its original tribal owners (the twelve tribes of Israel), and all human serfs (the Bible still had a form of serfdom) were to be freed. Whether the Jubilee year was ever actually kept is debated, not only by modern scholarship but by the Talmud itself (Arakhin 22b), but in theory, at least, it was to be announced by blowing the shofar on Yom Kippur (Leviticus 25:9)—the tenth day of the seventh month in the biblical calendar, but an apt time to announce an event that was agricultural in nature, because Yom Kippur immediately precedes Sukkot, the beginning of the agricultural year. Maybe, Hai speculates, we blow the shofar as Yom Kippur ends as a *zekher layovel*, a "recollection of the Jubilee."[6]

The custom of blowing the shofar at *N'ilah* was subsequently carried (along with Hai's reasoning) to Spain, where Isaac ibn Ghiyyat (1038–1089) considers it,[7] and to France as well, where *Machzor Vitry*, an encyclopedic compendium of French Jewish practice, enlarges upon it. Ibn Ghiyyat was a distinguished poet and legalist in the Golden Age that Jews enjoyed under Islam; his masterwork *Sefer Sha'arei Simchah* is an index of practice in the eleventh century. Dating *Machzor Vitry* is more difficult. Its author, Simchah of Vitry (about four miles from the center of Paris, nowadays), also wrote in the eleventh century, but the single printed edition we have has many later accretions, some as late as the thirteenth and fourteenth centuries (which the editors of the standard printed edition recognized and marked off as unoriginal to Simchah's work). But even the "original" may have undergone some scribal alterations after Simchah died—all the way into the twelfth century. The relevant passages on *N'ilah* are not the very late thirteenth- to fourteenth-century additions, however, so we can reliably date them to the eleventh century, with the proviso that they may be as late as the twelfth. They reflect Jewish practice in the school of thought begun by Rashi (pronounced RAH-shee, 1040–1105, the Hebrew acronym for *R*abbi *SH*lomo *Y*itzchak of Troyes), the most famous of all Jewish commentators to the Bible and the Talmud, a student of early Ashkenazi academies in the German Rhineland, and the spiritual progenitor of French and German interpretation thereafter.

Regarding the Yom Kippur sounding of the shofar, Ibn Ghiyyat (of Spain) simply repeats the geonic precedents from Amram and Hai. But Simchah (of Vitry) goes farther. He begins with Hai's idea that the shofar on Yom Kippur recollects the Jubilee year, but then wonders why the sounding of the shofar ten days earlier on Rosh Hashanah isn't sufficient for that purpose: why, that is, do we repeat it on Yom Kippur? As we saw above, Yom Kippur is the holy day most immediately preceding Sukkot, when the *Yovel* (an agricultural event) would have begun. But *Machzor Vitry* prefers a solution suggested by the Talmud itself (Rosh Hashanah 8b). As the Talmud sees it, the Jubilee year was sanctified on Rosh Hashanah but did not fully take effect right away. From Rosh Hashanah to Yom Kippur, serfs were free from labor, and land was rendered ownerless. But serfs did not return to their family homes and the land did not officially pass to the original tribal owners until the court blew the Yom Kippur shofar announcing it.

Turning to how the shofar is blown, Simchah acknowledges having "heard" that "Jews in the Land of Israel end Yom Kippur with *t'ki'ah, sh'varim, t'ru'ah, t'ki'ah,*" but "in our region of the diaspora [*hagolah shelanu*]" the prayer leader completes *N'ilah* "and blows just one *t'ki'ah* as a recollection of the Jubilee, except for Cologne [*koloniya*], where they blow [all four shofar sounds], *t'ki'ah, sh'varim, t'ru'ah, t'ki'ah.*"[8]

So a single *t'ki'ah* sufficed for the region of Paris represented by *Machzor Vitry* itself, but what about just a little farther away, the area that we now consider Germany but which, at the time, was still closely connected culturally to France? There were still no national entities called France or Germany, after all. Rashi himself had studied in the Rhineland, and by his time, the episcopal seat of the Holy Roman Empire was the Rhineland city of Cologne. *Machzor Vitry* apparently considers Cologne part of "our region of the diaspora" but with a different custom that he considers worth mentioning, in that it follows the practice of the Land of Israel.

And Cologne was not alone. One of the earliest German authorities, Eliezer ben Nathan from nearby Mainz (the RABaN, c. 1090–c. 1170), says also, "At the end of Yom Kippur, after *N'ilah*, we blow *t'ki'ah, sh'varim, t'ru'ah, t'ki'ah.*"[9] And we hear the same thing a bit later—at the end of the thirteenth century—from Meir Hakohen of Rothenberg (a bit farther west yet), a student of the most distinguished rabbi of the era (with a similar name), Meir of Rothenberg himself (otherwise known as the MaHaRaM). Meir Hakohen's work, known as *Hagahot Maimuniyot*, goes so far as to say, "The universal custom nowadays [*minhag ha'olam*] is to blow *t'ki'ah, sh'varim, t'ru'ah, t'ki'ah.*"[10]

But calling four blasts a *universal* custom, even in Germany, was an overstatement, since Rabbi Eliezer ben Yoel Halevi (the RAVIaH) of Bonn (c. 1160–1235) says expressly, "We blow a single simple *t'ki'ah* as a recollection of the Jubilee year."[11] The same practice arises obliquely from a discussion by his contemporary, German pietist Eleazar ben Judah of Worms (c. 1165–c. 1230). Eleazer is concerned about justifying the shofar as *N'ilah* ends, rather than waiting until the end of *Ma'ariv*. If *N'ilah* is just concluding, it might not yet be dark enough to be considered the next day, and the shofar can certainly not be scheduled for Yom Kippur itself, the reason being that the various sounds are hard to blow, and the person charged with the task might seek help from an expert who might be tempted to go home and transport his shofar to the synagogue—a breach in the rules of work, which include sanctions against carrying anything from the personal to the public domain. Eleazer says, however, "For a single *t'ki'ah*, we do not worry [about someone being tempted to seek out an expert]."[12] Obviously, one blast was still an option, even in Germany.

The debate over the number of blasts is chronicled by none other than Joseph Caro, one of the most distinguished rabbis of all time, living in sixteenth-century Safed. Although best known as the author of the code of Jewish law called *Shulchan Arukh* ("The Set Table"), he also wrote commentaries to earlier legal literature, including the thirteenth-century *Tur* by Jacob ben Asher (1269–1340)—a work to which we will return. Caro's discussion of the *N'ilah* shofar occurs in his commentary there (*Bet Yosef*). He actually does more than cite the various practices regarding the number of shofar blasts required. He also discusses the reasons behind the practice. Hai Gaon had offered two reasons: to confuse Satan and to recall the Jubilee year. Caro now adds opinions from the school of Rashi and Rashi's spiritual successors, Talmudists of France and Germany from the twelfth to the fourteenth century known as tosafists. Among them is Rabbi Isaac ben Samuel of Dampierre (d. c. 1185), who says he knows the Jubilee theory and has actually seen prayer books that explain the shofar that way. But he takes issue with them. "Why would we blow the shofar every single year?" he asks rhetorically. "Did the Jubilee occur every year?" Isaac offers a simpler reason: "To let people know that it is evening so they can go home and feed their children who have fasted and also prepare the meal for the end of Yom Kippur."[13] It is, we hear elsewhere, "a *mitzvah* to eat when Yom Kippur ends."[14]

Caro himself prefers a midrash to Ecclesiastes 9:7, according to which a heavenly voice reminded people to eat and to drink in gladness. Putting that together with Isaac of Dampierre, he concludes that the point of the shofar is just to let people know that Yom Kippur is over, so they can go home "and feed children [*banim*] who have fasted, and prepare dinner."

We frequently learn about social customs from debates such as this one. As an aside, therefore, we should look carefully at the word for "children"—*banim*—that Isaac of Dampierre chooses and Joseph Caro repeats. They must really mean "children," not just "members of the household," because they separate "feeding the children" from "preparing dinner." Presumably, adults can wait to eat until *Ma'ariv* is over, but children may not be able to. We learn, therefore, first of all, that not just the adults, but some children too fasted on Yom Kippur. Second, we already knew that men were expected to attend regular synagogue services, while women were not. We see now that women did, however, attend services on Yom Kippur; with the shofar blast at the end of *N'ilah*, they went home to feed their children and make dinner. The men, presumably, would stay through *Ma'ariv* before going home.

There were also significant Jewish populations in the towns of Provence, a region north of the Pyrenees (so not Sephardi) but well south of the Ashkenazi centers in Paris and the Rhineland (so not altogether Ashkenazi either). Jews there were developing their own stream of literature—perhaps best represented by *Sefer Hamanhig* by Abraham ben Nathan of Lunel (1155–1215), a book written expressly to survey the variety of Jewish custom everywhere and to accord all of it respect, so as to justify his own practices too as authentic, and to prevent Provençal Jewry from being overrun culturally by the twin behemoths of Spain in the south and Franco-Germany in the north. His account of the diversity regarding shofar blasts at *N'ilah* gives us a nice summary of the state of affairs at the time:

> Rav Amram, of blessed memory, wrote that after saying *Oseh Shalom* [the end of the *N'ilah Amidah*] we blow *t'ki'ah, sh'varim, t'ru'ah, t'ki'ah*, once, and then go back to our

homes in peace. So too, Hai of blessed memory wrote that it is the custom of all Israel to blow the shofar at the end of Yom Kippur, not because it is technically obligatory [a *chovah*] but as a recollection of the Jubilee [*zekher layovel*], as it is written [Leviticus 25:9], "On the Day of Atonement, you shall have the horn sounded throughout your land"; alternatively, it is to confuse Satan. It is explained explicitly in [the Talmud, Tractate] Rosh Hashanah [8b], "From Rosh Hashanah to Yom Kippur, serfs did not leave to go home and fields did not return to their owners. When the court blew the shofar for Yom Kippur, the serfs returned home and the fields went back to their owners." Therefore, we do this blowing of the shofar on Yom Kippur as a recollection of the Jubilee, because that is what they did in the days of the Temple—may it be rebuilt speedily and in our days, Amen! I have seen places where they blow only a single *t'ki'ah* alone and say a single *t'ki'ah* is sufficient to recollect the Jubilee. It seems to me, however, that whether to remember the Jubilee or to confuse Satan, we ought to blow *t'ki'ah, sh'varim, t'ru'ah, t'ki'ah.*[15]

This report by *Hamanhig* is confirmed a little later by Aaron ben Joseph Hakohen of Lunel, another Provençal town. Despite his name, he was actually from neighboring Narbonne and moved to Spain in 1306, when French Jews were expelled by King Philip IV. He too says, "We blow *t'ki'ah, sh'varim, t'ru'ah, t'ki'ah.*"[16] Given his history, it is hard to say whether he is describing the situation in Provence or in Spain (or in both), but (as we just saw) we know about Provence independently from *Hamanhig*, and as for Spain, the *Tur*, the law code that we mentioned earlier (by Jacob ben Asher, 1269–1340) confirms the fourfold shofar blast, as does a later commentary on prayer written in Seville in 1340 (*Sefer Abudarham*).[17]

Finally, in Italy too, they blew all four sounds, not just one. The most interesting account comes from Benjamin ben Abraham Anav Harofei ("the physician"; 1215–1295), cited in two works, one of them by Benjamin's brother, Zedekiah (*Shibbolei Haleket*) and the other by his first cousin once removed, Yekutiel ben Benjamin (*Tanya Rabbati*). After learning about the four shofar blasts, we get this colorful explanation behind it (certain to be appreciated by attorneys to this day):

Rabbi Benjamin ben Abraham Harofei wrote that the reason we blow the shofar on Yom Kippur is that the shofar is the defense attorney [when we are tried before God for our sins] on Rosh Hashanah, so that the Holy One of Blessing gets up from the seat of judgment to ascend to the seat of mercy and acquits them [the shofar's clients]—as it is written (Psalm 47:6), "God ascends at the sound of *t'ru'ah* . . . Adonai at the sound of the shofar."[18] When they [the worshipers] leave the court acquitted [on Yom Kippur], their verdict sealed positively, their defending attorney [the shofar] exits with them, letting its voice be heard in joy. It is common practice, after all, when litigants to a dispute win their case in court, they praise their attorney and rejoice with him.[19]

In sum, everyone had been blowing the shofar to end Yom Kippur at least as early as Amram Gaon (ninth century). Amram had advocated four blasts (*t'ki'ah, sh'varim, t'ru'ah, t'ki'ah*), a custom followed by Jews in the Land of Israel, as well. In France, however, ever since *Machzor Vitry* (eleventh century), a single *t'ki'ah* sufficed. The French custom spread to some places in Germany, but elsewhere (the rest of Germany, Spain, Provence, and Italy) *t'ki'ah, sh'varim, t'ru'ah, t'ki'ah* remained the rule. Explanations included recalling the Jubilee year, the need to confuse Satan, the desire to celebrate with the shofar (our attorney) after being pardoned in the courtroom on high, or just an announcement that it is time to go home and feed the family.

Adding Acclamations: The "French Connection"

Blowing the shofar on Yom Kippur, at least, had precedent in the Bible's Jubilee-year legislation. The acclamations (called *sh'mot*) did not. They seem to have been an early innovation in France, as we see from a return look at our eleventh- to twelfth-century French source, *Machzor Vitry*. But the report is not straightforward, because the topic is discussed not once but twice (call the two accounts A and B), in ways not altogether consistent. According to A, the prayer leader completes *N'ilah*, and then "blows one *t'kiyah* as a recollection of the Jubilee, and the congregation responds, *Adonai hu ha'elohim*, seven times."[20]

Report A thus gives us 1. The shofar right after *N'ilah* and 2. *Adonai hu* seven times—saying nothing about *Sh'ma* and *Barukh shem*, which must have been absent.

The very next paragraph (B) returns to the point. At first, it confirms A: "The *chazzan* says—and the people respond *Adonai hu ha'elohim* seven times." This is not exactly what A had to say, however, because here, the *chazzan* says the line first and the congregation responds, while in A, the congregation alone said it.

More substantively, however, B then objects to blowing the shofar before *Ma'ariv* (because we should be praying *Ma'ariv* to accompany the *Shekhinah* back home through the seven heavens); then, after *Ma'ariv*, B adds, "They say *Sh'ma yisra'el* once, although some say it three times, but I do not know the reasoning behind the two practices. They then say *Barukh shem* once. Some people say three times, *Adonai hu ha'elohim* and *Sh'ma* and *Barukh shem*. . . . Everyone says them aloud."[21]

The two passages reflect different customs. According to A, *N'ilah* was followed immediately by the shofar and the congregational recitation of *Adonai hu* seven times—once (presumably) for each of the seven heavens through which the *Shekhinah* had to travel. According to the end of B, however, *Adonai hu* (also seven times) was postponed until after *Ma'ariv*, but then followed by *Sh'ma* and *Barukh shem*. And the number of recitations varied from place to place.

Practice was obviously quite fluid from the ninth century (the period of Amram) to the eleventh (that of Hai in Baghdad, Isaac ibn Ghiyyat in Spain, and *Machzor Vitry* in France). Blowing the shofar was common to them all and went back the farthest, sometimes with one blast (*t'ki'ah*) and sometimes with four (*t'ki'ah, sh'varim, t'ru'ah, t'ki'ah*); sometimes too this shofar sounding concluded *N'ilah*, and sometimes it awaited the end of the *Ma'ariv* service that followed. And some French Jews, at least, were experimenting with adding *Adonai hu ha'elohim* seven times—and the *Sh'ma* and *Barukh shem* once. Yet others said all three verses, but three times for each.

The Ritual Solidifies: Part 1, Joseph Caro

How then did our verses get added? They began as an alternative custom in France with *Machzor Vitry* (eleventh to twelfth centuries) but were not said universally there and not the same number of times. From there, Joseph Caro picks up the story, in the commentary to the *Tur* that we looked at above, with regard to blowing the shofar:

> [The author of] *Sefer Mitzvot Gadol* [by Moses of Coucy—
> see below] wrote, I received from my teacher, Rabbi Judah

ben Rabbi Isaac [Sir Leon] that after completing the *N'ilah Amidah*, he would say *Kaddish* and then, seven times, *Adonai hu ha'elohim*, because the *Shekhinah* travels upward through seven heavens; and after that [he would say] *Sh'ma yisrael* once, and then right away, they would blow the shofar because it is written, "God ascends at the sound of *t'ru'ah*" (Psalm 47:6).[22]

We now have a complete chain of tradition, a genuine "French Connection": *Sefer Mitzvot Gadol* is the work of Moses of Coucy in France (thirteenth century, exact dates unknown). His teacher (from whom he learned his *N'ilah* customs) was Judah ben Isaac Sir Leon (1166–1224). The "Isaac" here (Judah's father) is Isaac ben Samuel of Dampierre (d. c. 1185—the same Isaac we encountered above); but Isaac's father was the son of Rabbi Simchah of Vitry, the author of *Machzor Vitry* in the first place! The custom of *Sh'mot* went from Simchah to his grandson, Isaac ben Samuel of Dampierre (d. c. 1185); then from Isaac to his son, Judah ben Isaac Sir Leon (d. 1224); and from Judah ben Isaac to his student Moses of Coucy.

Simchah of Vitry (eleventh century)
↓
Simchah's son, Samuel of Dampierre
↓
Samuel's son, Simchah's grandson, Isaac ben Samuel of Dampierre (d. 1185)
↓
Isaac's son, Samuel's grandson, Simchah's great-grandson,
Judah ben Isaac Sir Leon (1166–1224)
who taught
Moses of Coucy (thirteenth-century France, exact dates unknown)

⁖⁖⁖

But *Machzor Vitry* had two customs, not just one. Of our three verses, report A said just *Adonai hu ha'elohim*; report B said all three (*Adonai hu ha'elohim*, *Sh'ma*, and *Barukh shem*). Moses of Coucy follows neither precedent. He says *Adonai hu ha'elohim* and *Sh'ma* but not *Barukh shem*.

And none of these customs seems yet to have penetrated Germany.[23] We might have expected at least some reference to them in the *Tur*, for example, the thirteenth-century law code composed by Jacob ben Asher. Jacob lived in Spain, but his father, Asher ben Yechiel, had emigrated from Germany, and Jacob would have known and respected his father's customs. Also, we find no mention of it in *Sefer Roke'ach*, the pietistic work by Eleazar of Worms (c. 1165–c. 1230). And Abudarham (*Sefer Abudarham*, Seville, 1340) knows nothing of it in Spain.

How, then, did these verses become so universal? Critically, the "French Connection" charted above (with at least two of the verses, *Adonai hu ha'elohim* and *Sh'ma*) was passed along by Joseph Caro's commentary to the *Tur*, and Caro would go on to write the *Shulchan Arukh*, the last and most popular of our medieval codes. One would expect that by opening up Caro's *Shulchan Arukh*, we would find our verses there, a model for practice ever after. Problem solved!

But things are not that simple, because in his code, Caro says simply, "At the end of *N'ilah*, we say *Adonai hu ha'elohim* seven times; then we sound *t'ki'ah, sh'varim, t'ru'ah, t'ki'ah* on the shofar."[24]

With regard to the shofar, then, Caro's *Shulchan Arukh* followed the *Tur*, which had recommended four shofar blasts, especially because that was already the established custom in the Land of Israel where Caro lived—and a custom going all the way back to Rav Amram. But regarding the verses, Caro says nothing of *Sh'ma* and *Barukh shem*. It was one thing to report the customs of France in his commentary; it was another to advocate them in his code. So when it came to his own recommendation, he played it safe, following more established precedent. Why, however, did he recommend *Adonai hu ha'elohim*? Why omit the last two verses but not the first one?

For one thing, *Adonai hu* was far more established than *Sh'ma* and *Barukh shem*. Of the two *Machzor Vitry* traditions, both knew the custom of including *Adonai hu*; only the second added *Sh'ma* and *Barukh shem*. Also, *Adonai hu*, recited seven times, was linked to the well-known tradition of the seven heavens through which the *Shekhinah* had to pass on its post-*N'ilah* journey back to its heavenly abode.

There was probably more at stake for Caro, however. Although known best as a legalist, he was also a mystic, part of the kabbalistic efflorescence in sixteenth-century Safed. He had secured his halakhic reputation as a young man studying in Turkey, but his teachers there had steeped him in Kabbalah as well, so in 1534, he relocated to the emerging center of kabbalistic thought, Safed, where he emerged as the leading scholar—and not just in halakhah. He also authored a mystical journal in which he recorded nightly visits of the *Shekhinah*, appearing as the personification of the ancient Rabbinic law code the Mishnah and sharing mystical secrets with him. No wonder he was drawn to the image of the *Shekhinah* visiting Jews during Yom Kippur and then ascending after *N'ilah* to its proper place on high! No wonder also, he incorporated the sevenfold recitation of *Adonai hu ha'elohim* to accompany the *Shekhinah* back home.

In addition, the number seven had its own mystical importance to Caro. Kabbalists understood the universe as having come into being by an emanation of the Divine at the beginning of time—a sort of mystical "big bang" moment. The various stages of that emanation could be captured by the image of light diffusing from its divine origin until ultimately giving birth to the universe. The various stages of the emanation from divine source to created universe could be measured, because at certain stops along the way, the light congealed momentarily into a series of ten *sefirot*—holding pens, as it were, of the light at successive moments in primeval time. But the *sefirot* are emanations of God—hence part of God; they don't just disappear; they are all alive and well at any given moment. In God's dealing with the universe, God works through them. The entire working of the universe is, therefore, more than what it appears to be on the surface. It has also an esoteric component, in that it can be translated into the parallel state of the divine *sefirot* in action. Of the ten *sefirot*, the first three and the last seven exist semi-independently.

Kabbalists looked regularly for examples of sevens. Among other things, they overlaid the seven *sefirot* on such things as the days of week and the design of the Passover *seder* plate (six symbolic foods plus the plate itself); and also—of direct relevance here—the older tradition of seven heavens. For Caro, then, the practice of saying *Adonai hu ha'elohim* seven times was especially enticing. It fit perfectly into his kabbalistic understanding of reality.

So he loved the sevenfold *Adonai hu*. Not so the other two verses, which his code overlooks. Had Caro been the only translator of tradition, *Sh'ma* and *Barukh shem* at *N'ilah* would never have become commonplace. Something else was needed. And the *Shulchan Arukh* itself provides the clue to that "something else."

242 | Appendix B

The Ritual Solidifies: Part 2, Moses Isserles and the Minhagim Literature

Like all traditional Jewish texts, the printed text of Caro's *Shulchan Arukh* is surrounded by marginal commentaries of later authorities. In addition, Caro's own entries have been expanded by another halakhic giant, Moses Isserles of Cracow (1525 or 1530–1572), who sought to make Caro's Sephardi rulings palatable to Ashkenazi readers. So successful was he that he became known as the *Mapah* (the "Tablecloth") to Caro's *Shulchan Arukh* ("The Set Table").

Some of Isserles's glosses stand out because they are marked "*minhagim*" (literally, "customs"). So, here, Caro's omission of *Sh'ma* and *Barukh shem* is "corrected" by Isserles's note, "[We also say] *Sh'ma* once and *Barukh shem* three times—[from] *minhagim*."

The word *minhagim* denotes "customs" as opposed to "laws." These customs are not, strictly speaking, halakhah. But Judaism regards local custom very highly. In the eighth century, for example, when the first great *gaon*, Yehudai, attempted to force Babylonian rulings on communities in the Land of Israel, he encountered the objection *minhag m'vatel halakhah* ("custom nullifies law").[25] About the same time, an important book circulated called *Differences in Custom between Those in the East [Babylonia] and Those in the West [the Land of Israel]*. To be sure, as time went on and the geonic ideal of a centralized halakhah became more widely accepted, the authority of law (as opposed to custom) mounted. But still, long-standing custom was not just blithely dismissed. As we have seen in abundant detail here, the rabbis who established Jewish communities throughout Europe—whether France and Germany in the north, Spain and Italy in the south, or Provence in the middle—were intent on citing whatever customs they could find. Indeed, in his views on the shofar at *N'ilah*, Aaron ben Jacob of Narbonne (and Spain) says regularly, "Some places [follow one custom] and others [follow another] but everything follows custom [*hakol holekh achar haminhag*]."[26]

In the context of Isserles's gloss to the *Shulchan Arukh*, however, *minhagim* means more than "customs generally"; it refers to a distinctive body of literature that we have so far omitted from consideration—a set of books dedicated specifically to documenting customs of certain great rabbis in Ashkenaz, particularly the fourteenth- to fifteenth-century founders of Jewish life in Austria and Hungary, Jacob Klausner and Isaac Tyrnau, both of whom left us books entitled *Sefer Minhagim* ("The Book of Customs").

The more senior of the two, Klausner (who died in 1407/8), based his work on an older compendium of custom, one of the first in the genre, by the thirteenth-century French scholar Chaim Paltiel—another of the German rabbis of the time—known (among other things) for signing his responsa with the self-deprecatory epithet *tola'at* ("worm"). More significantly, he was yet one more student of the great Meir of Rothenberg (MaHaRaM, 1220–1293) whose name comes up so ubiquitously in the study of German Jewish jurisprudence. Like Meir, Chaim Paltiel represents those rabbis who moved eastward from the original Jewish settlements on the Rhine. Klausner himself had reached Vienna by 1380. His *minhagim* are actually marginal comments to Chaim Paltiel's work, which he included as the basis for his comments.

When we looked at report B of *Machzor Vitry* (eleventh to twelfth centuries), we encountered something that we passed over without lengthy comment: the fact that "some people say [all three verses] three times."[27] That might seem odd to readers today, since no one does it that way anymore. But *Machzor Vitry* was apparently reporting accurately, because some two centuries later, Chaim Paltiel knew the same custom! "We say *Sh'ma yisrael* three times, then *Barukh shem k'vod* three times, and *Adonai hu ha'elohim* three times." He knows also of the custom whereby "they say *Adonai hu ha'elohim* seven times, corresponding to the seven heavens . . . then *Sh'ma yisrael* once . . . and they blow a single *t'ki'ah* as a remembrance of the Jubilee year";[28] and that too we saw in *Machzor Vitry* (report B: "In France the cantor recites and the congregation repeats, *Adonai hu ha'elohim* seven times. . . . Then they say *Sh'ma yisrael* once").[29] Chaim Paltiel was connected in other ways to the French school of thought; he was a continuation of the Franco-German tradition going back to Rashi and the tosafists and had even studied with Eliezer of Touques, a man said by some to be head of the yeshivah in France. So the importance of Chaim Paltiel is, primarily, his confirmation of early French custom, seen earlier in *Machzor Vitry*.

Some two centuries later, in Vienna, Klausner wrote a commentary to Chaim Paltiel's treatise, tracing its customs back in time, and citing some of the literature that we have already looked at. His one sole personal addition arises because he does not like the "Jubilee year" reasoning for the shofar blast. Instead, he offers a midrash to the effect that when Moses descended Mount Sinai, it was Yom Kippur. He blew a single shofar blast then; so we do too.[30]

When Isserles cites *minhagim*, however, he probably means Klausner's student, Isaac Tyrnau (late fourteenth to fifteenth centuries), who left Vienna for nearby Tyrnau—whence his name. It is from Tyrnau that Isserles got the custom of reciting the *Sh'mot* in the manner that became standard Ashkenazi practice. Tyrnau says explicitly, "[We say] *Sh'ma yisrael* once, *Barukh shem k'vod* three times, and *Adonai hu ha'elohim* seven times, corresponding to the seven heavens; then a Full *Kaddish*, after which we blow a single *t'ki'ah* as recollection of the Jubilee year."[31]

Tyrnau's practice was not necessarily Austrian alone, of course. Customs circulate more fluidly than that—they hardly ever obey the arbitrary demarcations of political boundaries. In this case, for instance, the very same custom is reported of Tyrnau's contemporary Israel Isserlein (1390–1460) of Marburg and then Neustadt, in central Germany.[32]

The point of all of this is that Ashkenazi Jewry was slowly moving eastward. In the fourteenth and fifteenth centuries, it had reached Austria and Hungary. By the sixteenth century, its center of gravity had moved to Poland, where Moses Isserles was busy writing his Ashkenazi glosses on Joseph Caro's very Sephardi *Shulchan Arukh*. According to Caro, "We say *Adonai hu ha'elohim* seven times, then we blow *t'ki'ah, sh'varim, t'ru'ah, t'ki'ah*." Isserles corrects him. As to the shofar, he says, "According to some, we blow *t'ki'ah* alone, and that is the custom in these parts"; and as to the *Sh'mot*, Isserles (who had read Tyrnau) adds, "and *Sh'ma yisrael* once and *Barukh shem k'vod* three times."[33]

Confirmation of Isserles's opinion comes to us from two of Isserles's contemporaries. First, Joel Sirkes (1561–1640), a rabbi in several Polish communities, including Isserles's Cracow after 1619, provides a short commentary acknowledging the single shofar blast.[34] More interesting is Mordecai Jaffe (1535–1612), an extraordinary scholar whose long career took him from his native Prague, to Poland, back to Prague, then to Italy, back to Poland, then to Prague again, and finally to Poland (Poznan) a third time. Off and on for over fifty years, he worked on compiling his own "ashkenization" of Caro's *Shulchan Arukh*, putting it off when he heard that Isserles was writing just such a thing. He eventually published his work anyway, under the name *Sefer L'vush Malkhut*, usually shortened to *L'vush*.

Jaffe's version of the concluding *N'ilah* customs is fuller than what we get from Isserles, enough to be quoted in full here, especially since it sums up also the various strands of lore associated with them, most of which we have seen as themes running through the halakhic literature he inherited.

The prayer leader says *Sh'ma yisrael* once and the congregation repeats it once. Then he says *Barukh shem
k'vod* three times, corresponding to the idea that "God
has reigned, God does reign, and God will reign"—past,
present, and future. They then say *Adonai hu ha'elohim*
seven times, to accompany the ascent of the *Shekhinah*,
for now that Israel has completed its prayers, it embarks
on its ascent through the seven heavens. While Israel was
still praying, the *Shekhinah* dwelt among us, but now it
ascends to its place.

After we say *Adonai hu ha'elohim*, we say a Full *Kaddish*
and blow one *t'ki'ah*, a sign of the departing *Shekhinah*,
which leaves to ascend to the heavens as at the time of
the giving of Torah [on Sinai]—as it is written (Exodus
19:13), "When the ram's horn sounds a long blast, they
may go up the mountain"; and (Psalm 47:6), "God ascends
at the sound of *t'ru'ah.*"

The *t'ki'ah* is also a sign of joy and victory at our having vanquished Satan—who, in addition, is confused by
it, because it reminds him of the day of his death so that
he is not able to accuse us. We confuse him now [as *N'ilah*
ends], because now is the time when he has dominion over
us again—a lesson derived from the fact that the *gematria*
[the numerical equivalent] of [the four consonants that
make up the word] HaSaTaN[35] add up to 364, while a full
solar year has 365 days, suggesting that Satan's accusatory
reign lasts only 364 days a year, the exception being Yom
Kippur. But now [as Yom Kippur ends] he returns to his
accusatory regnancy, so we confuse him then.

Moreover the shofar's *t'ki'ah* is a sign of freedom, for
on this day our souls have become free of sin and our bodies have been liberated from the bondage of guilt.

Then too, it [the shofar blast] is a reminder of the
t'ki'ah that was sounded on Yom Kippur of the Jubilee
year.

So we blow the shofar.[36]

Ashkenazi tradition has followed the Isserles account ever since. It is, for
example, accepted as standard practice in *Mishnah B'rurah*, the influential commentary on the *Shulchan Arukh* written between 1894 and 1907
by the Hafetz Hayim, Israel Meir Hakohen Kagan (1838–1933).

The Final Touch: Next Year in Jerusalem

It is also around the time of the Hafetz Hayim that we first hear of the final verse in our ritual, "Next year in Jerusalem!" Since the period following the First Crusade, Jews have been saying that line to end the Passover seder, but its appearance at *N'ilah* is much more recent. While the Hafetz Hayim was composing his *Mishnah B'rurah*, another giant in Jewish law, Yechiel Michal Epstein (1829–1908) was summing up Jewish law after the *Shulchan Arukh* in his own monumental work, named, cleverly, the same words but in reverse, *Arukh Hashulchan* (not "The Set Table," but "The Table Setting"). His section on Yom Kippur was written sometime between 1903 and 1907. Both rabbis lived in modern-day Belarus, and given the timing, it is remotely possible that they penned their respective remarks the very same day! *Mishnah B'rurah* says, simply, "After blowing the shofar, the custom is for the prayer leader and the congregation to say, 'Next year in Jerusalem.'" *Arukh Hashulchan* concurs: "Our practice is to blow a single *t'ki'ah* as a good omen to announce that God has received our prayers; and we say 'Next year in Jerusalem.'"[37] The custom probably goes back no farther than *Mateh Ephraim*, a collection of customs for the High Holy Days composed by Ephraim Zalman Margolioth of Galicia (1762–1828), who says, "There are places where they blow the shofar before *Kaddish*, and then after blowing it, everyone responds, 'Next year in Jerusalem.'"[38]

We can only guess at the reason behind adding "Next year in Jerusalem," but the answer is probably implicit in the fact that the author of *Arukh Hashulchan* associates it with the shofar, which he considers a "good omen [*siman tov*] to announce [*l'vaser*] that God has received our prayers." The meaning of *siman tov* is straightforward enough but *l'vaser* has a deeper implication than just "to announce." As we shall presently see, it is not just any announcement, but the announcement, specifically, of good news. And it is not just any good news, but the ultimate good news of life after death, which the Rabbis saw as actual bodily resurrection.

To start with, already in the Mishnah (roughly 200 CE), the verb *l'VaSeR*, "to announce" (from the Hebrew root *B[or]V.S.R*) appears as a collective noun *B'SoroT*, in the technical term *b'sorot* tovot ("announcement of good news") along with its opposite *shmu'ot ra'ot* ("hearing bad news").

A. With the announcement of good news [*b'sorot tovot*] one says, "[Blessed is God] who is good and does good [*hatov v'hameitiv*]."

B. Upon hearing bad news [*shmu'ot ra'ot*], one says, "[Blessed is God] the judge of truth [*dayyan ha'emet.*]"[39]

A and B are polar opposites: good and bad, the whole point being that just as we normally praise God for good, we ought also to praise God for bad. Any good or bad news, presumably, can warrant the blessings in question, but we know from the blessing over bad news that the Mishnah means particularly the *ultimate* "bad news," news of a death (we still recite that blessing upon hearing that someone has died). Since the two sentences appear in apposition, it is probable that the "good news" is specifically the *ultimate* good news, the very opposite of death: life after death—resurrection, for the Rabbis. The idea seems to be that any bad or good news reminds us of the ultimate examples: death and resurrection.

When the author of *Arukh Hashulchan* calls the shofar a "good omen to announce that God has received our prayers," he means more than our prayers for the new year just beginning. He means also our prayers for the ultimate human hope, the paradigmatic case of good news: life after death.

The assumption that the "good news" in question denotes life after death (resurrection, for the Rabbis) is buttressed by the fact that the same blessing for good news ("who is good and does good") appears in our Grace after Meals (*Birkat Hamazon*), and is connected with the Hadrianic persecutions following the Bar Kokhba revolt of 135 CE. As the Talmud sees it, the Roman emperor, Hadrian, punished the Jewish rebels by forbidding the burial of those slain during the revolt. God performed the double miracle of keeping the bodies from decomposing in the hot sun (miracle 1) and then changing Hadrian's mind (miracle 2). The two-fold repetition of God's goodness ("who is good and does good") was applied to this double miracle.[40]

The story reads cogently only when one realizes that the point of burying the bodies before decomposition was to assure their resurrection; the blessing's "good news" is resurrection.

B'sorot tovot ("announcement of the good news") is the functional equivalent of what Christians call the Gospel, a word derived from the Middle English equivalent of "good" and "telling"—itself a translation from the earlier Greek *evangelion* ("good news"). But *evangelion* is just the equivalent of the Hebrew *b'sorot tovot*. The "good news" of life after death was central to Rabbinic Judaism and to Christianity.

Certainly in the context of *N'ilah*, when our sins are forgiven and we are said to be sealed in the "book of life," the verb *l'vaser* means, literally, to impart the "good news" that we will not die but live. Secular consciousness interprets that promise as the guarantee of another year of life on this earth—the equivalent of receiving a good report from our family doctor at our annual physical examination. Judaism was sufficiently "this-worldly" as to mean that as well—but traditionally speaking, that is not the *only* meaning inherent in the "good news" that follows upon our sins being forgiven. Judaism also insisted on the promise of overcoming death—exactly as Christianity did. Yes, we all die; but yes, as well, we all can hope for the good news of life after death.

For the Mishnah, this life after death was bodily resurrection, but Jewish tradition retained other interpretations also: a messianic era, the world to come, rebuilding Jerusalem, and eternality of the soul. Unlike Christianity, which took great care to unpack each concept's implications and the way they all cohere in a single theological construct, Rabbinic Judaism let them all exist simultaneously without determining just how they all applied to one another: what happened first, what next, and so on. The philosophically inclined Maimonides did his best to sort it out but admitted that "in all such matters, no one knows how they will come about until· they do."[39] Still, belief in it all remained. At various times one promise took precedence over another, but none of them was ever officially abrogated in traditional circles.

When, therefore, the author of *Arukh Hashulchan* calls the shofar of *N'ilah* "a good omen to announce that God has received our prayers," and when he follows that immediately by the words "and we say 'Next year in Jerusalem,'" we have reason to believe that he saw an eschatological connection between the shofar, on the one hand, and the age-old promise of ultimate redemption, on the other. We cannot know exactly when and why "Next year in Jerusalem" was added, but we have at least some grounds for saying that by the eighteenth century, Jews increasingly saw forgiveness at *N'ilah* as implying good news not just for another year of life and health, but for life after death and a return to Zion as well.

In some traditions (although not in the original sources that give us the custom), *L'shanah haba'ah* is said three times and placed in the middle of the final *Kaddish* (with the blowing of the shofar placed there as well). In such cases, an accompanying note can often be found emphasizing this universal dream of messianic times:

Upon hearing the sound of the *t'ki'ah g'dolah* on the shofar, one is overcome by the strong yearning for the time when we are worthy of hearing the shofar sound of the future, the time of the messiah. The essence of the yearning is in these very words [of the *Kaddish*]—"God's name will be glorified and sanctified throughout the world," and this is what one should focus on also during the words "Next year in Jerusalem."[40]

Throughout the High Holy Day period, insertions in the *Amidah* request that we be "*written* in the book of life." At *N'ilah*, however, the verb changes, as we ask to be "*sealed* in the book of life." It is the time for the gates to close and the book to be sealed. We pass through the gates with our fates sealed for good—for life, that is. We have seen how Judaism values life on this earth, not just life thereafter; how God "extends a hand" to pull us up from the morass of sin to life reborn, as signaled by the *t'ki'ah g'dolah* that heralded our births on Rosh Hashanah. But the hope for life is equally the age-old Jewish promise of a better time to come, life after death, resurrection, the soul eternal, and "Next year in Jerusalem"—not the Zionist dream, traditionally speaking, but the eschatological one, the possibility of a messianic return to the place the Jewish soul has ever called home.

Both remain part of *N'ilah*'s promise: life here and now, and life in the hereafter. As to the first, *N'ilah* envisions Yom Kippur completed, our shroud-like *kittel* put away for another year, our *tallit* reserved for morning worship alone, the normal practice for another year of living normally. But equally, *N'ilah* holds out the ultimate hope that all who have come into the world will turn again to God, remembering the universal moral message revealed first to Adam and to Eve, the progenitors of us all—that all may merit a personal life after death, a life that death cannot steal away; and a better time beyond history that Jews call messianic.

ணையை

Notes

The History and Symbolism of *N'ilah*: A Thick Description of Life and Death, by Rabbi Lawrence A. Hoffman, PhD

1. Jerusalem Talmud, Berakhot 4:1.
2. Ibid.; the view of Rabbi Yochanan.
3. Ibid.; the view of Rav, now the halakhah. Cf., Maimonides, *Mishneh Torah*, Laws of Prayer 1:7.
4. Talmud, Yoma 87b.
5. Ibid.
6. Clifford Geertz, *The Interpretation of Cultures* (New York: Basic Books, 1973), 9, 10.
7. Helaine Ettinger, "Sacred Art: Appreciating *Ne'ilah* as Literature and Ritual" (rabbinic thesis, Hebrew Union College–Jewish Institute of Religion, New York, 1991).
8. Eleanor G. Smith, "On the Eve of Yom Kippur: Preparing the Soul for Death" (rabbinic thesis, Hebrew Union College–Jewish Institute of Religion, New York, 1993).
9. Lisa A. Edwards, "A Horn of Plenty: The Re-Vision of the Shofar Service for Rosh Hashanah" (rabbinic thesis, Hebrew Union College–Jewish Institute of Religion, New York, 1994).
10. Cantor Benjie Ellen Schiller, private communication, May 25, 2017.

Closing Lines, Closing Gates: How the Yom Kippur Drama Ends, by Rabbi Helaine Ettinger

1. Chaim Joseph David Azulai (*Midbar K'demot*, eighteenth century), cited in S. Y. Agnon, *Days of Awe* (New York: Schocken Books, 1948), 217.
2. Arnold van Gennep, *The Rites of Passage* ([1908]; Chicago: University of Chicago Press, 1960), 189.

God's Plea: A Wordless Gesture and a Still Small Voice, by Rabbi Margaret Moers Wenig, DD

1. Similarly "opening heaven's gates" (*pote'ach sh'arim*) means bringing on the morning.
2. *Ad yom moto t'chakeh lo, im yashuv miyad t'kablo*, from *Ki kh'shimkha* in the liturgical poem *Un'taneh Tokef*. See Lawrence A. Hoffman, ed., *Who by Fire,*

Who by Water—Un'taneh Tokef, Prayers of Awe (Woodstock, VT: Jewish Lights, 2010), 31.

3. The opening words of the liturgical poem (*piyyut*) *V'khol Ma'aminim*, based on Deuteronomy 32:41. See Lawrence A. Hoffman, ed., *All The World: Universalism and Particularism in the High Holy Days*, Prayers of Awe (Woodstock, VT: Jewish Lights, 2014), 135, 136n1.

4. From the medieval poem *Adon Olam*. See Lawrence A. Hoffman, ed., *My People's Prayer Book*, vol. 5, Birkhot Hashachar *(Morning Blessings)* (Woodstock, VT: Jewish Lights, 2001), 96.

5. From the liturgical poem (*piyyut*) *Ki Hinei Kachomer*. See Lawrence A. Hoffman, ed., *Naming God:* Avinu Malkeinu—*Our Father, Our King* (Woodstock, VT: Jewish Lights, 2015), 61–63.

6. The closest image to this one comes in the liturgical poem (*piyyut*) by Samuel ben Kalonymus, *Shir Hayichud L'yom Rishon*: "To this day you have taken me by the hand [*Ad hayom hazeh hechazakta b'yadi*]." See Philip Birnbaum, ed., *High Holiday Prayer Book* (New York: Hebrew Publishing Company, 1951), 101.

7. From Talmud, Yoma 87b, as a prayer for Yom Kippur, then eventually added to the preliminary morning service for weekdays, Sabbaths, and festivals. *N'ilah* is the only occasion when we recite these words at night.

Goodbye Yom Kippur, Hello Sukkot!, by Rabbi Asher Lopatin

1. *Eccesiastes Rabbah* 9:7, beginning.
2. *Tur, Orach Chayim* 624.
3. *Zohar* 1:172b.
4. R'ma, *Orach Chayim* 624:5.

Recapturing *Piyyut*: Music and Poetry in Jewish Tradition, by Cantor David Lefkowitz

1. For *Un'taneh Tokef*, see Lawrence A. Hoffman, ed., *Who by Fire, Who by Water*—Un'taneh Tokef, Prayers of Awe (Woodstock, VT: Jewish Lights, 2010).

2. For the Thirteen Attributes of God, see Lawrence A. Hoffman, ed., *Encountering God:* El Rachum V'chanun—*God Merciful and Gracious*, Prayers of Awe (Woodstock, VT: Jewish Lights, 2016).

3. For *B'rosh Hashanah*, see Hoffman, *Who by Fire, Who by Water*—Un'taneh Tokef, 40–43. For *Avinu Malkeinu*, see Lawrence A. Hoffman, ed., *Naming God:* Avinu Malkeinu—*Our Father, Our King*, Prayers of Awe (Woodstock, VT: Jewish Lights, 2015).

There and Back Again, by Catherine Madsen

1. An Inuit shaman.
2. Paula Saffire, *Tender Miscarriage: An Epiphany* (Tucson: Harbinger House, 1989).

To the Point of No "Return"—and Back Again, by Rabbi Nicole K. Roberts

1. Carolita Johnson, published April 28, 2014.
2. *El Nora Alilah*; see liturgy, p. 98–100.
3. Rabbi Leon A. Morris, "Possibilities for Reconceptualizing *N'ilah*," in *Machzor: Challenge and Change*, vol. 2, *Preparing for the New Machzor and for the High Holy Days* (New York: CCAR Press, 2014), 190.
4. *Sha'arei Armon*; see liturgy, p. 102–103.
5. *El Nora Alilah*; see liturgy, p. 98–100.
6. *Tei'anu V'tei'atru*; see liturgy, p. 106–108.
7. See liturgy, p. 174.

Come Back to Life: The Resurrecting Power of the Days of Awe, by Rabbi Elaine Zecher

1. *Mishnah B'rurah*, 225:4.
2. For the same reason, the *kittel* is also worn traditionally by the groom at his wedding, for making the pre-wedding confession that symbolically "buries" him to his old life.
3. The *G'vurot* (second blessing in the *Amidah*).

"Heart Surgery" in the Bible: God Is on Our Side, by Dr. Marc Zvi Brettler

1. All translations are my own, often a modification of the NJPS translation, which understands many of the verses cited differently.
2. For my understanding of this passage, see http://thetorah.com/is-israels -repentance-a-foregone-conclusion/

Please Remove Your Shoes, by Rabbi Joshua M. Davidson

1. From *Itturei Torah*, 3:28, in *The Torah: A Modern Commentary*, ed. W. Gunther Plaut (New York: Union of American Hebrew Congregations, 1981), 407.
2. Moshe ben Yisrael of Kobryn, in Martin Buber, *Tales of the Hasidim, Book Two: The Later Masters* (New York: Schocken Books, 1975), 170.
3. *Genesis Rabbah* 60:14.
4. *Parashat Sh'mini Mekhilta deMiluim*.
5. Ibid.

"You Extend Your Hand," by Rabbi Edwin Goldberg, DHL

1. Translated in this book as "your arm reaches out." See J. Hoffman, p. 67.
2. See Abraham J. Karp, *From the Ends of the Earth: Judaic Treasures of the Library of Congress* (New York: Rizzoli/Library of Congress, 1991), 182–84.

The Guy with the Butter, by Rabbi Shira Stutman

1. Alan Lew, *This Is Real and You Are Completely Unprepared: The Days of Awe as a Journey of Transformation* (Boston: Little, Brown, 2003), 259–60.

The Metaphor of Gates: Editor's Introduction, by Rabbi Lawrence A. Hoffman, PhD

1. *Orchot Chayim, Hilchot Yom Hakippurim*, end, 108a.

Our Challenge: It's Unlawful and Unjust to Close the Gates, by Rabbi Tony Bayfield, CBE, DD

1. Elie Wiesel, *Night* (London: Fontana Books, 1972), 57.
2. *Forms of Prayer*, vol. 3, 8th ed. (London: RSGB, 1985), 616–21.
3. The phrase refers to the radical individualization of identity prevalent across modern Western society and debated by sociologists such as Robert Putnam, Steven M. Cohen, Robert Bellah, and Zygmunt Bauman.
4. The recognition that we are irrevocably connected—to family, community, and society.
5. Ecclesiasticus 44:1–9. Not to be confused with Ecclesiastes, Ecclesiasticus is part of the Apocrypha (c. second century BCE).
6. *Forms of Prayer*, 3:620.
7. The image of the closing of the gates of mercy goes back to the closing of the Temple gates at the end of the Yom Kippur sacrificial rite.
8. Jacob is characteristically brazen: "Do this for me and I'll do that for you" (Genesis 28:20–22).
9. See Jack R. Lundbom, *Jeremiah 1–20*, Anchor Yale Bible (New Haven: Yale University Press, 2009), 12:1, p. 640.
10. E.g., Proem 24 to *Lamentations Rabbah*.
11. Anonymous; quoted in *Forms of Prayer*, 3:796.
12. Quoted in Samuel H. Dresner, *Levi Yitzhak of Berditchev: Portrait of a Hasidic Master* (Bridgeport: Hartmore House), 1974, 86–87.
13. "Alte Kashe" was used by Maurice Ravel, "L'énigme éternelle," no. 2 of *Deux melodies hébraiques*, written in 1914, supporting a nineteenth-century Hasidic attribution.
14. Alter Brody, "The Holy Ledger."

Help Us Stay Open, by Rabbi Shai Held, PhD

1. I am grateful to Rabbi Melissa Weintraub, whose sermon many years ago first led me to think of Amichai's poem in this context.
2. Robert Alter, *The Five Books of Moses: A Translation with Commentary* (New York: W. W. Norton, 2008), 933. See also Moshe Weinfeld, *Deuteronomy 1–11* (New York: Doubleday, 1991), 438. This paragraph is taken, with very minor adaptations, from Shai Held, "Will and Grace: Or, Who Will

Circumcise Our Hearts?" in *The Heart of Torah: Essays on the Weekly Torah Portion* (Philadelphia: Jewish Publication Society, 2017).
3. See Held, "Will and Grace."

The Shifting Presence of God, by Rabbi Elie Kaunfer, DHL

1. Jules Harlow, ed., *Mahzor Layamin Hanora'im* (New York: Rabbinical Assembly, 1972), 699.
2. *Deuteronomy Rabbah* 2. Cf. *Lamentations Rabbah* 3; *Midrash to Psalms* 65.
3. Cf. Maimonides, *Mishneh Torah*, Laws of Prayer 1:7, 3:6; *Kesef Mishneh* to 1:7.
4. Cf. Louis Ginzberg, *Perushim V'chidushim Birushalmi*, 3:67.
5. *L'vush* 623:5.
6. Cf. *Encyclopedia Talmudit, Machzor*, 355; and Daniel Sperber, *Minhagei Yisrael*, 7:298–324.
7. SMaG, Negative Commandments 68; SMaK, Rabbenu Peretz 221:5; *Taz, Orach Chayim* 523:2; *Mishnah B'rurah, Orach Chayim* 523:13.
8. Ibn Shuab, D'rashah Leyom Kippur (Spain, 1280–1340), quoted in Sperber, *Minhagei Yisrael*, 7:310.
9. *Shibbolei Haleket*, #322, quoting a midrash from *Pirkei D'rabbi Eliezer*, but not our editions. Cf. *Siddur of R. Shlomo of Worms*, ed. Hershler, p. 239; Sperber, *Minhagei Yisrael*, 7:312, 315–16.

Openings at Closing Time, by Rabbi Jan R. Uhrbach

1. Martin Buber, *Ten Rungs* (New York: A Citadel Press Book, published by the Carol Publishing Group, 1955), p. 51. Throughout my citations, I have tried as much as possible to emend androcentric language to provide gender inclusivity—in this case, "We are" instead of "Man is" and so forth.
2. Soloveitchik.
3. *Deuteronomy Rabbah* 2:12.
4. Talmud, Bava Metzia 59a; cf. Talmud, Berakhot 32b.
5. The other four are eating and drinking, washing, anointing oneself, and engaging in sex. Cf. Mishnah Yoma 8:1; Talmud, Yoma 73b.

The Sliding Doors of *N'ilah*, by Dr. Wendy Zierler

1. Yehuda Amichai, *Lo Me'akhshav Lo Mikan* (Jerusalem: Shocken, 1963). All translations from the novel are my own.

El Nora Alilah and the Two Faces of the Day of Atonement, by Rabbi Dalia Marx, PhD

1. I thank Rabbi Lawrence A. Hoffman, PhD, and Cantor Eliyahu Schleifer for their helpful comments on this essay.
2. A medieval story connects *Un'taneh Tokef* to a certain Rabbi Amnon, said to be tortured for refusing to convert to Christianity. Although not historical,

the story is well known and influential. See Lawrence A. Hoffman, ed., *Who by Fire, Who by Water*—Un'taneh Tokef (Woodstock, VT: Jewish Lights, 2010), 26–28.

3. This verse, absent from the medieval original and not part of the acrostic, was added later by cantors. Professor Eliyahu Schleifer recalls it as a late popular addition that was accepted anonymously, at least in Israel.
4. The response to "May you merit many years [of life]" is *Tizku v'tichyu v'ta'arikhu yamim* ("May you merit life and length of days"). The content and style of this strophe is different from that of the entire poem, since here it is not what the cantor says to God but what the cantor says to the community. In this sense, it is similar to *Mi Sheberakh*, the prayers for blessing that are recited in the framework of the Torah service.
5. In Israel as in some other places in contemporary Judaism, the wish "Next year in Jerusalem" is rendered "Next year in Jerusalem *rebuilt.*"
6. As far as I know, the first to include this poem in the Liberal service was Cantor David Meldola (1780–1861), who brought a myriad of Sephardi *piyyutim* to the Hamburg Temple. Later, David Einhorn, a founding rabbi for North American Reform Judaism, included it in his 1858 *Olat Tamid*, and from there, it became standard Reform practice. Marcus Jastrow and Benjamin Szold included it for their Conservative Movement prayer book of 1873, and it is now part of Conservative liturgy too. Mordecai Kaplan omitted it from his original Reconstructionist liturgy, but Reconstructionist synagogues say it now. Progressive congregations in the UK also include it—see, e.g., comments by Rabbi Andrew Goldstein, p. 147–150. *Kavanat Halev*, the Israeli Reform *machzor* added *El Nora Alilah* in the late 1980s.

Endings and Beginnings: *N'ilah* "Commencement Address," by Rabbi Sonja K. Pilz, PhD

1. See *El Nora Alilah*, especially the "traditional" Sephardi melody, in Cantor Jeffrey Shiovitz, ed., *Zamru Lo: The Next Generation*, vol. 2, *Congregational Melodies for the High Holidays* (New York: Cantors Assembly, 2006), 276–79.
2. Attributed to Rabbi Moses ibn Ezra, twelfth century, Spain.
3. *El Nora Alilah* quotes the messianic visions of Ezekiel 23:4 and Daniel 10:21, 12:1.

Childhood Memories and Life's Gates, by Rabbi Dennis C. Sasso, DMin

1. Peter Cole, *The Dream of the Poem: Hebrew Poetry from Muslim and Christian Spain 950–1492* (Princeton, NJ: Princeton University Press, 2007), 127.
2. Ibid., 132.
3. Abraham Lopes Cardozo, *Sephardic Songs of Praise* (Cedarhurst, NY: Tara Publications, 1987), 75.

The Grand Conclusion: Editor's Introduction, by Rabbi Lawrence A. Hoffman, PhD

1. Sometimes, *Lashanah* not *L'shanah*—adding the definite article, that is. Technically, *Lashanah* is correct because the modifying word following (*haba'ah*) contains the definite article. *L'shanah* ought to be followed by just *ba'ah*, not *haba'ah*. Some scholarly publications therefore prefer *Lashanah*. But the overwhelming propensity of liturgies say *L'shanah* specifically.

(Not) Last Words, by Dr. Annette M. Boeckler

1. I am grateful to Rabbi Lawrence A. Hoffman, PhD, whose comments and questions helped direct me in my research and thinking.
2. Traditionally, chanted by cantor and repeated line by line by the congregation.
3. According to the Eastern Ashkenazi tradition (*Minhag Polin*) the phrase *L'shanah haba'ah birushalayim* ("Next year in Jerusalem") is chanted after the shofar sound; see, e.g., the U.S. Conservative *Mahzor Lev Shalem*, ed. Edward Feld (New York: Rabbinical Assembly, 2010), 429. Many progressive *machzorim*, however, follow the Western Ashkenazi tradition (*Minhag Rinus*)—the dominant tradition in nineteenth-century Germany—and omit it.
4. Gotthard Deutsch, "Ne'ilah," in *The Jewish Encyclopedia* (New York: Funk and Wagnalls, 1906), 9:215, http://www.jewishencyclopedia.com/articles /11432-ne-ilah; cf. Macy Nulman, *The Encyclopedia of Jewish Prayer: Ashkenazic and Sephardic Rites* (Northvale, NJ: Jason Aronson, 1996), 300–301.
5. The three statements are mentioned for the first time as a custom in *Tosafot* to Berakhot 34a (s.v., *amar p'suka p'suka*). On the thirteenth-century origins see Deutsch, "Ne'ilah," 215. *Machzor Vitry* does not yet know the custom of saying *Sh'ma* at the end of Yom Kippur. It concludes *N'ilah* with one *t'ki'ah* recalling the Jubilee year, after which the congregation replies seven times: *Adonai hu ha'elohim* (S. Hurwitz, ed., *Machzor Vitry Lerabbeinu Simcha*, 2nd ed. (Nuremberg: M'kitsei Nirdamim, 1923), 395 [end of third passage starting with *v'shaliach*]).
6. See Ephraim Kanarfogel, *"Peering through the Lattices": Mystical, Magical, and Pietistic Dimensions in the Tosafist Period* (Detroit: Wayne State University Press, 2000), 144f., 180f.
7. *L'vush* 623:5. Another explanation relates the threefold repetition to the traditional division of priests, Levites, and Israelites (M. Nulman).
8. According to *Tosafot* to Berakhot 34a (s.v. *amar p'suka p'suka*, end). Cf. Elie Munk (*Die Welt der Gebete, Zweiter Band: Die Sabbat- und Festgebete*, 3rd ed. [Frankfurt/Main: Hermon, 1938], 288), who refers to Moses ben Abraham of Przemsyl's *Matteh Moshe*, § 884 and also *Beth Jacob*, 624; *Shulchan Arukh*, *Orakh Chayyim* 61:12. Sephardim end *N'ilah* slightly differently. They cite these verses toward the end but repeat seven times the double statement *Adonai hu ha'elohim, Adonai hu ha'elohim*—this double form actually is the biblical quotation. Thus Sephardim, too, have a sevenfold repetition even if *Adonai hu ha'elohim* is heard fourteen times.

9. The *Vidui* is found, e.g., in the following: (1) Jonathan Sacks, ed., *The Authorized Daily Prayer Book of the United Hebrew Congregations of the Commonwealth*, 4th ed. (London: Collins, 2007), 828–31, with the following order: *Adonai melekh, Adonai malakh, Adonai iimlokh l'olam va'ed* (three times); *Barukh shem . . .* (three times); *Adonai hu ha'elohim* (seven times); *Sh'ma* (once). It is not part of the confession but is introduced with "When the end is approaching, the following should be said" (not specified by whom, probably the bystanders), while the confession is "said by one near death." (2) *Seder Ha-T'fillot: Forms of Prayer I*, 8th ed. (London: Movement for Reform Judaism, 2008), 420, with the following order: *Adonai melekh . . .*; *Barukh . . .*; *Adonai hu . . .*; *Sh'ma*. Here the lines appear as the end of "A prayer during dangerous illness (a deathbed confession)" formulated in the first-person singular and thus clearly meant to be said by the dying person. (3) Jules Harlow, ed., *Siddur Sim Shalom* (New York: Rabbinical Assembly, United Synagogue of America, 1985), 256 with the following: *Sh'ma* followed by *Adonai hu* twice if spoken by the dying person and only *Sh'ma* at the end of the alternative prayer spoken by those present if the dying person is unable to say it. (4) *Seder Tov Lehodot* (Amsterdam: Verbond van Liberaal-Religieuze Joden in Nederland, 2001), 611 with the following order: *Sh'ma* (once); *Barukh . . .* (three times); *Adonai hu ha'elohim* (seven times); *Adonai melekh, Adonai malakh, Adonai yimlokh l'olam va'ed* (once) followed by a remark in Dutch: "If it turns out that this breath actually was not the last, you can repeat the first sentence of the *Sh'ma* several times." This order follows the prototypical *Ma'avar Yabok* (1626).
10. It may be that this line was added because of its being mentioned in *L'vush* 623:5 as explanation for the threefold *Barukh*.
11. B. H. Ascher, *The Book of Life; being a complete formula of The Service and Family Devotion adapted for the use of the sick and for those who attend them in their dying moments . . .* (London: Meldola, Cahn & Co, 1847), 190–91. For similar later editions, see H. Vidaver, *The Book of Life: A Complete Formula of the Service and Ceremonies Observed at the Death-bed, House of Mourning and Cemetery together with Prayers on Visiting the Graves* (Brooklyn: Hebrew Publishing Co., 1901), 64; H. Rabinowicz, A *Guide to Life: Jewish Laws and Customs of Mourning* (New York: Ktav, 1964), 18: "When the end is approaching the last paragraph of the Confession should be recited, especially the 'Hear O Israel'"; I. M. Levinger, *Der letzte Weg. Vorschriften, Gebete und Gedanken zum Thema Tod und Trauer* (Basel: 1991), 84–85; S. G. Blogg, *Sefer Hachajjim: Israelitisches Gebet- und Erbauungsbuch. Gebete bei Krankheitsfällen, in einem Sterbehause und bei dem Besuche der Gräber von Verwandten . . .*, 11th ed. by A. Sulzbach (Basel: Goldschmidt, 1905), 62—a note says that in Frankfurt am Main the order differs: *Adonai hu . . .* (seven times), *Sh'ma, Barukh shem* (once), the last statement said very softly. In the Spanish-Portuguese tradition the *Sh'ma* comes first, followed by a variety of other statements; see M. Gaster, *The Book of Prayer and order of*

service according to the custom of the Spanish and Portuguese Jews . . . (London: Humphrey Milford, 1939), 197 (unchanged in the latest edition revised by S. Gaon [London: Spanish and Portuguese Synagogue, 2010], 196).

12. Vidaver, *The Book of Life* (1901), 65.

13. I. M. Levinger, *Der letzte Weg*, 84. The idea to take care to die saying the word *echad* stems from the Crusade era when people reinterpreted the story about Rabbi Akiva's death (Talmud, Berakhot 61a) to imply that saying the *Sh'ma* as he did is the martyr's way to die. See Elliott Horowitz, "The Jews of Europe and the Moment of Death in Medieval and Modern Times," *Judaism* 44 (1995): 271–81, esp. 276–78.

14. The idea to say a confession on the deathbed is Talmudic (Shabbat 32a), but without verses of sacred names. Nachmanides (*Torat Adam*, in H. Chavel, ed., *Kitve Ramban*, 2:47) quotes a deathbed confession from *chasidim v'anshei ma'aseh*, a term for *Chasidei Ashkenaz* (Karnafogel, *Peering through the Lattices*, 46n35). Da Modena (*Tzori Lanefesh* . . ., folio, 6b, starting with *modeh ani*) quotes a version of Nachmanides's *Vidui* (with some minor variants), so must have known this tradition, but nowhere explicitly discusses it. He draws from the Yom Kippur liturgy and mentions Christian deathbed customs that inspired him. Note that in the Catholic tradition the extreme unction by a priest on the deathbed counts as one of the seven sacraments.

15. From the preface of Leon da Modena, *Tzori Lanefesh Umarpe La'etsem*, translation quoted from Avriel Bar-Levav, "Leon Modena and the Invention of the Jewish Death Tradition," in David Malkiel, ed., *The Lion Shall Roar: Leon Modena and His World* (Jerusalem: Magnes, 2003), 89.

16. The Venice 1619 edition is available online: http://www.hebrewbooks.org /19672. For detail, see Bar-Levav, "Leon Modena," 85n102.

17. Online: http://www.hebrewbooks.org/11774.

18. It gives the following seven verses: Psalm 18:11; Song of Songs 1:1; Psalm 50:1; Psalm 50:2; Deuteronomy 6:4 (*Sh'ma*); 1 Kings 18:39 (*Adonai hu ha'elohim, Adonai hu ha'elohim*); *Adonai melekh, Adonai malakh, Adonai yimlokh l'olam va'ed.*

19. For a history of deathbed rituals, see Horowitz, "The Jews of Europe," 271–81; Stefan C. Reif, Andreas Lehnardt, and Avriel Bar-Levav, eds., *Death in Jewish Life: Burial and Mourning Customs among Jews of Europe and Nearby Communities* (Berlin: De Gruyter, 2014); Bar-Levav, "Leon Modena," 85–102; and the blog post by Avriel Bar-Levav, *Manuals for the Dying*, http:// www.jewishideasdaily.com/docLib/20100219_ManualsfortheDying.pdf.

The Final Moments of *N'ilah*: Meeting Elijah, Once Again, by Rabbi Jeffrey K. Salkin

1. For historical detail comparing the deathbed *Sh'ma* and the *Sh'ma* at the end of *N'ilah*, see Boeckler, "(Not) Last Words," pp. 177–181.

2. Alex Israel, *I Kings: Torn in Two* (Jerusalem: Maggid Books, 2013), 250.

"Go Forth Joyfully, Eat Your Meal, and Drink Your Wine," by Rabbi Edward Feld

1. *Elohim [Ha]dar Bimro'm'kha*, "O God who dwells on high." See *Machzor Roma* (Luzzatto ed.), 2:156.

A Love Affair at *N'ilah*, by Rabbi Aaron Goldstein

1. *Siddur Lev Chadash*, 122.

Denouement or Entwinement?, by Rabbi Delphine Horvilleur

1. Yuval Noah Harrari, *Sapiens: A Brief History of Humankind* (New York: HarperCollins, 2015), 125.
2. "La *solutio* et la *resolutio* ont à la fois le sens de la dissolution, du lien dissous, du dégagement, du désengagement ou de l'acquittement (par exemple de la dette) *et* de la solution du problème"; Jacques Derrida, *Résistances—de la psychanalyse* (Paris: Galilée, 1996), 15.

Ending with a Bang or a Whimper? What Do We Take Home with Us?, by Rabbi Jonathan Magonet, PhD

1. It is sad but appropriate to mark here the passing of Rabbi Lionel Blue *z'l* (6 February 1930–19 December 2016) who was the main architect and inspiration for the re-envisaging of the prayer books of the Reform Synagogues of Great Britain (a.k.a. Movement for Reform Judaism) in the closing decades of the twentieth century, and whose influence is evident in all contributions I have made to the volumes of Prayers of Awe. As he wrote in the opening of the prayer quoted here, for Lionel 'Neilah has come.'
2. *Forms of Prayer for Jewish Worship, vol. 3, Prayers for the High Holydays*, (8th edition), ed. The Assembly of Rabbis of the Reform Synagogues of Great Britain (The Reform Synagogues of Great Britain, 1985), p. 635.
3. *Ibid.*, pp. 659–661.

Closing Time, by Rabbi Janet Marder and Rabbi Sheldon Marder

1. The translation of *Ad Yom Moto* is adapted from *Mahzor Lev Shalem*, ed. Edward Feld (New York: Rabbinical Assembly, 2010), 393.
2. From Archibald MacLeish, "You, Andrew Marvell," in *Collected Poems: 1917–1952* (Houghton Mifflin, 1954).
3. *Mishkan HaNefesh: Machzor for the Days of Awe*, vol. 2, *Yom Kippur*, ed. Edwin Goldberg, Janet Marder, Sheldon Marder, and Leon Morris (New York: CCAR Press, 2015), 640.
4. Yehuda Amichai, *Open Closed Open*, trans. Chana Bloch and Chana Kronfeld (New York: Harcourt, 2000), 6.
5. Alan Lightman, *The Accidental Universe* (New York: Vintage Books, 2014), 24–25.
6. *Mishkan HaNefesh*, 660.

7. Ibid., 614–15.

Yom Kippur Is Almost Over: What Will Happen to the Wine?, by Rabbi Jacob J. Schacter, PhD

1. Leon Wieseltier, *Kaddish* (New York: Alfred A. Knopf, 1998), 61.

Appendix B: The Climactic End to *N'ilah*, by Rabbi Lawrence A. Hoffman, PhD

1. E.g., Koren *Machzor*, ed. Jonathan Sacks (2012), 1194–97; ArtScroll *Machzor*, ed. Meir Zlotowitz and Avie Gold (1986), 762–63; Birnbaum *Machzor*, ed. Philip Birnbaum (1951), 1,017. Cf. E. D. Goldschmidt, *Machzor Layamim Hanora'im*, vol. 2 (Yom Kippur) (Jerusalem: Koren Press, 1970), 790 and (in the Hebrew introduction) 32; and Shlomo Zevin, ed., *Entsiklopediah Talmudit*, vol. 23 (*Machzor Yom Hakippurim*).

2. E.g., Bevis Marks *Machzor*, ed. D. A. De Sola (1837); Bevis Marks *Machzor*, ed. Moses Gaster (1904).

3. *Seder Rav Amram*, part 2, section 31; Goldschmidt, *Machzor Layamim Hanora'im* 2:171.

4. *Sha'arei T'shuvah*, section 67.

5. The term "Jubilee year" is something of a misnomer. The Latin translation for the Hebrew *sh'nat hayovel* was rendered as *annus jubilaeus* (*jubilaeus* sounding something akin to *yovel*), whence the King James Version of the Bible gave us "Jubilee year."

6. *Sha'arei T'shuvah*, section 67. The translation of *zekher* (from the Hebrew root *z.kh*.r) is difficult. More properly (like *zikaron*, a parallel term), it means "pointer," in the sense of "pointing out" or "drawing attention to." In liturgy, it usually functions theologically to denote a means of drawing God's attention to something. See Lawrence A. Hoffman, *"Zekher* and *Zikaron*: A Liturgical Theology of Memory," in *Memory in Jewish and Christian Traditions*, ed. Michael S. Signer (Notre Dame: University of Notre Dame Press, 2001). Here it may only mean a "recollection" of what once occurred in Temple times.

7. Isaac ibn Ghiyyat, *Sefer Sha'arei Simchah, Hilkhot Yom Hakippurim*.

8. *Machzor Vitry*, Berliner ed., 1:381; repeated, 1:395. The same report is given verbatim in two other books that come from the school of Rashi, *Siddur Rashi*, section 204, and *Sefer Hapardes*, section 183.

9. *Sefer HaRaban [Even Ha'ezer], Massekhet Yoma* (Prague ed., reprinted Jerusalem, 1957), 170a.

10. Carried also in *Bet Yosef* by Joseph Caro, *Orach Chayim* 624.

11. *Sefer Raviah*, part 2, *Massekhet Yoma*, M'kitzei Nirdamim, ed., 2: 198.

12. *Sefer Roke'ach, Hilkhot Yom Hakippurim*, end. Cf. Daniel Goldschmidt, "Machzor APaM [the *machzor* from the northern Italian cities of Asti, Fossamo and Montcalvo]," in Goldschmidt, *Mechkarei T'fillah Ufiyyut*

(Jerusalem: Magnes Press, 1979), 120–21. These communities retained French custom in their High Holy Day worship but blew all four blasts as well. The same practice is found in *Sefer Hamachkim* and *Siddur Troyes*, both of them from France (see n. 122).

13. *Tosafot* to Shabbat 114b; s.v. *v'ama'i.*
14. *Tosafot* to Shabbat 117a; s.v. *aval.*
15. *Sefer Hamanhig*, ed. Isaac Rafael (Jerusalem: Rav Kook, 1978), part 1, *Hilkhot Tzom Kippur*, 359–60.
16. *Orkhot Chayim*, *Hilkhot Yom Hakippurim*, end.
17. *Tur, Hilkhot Yom Hakippurim, Orach Chayim* 624; *Abudarham*, Wertheimer ed., p. 290.
18. JPS translation: "God ascends amidst acclamation [*bit'ru'ah*], the Lord to the blast of the horn [*b'kol shofar*]." I cite the verse the way Benjamin read it.
19. Cf. *Shibbolei Haleket*, section 322; *Tanya Rabbati*, section 81, end.
20. *Machzor Vitry*, 395.
21. Ibid., 395–96.
22. *Bet Yosf* to *Tur, Orach Chayim* 624, s.v. *v'yesh nohagin.*
23. Although, oddly enough, it is found in a manuscript of *Machzor APaM* from northern Italy. See Goldschmidt, "Machzor APaM," 121n12.
24. *Shulchan Arukh, Orach Chayim* 623:6.
25. Louis Ginzberg, *Ginzei Schechter*, 2:559–560.
26. E.g., *Orchot Chayim, Hilkhot Yom Kippurim*, on the shofar.
27. *Machzor Vitry*, 395–96.
28. *Sefer Minhagim L'rabbenu Avraham Klausner*, section 41, ed. Jonah Joseph Dissin (Jerusalem: 1978), 37–38. For Paltiel, cf. Daniel Goldschmidt, *Mechkarei T'fillah Ufiyyut* (Jerusalem: Magnes Press, 1979), 44–45.
29. *Machzor Vitry*, 395–96.
30. *Sefer Minhagim L'rabbenu Avraham Klausner*, section 41, pp. 44–45.
31. *Sefer Haminhagim L'rabbenu Isaac Tyrnau*, Yom Kippur, *N'ilah*, ed. Solomon Spitzer, (Jerusalem: 1979), 116.
32. *Leket Yosher* (Freiman ed. [Berlin, 1903], 142), the book by Rabbi Joseph ben Moses, celebrating the customs of Isserlein, his teacher.
33. *Shulchan Arukh, Orach Chayim* 723. Isserles's words for "in these parts" is, literally, "in these countries," referring to the various independent entities into which present-day Poland was then divided.
34. *Bayit Chadash (BaCH)* to *Tur, Orach Chayim* 724, s.v. *Ma'i shekatav v'tok'in.*
35. In Hebrew, Satan is normally referred to as "The Satan"—HAsatan, not just Satan.
36. *L'vush, Hilkhot Yom Kippur, Orach Chayim* 723.
37. *Mishnah B'rurah, Orach Chayim* 623:13; *Arukh Hashulchan, Orach Chayim* 623:8.
38. *Mateh Ephraim Hashalem, Orach Chayim* 623:7 (end). Cf., note to *Mateh Ephraim* in Shlomo Zevin, ed., *Entsiklopediah Talmudit: Machzor Layom Hakippurim*, 457n47.

39. M. Ber. 9:2
40. Ta'anit 31a.
41. Cf., e.g., *Machzor Hashalem*, Yom Kippur [*Machzor Mateh Levi*] (Lemberg, 1907; reissued, Brooklyn: Chevrat M'orer Y'shanim, 1965), 492; *Entsiklopediah Talmudit, Machzor Layom Hakippurim*, 454; and Jacob Weingarten, ed., *Hamachzor Ham'forash*, Yom Kippur (Jerusalem: Gefen, 1987), 852.

Glossary

Amidah (pronounced ah-mee-DAH or, commonly, ah-MEE-dah): Literally, "standing." Hence the "prayer said standing," the second of two central units in the worship service, the first being the *Sh'ma* and Its Blessings.

Ashkenaz (pronounced ahsh-k'-NAHZ or, commonly, AHSH-k'-nahz): The geographic area of northern and eastern Europe. The adjective "Ashkenazi" (pronounced ahsh-k'-nah-ZEE or ahsh-k'-NAH-zee) describes the liturgical customs practiced there or the people and communities that follow them, as opposed to "Sepharad" and "Sephardi," the parallel terms for Spain (see **Sepharad**).

Blessing: Used liturgically as the English for the Hebrew *b'rachah* (pronounced b'-rah-KHAH or, commonly, b'-RAH-khah), the technical term for the Rabbis' favored prose pattern of liturgy. "Short blessings" are one-liners recited upon enjoying God's bounty (tasting specific foods, perhaps, or observing nature's beauty); "long blessings" are extended treatments of themes that constitute much of Jewish prayer books.

Eleh ezk'rah (pronounced AY-leh ehz-k'-RAH, but, commonly, AY-leh EHZ-k'-rah): Literally, "These, I remember," the opening words of the martyrology recited on Yom Kippur, a recollection, largely, of the Rabbis martyred by Hadrian following the abortive Bar Kokhba revolt of 135.

Gaon (pronounced gah-OHN; plural: *geonim*, pronounced g'-oh-NEEM): Title for the leading Rabbis in Babylonia (present-day Iraq) from about 750 to 1034. From a biblical word meaning "glory," and equivalent to "Your Excellency."

Gematria (pronounced g-MAHT-ree-yah): The system of assigning a numerical value to each Hebrew letter, then matching the total value of a word or phrase to another word or phrase of the same value, and applying the meaning implicit in one word or phrase to the other.

Halakhah (pronounced hah-lah-KHAH or, commonly, hah-LAH-khah): The Hebrew word for "Jewish law." From the Hebrew word meaning "to walk" or "to go," denoting the way in which a person should walk through life.

Halakhic (pronounced hah-LAH-khic): "Legal," the anglicized adjective from "halakhah" ("Jewish law"); see **halakhah**.

Hatov v'hameitiv (pronounced hah-TOHV v'-hah-mei-TEEV): Literally, "the one who is good and does good." The concluding words of the blessing (see **blessing**) recited upon hearing good news (also the fourth blessing in the Grace after Meals); the name, therefore, for those two blessings.

Havdalah (pronounced hahv-dah-LAH or, commonly, hahv-DAH-lah): Literally, "separation," hence, the name of the prayer that separates Shabbat from the following week, said as an insertion into the Saturday evening *Amidah* and then again at home, later in the evening. Recited also at conclusion of holy days—after *N'ilah*, for example, when darkness sets in to end Yom Kippur day.

Kabbalah (pronounced kah-bah-LAH or, commonly, kah-BAH-lah): A general term for Jewish mysticism, but used properly for a specific type of mystical approach that emerged first in Provence (twelfth century); then expanded into Spain (thirteenth and fourteenth centuries) where its primary document, the *Zohar,* was composed; then took on new life again after the expulsion of Jews from Spain and Portugal (1492, 1497), when emigres elaborated new forms of it, particularly in Safed (Hebrew, *Tsfat*) in northern Israel. From a Hebrew word meaning "to receive" or "to welcome," and, secondarily, "tradition," implying the receiving of tradition from one's past.

Kaddish (pronounced kah-DEESH or, commonly, KAH-dish): From the Hebrew word meaning "holy"; hence, the name of a prayer declaring the holiness of God. Used in many contexts, the best known being a "Mourner's *Kaddish*," a prayer recited in memory of those who have died; but used also to separate large prayer units from one another.

K'dushah (pronounced k'-doo-SHAH or, commonly, k'-DOO-shah): From the Hebrew word meaning "holy," and therefore, one of several prayers from the first or second century occurring in several places

and versions, all of which have in common the citing of Isaiah 6:3—
Kadosh, kadosh, kadosh . . . , "Holy, holy, holy is the Lord of hosts. The
whole earth is full of his glory."

K'dushta (pronounced k'-doosh-TAH or, commonly, k'-DOOSH-tah):
The most famous genre of *piyyut* (liturgical poetry) from late antiquity
(see **piyyut**). It has nine parts inserted throughout the first three blessings of the Shabbat or holiday *Amidah*; the last seven occur within the
third benediction, the *K'dushah*, where the poem reaches its climax
(see **K'dushah**). Hence, the title *K'dushta*, Aramaic for *K'dushah*.

Kittel (pronounced KIH-t'l): The Yiddish word for the white garb traditionally worn on Yom Kippur, symbolic of the shrouds in which one
is buried.

Kol Nidre (pronounced KOHL need-RAY or, commonly, kohl NIHD-
ray): Literally, "all vows," the initial words of a Yom Kippur prayer
annulling improperly made vows; by extension, the name given to the
evening service inaugurating Yom Kippur, the service in which *Kol
Nidre* is said.

Ma'ariv (pronounced mah-ah-REEV or, commonly, MAH-ah-riv): From
the Hebrew *erev* (pronounced EH-rev), meaning "evening." Hence, the
title of the evening worship service.

Machzor (pronounced mahkh-ZOHR or, commonly, MAHKH-z'r):
From the Hebrew root *ch.z.r*, "to come round" or "return"; hence, the
name given to prayer books for holy days, the occasions that "come
round" once a year. The High Holy Days feature a Rosh Hashanah
machzor and a Yom Kippur *machzor*.

Midrash (pronounced meed-RAHSH or, commonly, MID-rahsh):
From a Hebrew word meaning "to ferret out the meaning of a text,"
and, therefore, a Rabbinic interpretation of a biblical word or verse. By
extension, a body of Rabbinic literature that offers classical interpretations of the Bible.

Mikveh (pronounced mik-VEH but, popularly, MIK-v'h): A "ritual bath"
used (1) in a variety of cases (a menstruant, for example) as a transfor-
mational agent from the state of *t'umah* to *tohorah* ("ritual impurity" to
"ritual purity"); (2) for purposes of conversion; (3) generalized, through
time, for other ends, such as preparing for Shabbat.

Minchah (pronounced meen-KHAH or, commonly, MIHN-kh'h): Literally, "afternoon"; hence, the title of the afternoon worship service.

Minhag (pronounced meen-HAHG or, commonly, MIN-hahg): The Hebrew word for "custom" and, therefore, the customary way that Jews of different traditions pray. By extension, *minhag* means a "rite," as in *Minhag Ashkenaz*, meaning "the rite of prayer" or "the customary way of prayer for Jews in Ashkenaz"—that is, northern and eastern Europe.

Mishnah (pronounced meesh-NAH or, commonly, MISH-n'h): The name of the definitive six-volume statement of Jewish law from the Land of Israel, c. 200 CE.

Musaf (pronounced moo-SAHF or, commonly, MOO-sahf): Literally, "extra" or "added"; hence, the title of the additional service of worship appended to the morning service on Shabbat and holy days.

Nusach (pronounced noo-SAHKH or, commonly, NOO-sahkh): Literally, "form" or "formula"; hence, the form (or wording) in which a prayer appears; but also the form in which a prayer is sung and, by extension, the word used to denote the various cantorial styles by which prayers are traditionally sung.

Piyyut (pronounced pee-YOOT; plural: *piyyutim*, pronounced pee-yoo-TEEM): Literally, "a poem," but used technically to mean a liturgical poem composed in classical or medieval times and inserted into the standard prayers on special occasions.

Sefirot (pronounced s'-fee-ROTE; singular: *sefirah*, pronounced s'-fee-RAH or, commonly, s'-FEE-rah): Literally, "countings," but also "spheres," the kabbalistic term for the spheres of light said to have emanated from God, out of which the universe came into being.

Sepharad (pronounced s'-fah-RAHD): The geographic area of modern-day Spain and Portugal. The adjective "Sephardi" (pronounced s'fahr-DEE or, commonly, s'-FAHR-dee) describes the liturgical customs practiced there prior to the expulsion from Spain and Portugal in 1492 and 1497, respectively; or the people and communities that follow those practices to this day; as opposed to "Ashkenaz" and "Ashkenazi," the parallel terms for northern and eastern Europe. One stream of Sephardi tradition emerged from emigres who left Spain for the Netherlands, and then places like England and the Americas. Another emerged from those who went to the Ottoman Empire (including the Land of Israel).

Shabbat (pronounced shah-BAHT): The Hebrew word for "Sabbath," from a word meaning "to rest."

Shacharit (pronounced shah-khah-REET or, commonly, SHAHKH-reet): From the Hebrew *shachar* (SHAH-khar), meaning "morning." Hence, the title of the morning worship service.

Shekhinah (pronounced sh'-khee-NAH or, commonly, sh'-KHEE-nah): From the Hebrew root *sh.kh.n*, "to dwell"; hence, the aspect of God (usually identified as feminine) that "dwells" among us.

Sh'ma (pronounced sh'-MAH): Literally, "Hear!"; hence, the shorthand term for Judaism's primary statement of faith (from Deuteronomy 6:4), "Hear, O Israel, Adonai is our God; Adonai is One." By extension, the title for a lengthier prayer, composed of three biblical citations (Deuteronomy 6:4–9; Deuteronomy 11:13–21; Numbers 15:37–41) that begin with that line. Along with its surrounding blessings, the *Sh'ma* and Its Blessings is the first of two central units in the worship service, the second being the *Amidah* (see ***Amidah***).

Shofar (pronounced shoh-FAHR or, commonly, SHOH-fahr): A ram's horn, blown ritually during Rosh Hashanah services and at the close of Yom Kippur *N'ilah*.

Sh'varim (pronounced sh'-vah-REEM or, commonly, sh'-VAH-reem): One of three traditional shofar sounds (see **shofar**), consisting of three somewhat extended blasts that sounds like wailing.

Siluk (pronounced see-LOOK): The climactic and final part of the genre of liturgical poem known as *K'dushta* (see ***K'dushta***).

S'lichah (pronounced s'-lee'KHAH or, commonly, s'-LEE-khah): From the Hebrew root *s.l.kh*, meaning "pardon." Hence, the name of a benediction in the *Amidah* (see ***Amidah***) that requests God's pardon, and a liturgical poem (*piyyut*) on the theme of God's pardoning our sins.

Tallit (pronounced tah-LEET or, by some, the Yiddish version, TAH-lis): A prayer shawl customarily worn for morning services, but on Yom Kippur, worn also at the inaugural evening service the night before, and then at all services throughout Yom Kippur day, until the concluding service, *N'ilah*, for which it is removed.

Talmud (pronounced tahl-MOOD or, commonly, TAHL-mud): The name given to each of two great compendia of Jewish law and lore compiled over several centuries and, ever since, the literary core of the Rabbinic heritage. The *Talmud Yerushalmi* (pronounced y'-roo-SHAHL-mee), the "Jerusalem Talmud," is earlier, a product of the Land of Israel generally dated about 400 CE. The better-known *Talmud Bavli* (pronounced BAHV-lee), or "Babylonian Talmud," took shape in Babylonia (present-day Iraq) and is traditionally dated about 550 CE. When people say "the" Talmud without specifying which one they mean, they are referring to the Babylonian version. *Talmud* means "teaching."

T'ki'ah (pronounced t'-kee-AH or, commonly, t'-KEE-ah): One of three traditional shofar sounds (see **shofar**), consisting of a single lengthy blast.

T'ki'ah g'dolah (pronounced t'-kee-AH g'doh-LAH or, commonly, t'-KEE-ah g'DOH-lah): Literally, "a great *t'ki'ah*," that is, an extensively drawn out *t'ki'ah*.

T'ru'ah (pronounced t'-roo-AH or, commonly, t'-ROO-ah): One of three traditional shofar sounds (see **shofar**), consisting of nine staccato-like blasts.

T'shuvah (pronounced t'-shoo-VAH or, commonly, t'-SHOO-vah): Literally, "repentance," from the Hebrew *shuv* (pronounced SHOOV), meaning "return."

Tzitzit (pronounced tzee-TZEET): The Hebrew word for "tassels," or "fringes," denoting the tassels affixed to the four corners of the *tallit* (the prayer shawl; see *tallit*), as Numbers 15:38 instructs.

Yizkor (pronounced yeez-KOHR or, commonly, YIHZ-k'r): Literally, "He [God] will remember" or "May He [God] remember"; hence, the name of a memorial prayer recited, among other times, on Yom Kippur.

Z"l (pronounced with an assumed "a" in the middle, ZAHL): A contraction of the initials for the two Hebrew words *Zichrono/ah livrachah* (pronounced zikh-roh-NOH/AH liv-rah-KHAH, "May his/her name be a blessing"). A term of respect used for people who have died.

Zohar (pronounced ZOH-hahr): A shorthand title for *Sefer Hazohar* (pronounced SAY-fer hah-ZOH-hahr), literally, "The Book of Splendor," which is the primary compendium of mystical thought in Judaism; written mostly by Moses de Leon in Spain near the end of the thirteenth century and, ever since, the chief source for the study of Kabbalah (see **Kabbalah**).

Prayers of Awe Series

An exciting new series that examines the High Holy Day liturgy to enrich the praying experience of everyone—whether experienced worshipers or guests who encounter Jewish prayer for the very first time.

Edited by Rabbi Lawrence A. Hoffman, PhD

Who by Fire, Who by Water—*Un'taneh Tokef*
6 x 9, 272 pp, Quality PB, 978-1-58023-672-0   **$19.99**; HC, 978-1-58023-424-5   **$24.99**

All These Vows—*Kol Nidre*
6 x 9, 288 pp, HC, 978-1-58023-430-6   **$24.99**

We Have Sinned—Sin and Confession in Judaism: *Ashamnu* and *Al Chet*
6 x 9, 304 pp, HC, 978-1-58023-612-6   **$24.99**

May God Remember: Memory and Memorializing in Judaism—*Yizkor*
6 x 9, 304 pp, HC, 978-1-58023-689-8   **$24.99**

All the World: Universalism, Particularism and the High Holy Days
6 x 9, 288 pp, HC, 978-1-58023-783-3   **$24.99**

Naming God: *Avinu Malkeinu*—Our Father, Our King
6 x 9, 336 pp, HC, 978-1-58023-817-5   **$27.99**

Encountering God: *El Rachum V'chanun*—God Merciful and Gracious
6 x 9, 250 pp, HC, 978-1-58023-854-0   **$27.99**

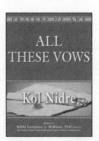
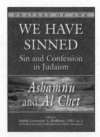

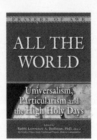
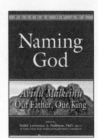